RUNNING THE WAR IN IRAQ

RUNNING THE WAR IN IRAQ

An Australian general, 300,000 troops, the bloodiest conflict of our time

Major General Jim Molan

HarperCollins*Publishers*

HarperCollins*Publishers*

First published in 2008
by HarperCollins*Publishers* Australia Pty Limited
ABN 36 009 913 517
www.harpercollins.com.au

Copyright © Major General Jim Molan 2008

The right of Major General Jim Molan to be identified as the
author of this work has been asserted by him in accordance with
the *Copyright Amendment (Moral Rights) Act 2000.*

HarperCollins*Publishers*
25 Ryde Road, Pymble, Sydney, NSW 2073, Australia
31 View Road, Glenfield, Auckland 10, New Zealand
1–A, Hamilton House, Connaught Place, New Delhi – 110 001, India
77–85 Fulham Palace Road, London, W6 8JB, United Kingdom
2 Bloor Street East, 20th floor, Toronto, Ontario M4W 1A8, Canada
10 East 53rd Street, New York NY 10022, USA

National Library of Australia Cataloguing-in-Publication data:

Molan, Andrew James, 1950–
   Running the war in Iraq / Major General Jim Molan.
   ISBN: 978 0 7322 8781 8 (pbk.)
   Coalition Provisional Authority.
   Iraq War, 2003– – Strategic aspects.
   Postwar reconstruction – Iraq.
   Administrative agencies – Iraq
   Iraq – Politics and government – 2003–
956.704431

Cover design: Michael Donohue
Cover image: Ian Waldie/Getty Images. NB Attempts to discover the identity
   of the soldier pictured were unsuccessful.
Typeset in Bembo 11.5/16.5pt by Kirby Jones
Printed and bound in Australia by Griffin Press.

79gsm Bulky Paperback used by HarperCollins*Publishers* is a natural, recyclable product made
from wood grown in a combination of sustainable plantation and regrowth forests. It also contains
up to a 20% portion of recycled fibre. The manufacturing processes conform to the
environmental regulations in Tasmania, the place of manufacture.

6 5 4 3 2 1   08 09 10 11

In memory of an angel,
our granddaughter
Emily Charlotte Sutton,
who died and was born on 12 October 2007.
Like so many souls in so many lands,
a life ended before it began.

Contents

Acknowledgments

Almost every document I dealt with in Iraq was classified and so, quite rightly, could not be removed from US computer systems. This account of my year in Iraq, then, is the product of memory jogged only by notes I took both in Iraq and soon after my return home in April 2005. I have also relied on personal emails, media reports and some other unclassified sources. When the opportunity arose, I reinforced my memory by talking with my US, British and Australian comrades from Iraq.

It is therefore inevitable that errors of historical fact — particularly pertaining to names, dates, unit roles and titles — will have crept into this book. I accept that, and apologise in advance.

There are many people I should acknowledge. Peter Cosgrove had enough faith to send me to Iraq, and supported me when being chief of operations of the biggest deployed force in the biggest war of its day turned out to involve much more than just humanitarian operations.

Both Peter and his successor as Chief of the Australian Defence Force, Angus Houston, encouraged me to write a book — I suspect as much to keep me and my obsession with Iraq out of their hair as to produce a record!

I was ably assisted by the two Australian Army majors who, one after the other, were my right-hand men in Iraq: Steve Summersby and Steve Gliddon. Steve Summersby suffered me for longer, but kept me both sane and focused, tidied up the egos that I bruised in doing my job, and restored the human relationships that are critical in war. Steve Gliddon had a hard act to follow, but did so admirably and saw me through to the end of my time in Iraq. It is surprising what you remember of torrid times, but the constant stream of tea and coffee and the companionship in our armoured vehicles in the small hours of the morning were disproportionately important to me.

I cannot say enough about my bodyguard: Australians who came and went in three- or four-monthly intervals. I started with two Special Forces soldiers protecting me, had six at times, but mostly had four. They headed a team of three to eight US soldiers whom we begged, borrowed or just stole from others. Acknowledging their anonymity, the Australians were: Drew, Whitey, Ryan, Mac, Paul, Lockey, Harry, Thommo, Kaz, Dave, Stodds and Henry. All of them regularly put themselves between me and threats, accepting all consequences, and I thank them again.

Several of these men have since left the military, and that is our loss. Others have gone on to more direct combat action in Afghanistan. The courage of Sergeant Locke was publicly recognised with a Medal of Gallantry before he was killed in action in Oruzgan province. Dave was tragically killed in an accident at Swan Island which I did not know about until much too late. Drew is special because he set up — with little assistance — the security system that served us so well, and he and Whitey taught me about pistols.

These men were true Australian soldiers, and all had a sense of humour that kept me sane. We lived intimately together. Not only did they defend my life, but they did my housekeeping. On our departure, Thommo sent me a note saying, 'Boss, it has been great working for you, but never again will I wash and fold another man's underwear.' Greater love hath no man.

Words do not often fail me but they do in thanking my wife, Anne. She has been with me forever in a way that I never deserved and I have often rewarded her with absence and worry. She is a hopeless editor of manuscripts because she thinks that everything I do is good, but she is the strength of our family. When I was in Iraq our four children, Sarah, Erin, Felicity and Michael, noticed that I was gone again, but perhaps did not fully realise the circumstances. They were pragmatic, stoic and supportive, knowing that this absence was somewhat out of the ordinary. It affected each in their own way, especially when the news from Iraq was not good. It has taken me until about now to realise that they are what life is about.

An extraordinary number of people reviewed this manuscript when it was considerably longer than it is now, and they all took it seriously. In particular I mention Craig Burn, Ken Brownrigg, Steve Gliddon and Mike Kelly. I thank them and apologise that so much of what they commented on has been cut by merciless editors.

The book leapt ahead under the advice of Dr Bob Breen, who did the first gross edit, and the eminent Australian military historian Professor David Horner, who did the first fine edit. I thank the Army History Committee under Major General John Cantwell for sponsoring this first series of edits. Finally, due to the intercession of its initial editors and Robert Joske, it caught the attention of HarperCollins, who have assisted me by providing Malcolm Knox's editorial expertise and Amruta Slee's commercial management. Finally, I thank Peter Jennings for the miracle of convincing the Australian Department of Defence to approve its release.

There are too many of my comrades in Iraq to thank, as much for their comradeship as for the content they provided for this book. My experience in Iraq was a US experience. I replaced a US general and was replaced by a US general. In the year I was in Iraq, I hardly saw any Australians outside my personal staff. I grew to admire US generalship despite the uninformed criticism and search for scapegoats that went on for a while in 2006 and 2007. I worked for Lieutenant General Ricardo (Ric) Sanchez for four months and for General George Casey for eight months, and I believe that the US generals commanding the major combat elements in Iraq were as good as any country has ever produced and far better than most. They were technically competent, clever, adaptable, moral and courageous. Unfortunately, this has never guaranteed victory.

In particular I thank George Casey for the faith he had in me. I imagine he could have had any US general he wanted as his chief of operations, but he took a chance with an Australian. I learnt more about generalship from him than I can ever acknowledge. I also want to mention Major General Joe Weber, a US Marine who speaks fluent Texan and was the chief of staff, the boss of all the generals in the headquarters. Joe's intercession on my behalf on a number of occasions was, I believe, instrumental in any success I may have had. Joe's son and son-in-law followed him to Iraq and are serving there in combat positions as I write. This is a serious war for Americans.

I should also mention John Negroponte. He was the US Ambassador to Iraq for most of the time I was there, and a man of extraordinary ability. The relationship between Negroponte and Casey provides a case study in how counterinsurgency management improved during this vital phase of the war. I also worked closely with the US Deputy Head of Mission, James Jeffrey, who became as much of a friend as you can have in such turmoil.

I also acknowledge some of the many Iraqis with whom I had regular contact: Prime Minister Iyad Allawi; Deputy Prime Minister Barhem Saleh; National Security Adviser Mowaffak al Rubaie; the commander of the Iraqi Army, Lieutenant General Abdul Kadr; the Chief Electoral Officer in the Independent Electoral Commission of Iraq, Dr Adil Al-Lami; and Major General Ayden Khaled Qadir, chief of operations of the Iraqi Police. History will judge us all, but to me these Iraqis appeared to be true patriots.

I would particularly like to acknowledge the US Soldiers, Sailors, Airmen and Marines I worked with. I gained a great understanding about generalship, leadership and soldiering simply from being exposed to US comrades such as Mark McQueen, Casey Haskins, Garrick Kelly, Don Jackson, Bob Pricone, Brian Boyle, Mark Lowe, Tom Duhs, 'Bear' Byrd, James Maxwell and many more. My closest friends in the UK camp were John McColl and the three Andrews — Farquhar, Graham, and Sharpe — all of whom had an immense impact on the campaign. The only Canadian soldier in Iraq was Brigadier General Walt Natynczyk, who held a two-year position in the American headquarters. As Commonwealth colonials, we had much in common.

In particular, I would like to mention the US one-star officers who worked for me: Peter Palmer, Sandy Davidson, Steve Hashem and Erv Lessel.

I need to respond pre-emptively to a view I have struck a number of times since returning from Iraq. I have been accused of being 'captured' by the might of the American war machine. I deny that my respect for the US military stems from a fascination with their 'shiny toys of war', and I hope that the facts in this book will show what a demeaning accusation that is. Having worked in the 'belly of the beast' for a year, and having been exposed to the US military for a far longer period, I know its imperfections intimately. But I do not subscribe to some of the myths that exist in relation to our great and powerful friend. From a purely military point of view, no-one can do what the US military does around the world, and not just because of its size. I find it hard to see many functions that any other military, including the Australian Defence Force, performs better than the US military.

My view of both the Australian and US militaries is brutally realistic. Despite my admiration, I know better than most that all militaries are made up of fallible humans. And as the lone superpower, the US is tested so often that its failures are very public. Many militaries around the world do not do much of consequence. If you don't do much, you will rarely fail.

But most of all I wish to acknowledge the courage of the soldiers of the coalition and the emerging Iraqi Security Force. I was aware minute by minute that they were being asked to do things that were, by any society's standards, extraordinary. These tasks included: spending four-hour shifts on roadblocks in the middle of Ramadi or on the edge of Sadr City; conducting raids from helicopters in the dark of night on a booby-trapped farmhouse full of insurgents; conducting assaults on buildings full of jihadists in the middle of a hostile city; driving fuel trucks as part of a convoy on a major highway; participating in routine patrols in apparently quiet areas; and building schools in the suburbs of the most dangerous capital city in the world. In all of these endeavours, death is only a second away and any error of judgment or lack of discipline has dire consequences. The passing threats that I personally faced disappear into total insignificance compared with the most boring day in the life of many of these soldiers.

Lieutenant General Des Mueller, who retired as the Vice Chief of the Australian Defence Force and whose advice I have valued since I worked for him many years ago, pointed out that Henry David Thoreau, a US essayist, poet and philosopher, once said, 'How vain it is to sit down to write when you have not stood up to live.' I would like to think that I stood up and lived before I wrote.

Australia has been America's ally in every war we have fought since World War I – something no other country can claim. There can be no doubt that our countries' relationship is a special one. It is a relationship reflected in years of shared service and sacrifice in defense of our shared interests. Upon arriving in Iraq in July 2004, I was reminded daily of this special relationship serving side-by-side Major General Jim Molan, a dedicated and professional soldier.

Jim's service with the Multi-National Force in Iraq was magnificent in every respect. His contributions, including time as my Operations Officer, covered such challenging and historic events the November 2004 Battle of Fallujah and the inspiring elections in January 2005. Yet while Jim provides a fascinating *insiders* account of these and other events, this book is more than a history.

As a soldier with years of experience, Jim Molan knows that war, especially "war among the people", requires more than simply tactical and operational victories by men and women in uniform – victories Jim describes in this book. It requires substantial strategic patience and support from our domestic populace. In this respect, Jim's service in Iraq, against a dangerous enemy, is really continued here in this book. His experience-based explanation, in unambiguous terms, of what is at stake in the fight against violent extremism; of the nature of a war in which "victory" is both difficult to define and achieve; and of the costs and long term commitment required by free peoples to prevail in this struggle will contribute to our shared efforts in this and future wars.

Jim Molan is right, "freedom is not free."

General George W. Casey, Jr.
United States Army

The views presented in this foreword are my own and do not necessarily represent the views of the Department of Defense or its components.

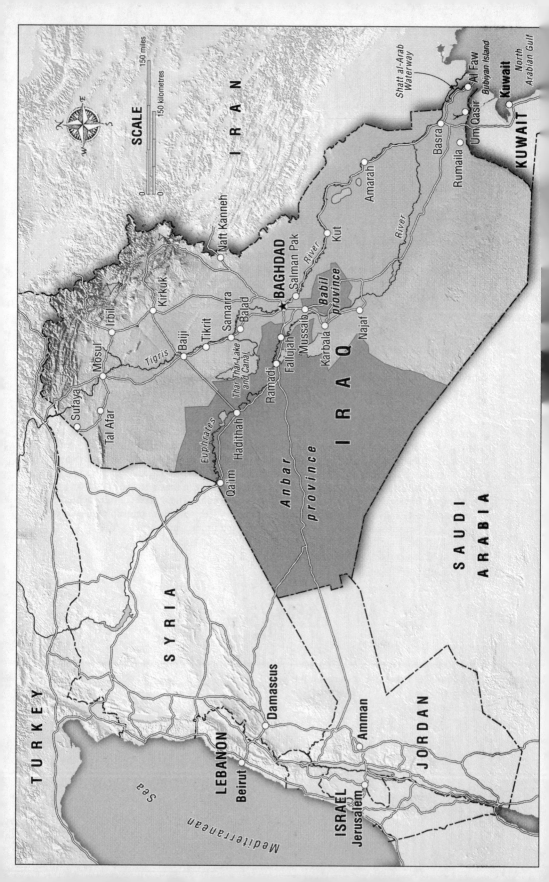

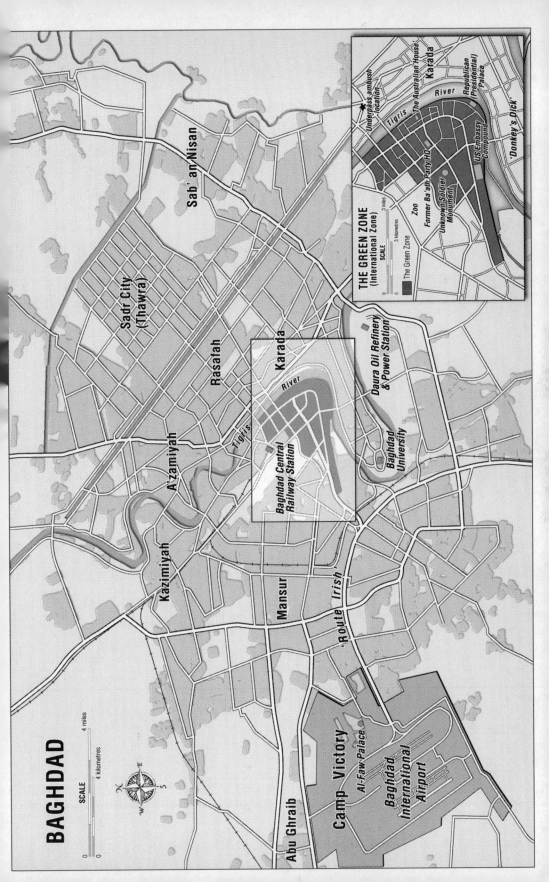

BAGHDAD

SCALE

0   4 miles

0   4 kilometres

Abu Ghraib

Camp Victory
Al-Faw Palace

Baghdad
International
Airport

Kazimiyah

Mansur

'Route Irish'

A'zamiyah

Rasafah

Sadr City
(Thawra)

Sab' an-Nisan

Karada

Tigris

River

Baghdad Central
Railway Station

Daura Oil Refinery
& Power Station

Baghdad
University

THE GREEN ZONE
(International Zone)

SCALE

0   3 kilometres

0   3 miles

The Green Zone

Underpass ambush
location

Karada

The Australian House

Tigris

River

Former Ba'ath Party HQ

Republican
(Presidential)
Palace

US Embassy
Compound

'Donkey's Dick'

Zoo

Unknown Soldier
Monument

RUNNING THE WAR IN IRAQ

CHAPTER 1

People, oil, history, suffering and dirt

Flying into Baghdad, April 2004

A hot slipstream blew through the open door as the Blackhawk helicopter swept over the dun-coloured buildings. This was certainly not Jakarta, where I had spent much of my adult life. This city had no high rises, no ultra-modern glass and metal, and little greenery. All it had in common with that great tropical city was the smog: a thickening grey as the evening set in.

Laid out before me was Baghdad, and Baghdad was the colour of the desert. I was apprehensive and could feel a knot in my stomach because I was now seeing it for the first time.

The footage of the first bombings of the invasion, now a year ago, had brought this cityscape into my lounge room as it had for millions of other people around the world. Now I looked upon it with an intense personal curiosity. We flew past a major highway that ran relatively straight from the airport to the city: the infamous Route Irish, referred to by journalists — with some justification — as the most dangerous road in the world. 'Route Irish' was a strange name for a road in Iraq, but the first US forces had renamed the major roads so they could actually pronounce them, usually after US States, cities, sporting teams or cars. For a second I wondered if Route Irish was named after the 'Fighting Irish', the famous Notre Dame University football team, but then the road was quickly behind me and I never remembered to ask anyone. As I was to find out, life moved fast here.

I had been in Iraq for less than a week, living at Camp Victory, a sprawling military complex on the outskirts of the city near Baghdad International Airport. Already I had observed some of the heaviest fighting since the end of major combat operations in April 2003 — the 'major combat operations' that now seemed only to have been an overture to the real war.

Our Blackhawk and another were flying to the Green Zone in the centre of Baghdad for a meeting. For safety, Blackhawks always flew in pairs. To confuse any potential attackers lying among the buildings below us, the pilots flew low and fast. Helicopters were often fired at by small arms or the devastating surface-to-air missile launchers which could be fired from a man's shoulder. The gunners on each side of me were calmly alert. I could hear the pilots' patter in my headset, professional and businesslike for the short trip.

Most Baghdad buildings were squat, I noticed, with an open and flat roof. Air conditioners hung off just about every one, as did satellite dishes — a major change from Saddam Hussein's rule, when satellite TV was banned. In the 12 months since their leader had been deposed by the US-led invasion, the Iraqis had been buying up big: even on buildings that you would think housed only one family there were two or three satellite dishes. A couple of times, as we briefly swooped below the tops of the higher buildings, I glimpsed the flicker of televisions.

Evidently the roof was an essential part of the typical Iraqi family's living space. Often there were several beds on the roof, or at least one large bed or couch, with carpets scattered around. The coalition watched roofs intently from high up in the sky, and sometimes the activity yielded a surprise. My staff told me that one night they watched two male Iraqi guards having sexual intercourse on a roof, courtesy of the TV feed from an unmanned drone flying silently far above. It was a great story, growing better at each telling, and may even have been true. The spy cameras were good, but their performance might have been enhanced by the human imagination. I retold the story many times over the next year, the duty one performs for the true apocryphal story.

The two helicopters banked out to the north of Route Irish, varying their approach to avoid ambush. We passed over a large date palm plantation, a surprise splash of green so close to the centre of a city of five and a half million. In the slum areas I could see what I knew to be sewage — big pools of standing water — a constant reminder to Iraqis of our failure to provide basic services.

In a straight line, the journey was no more than 10 kilometres, but our route covered at least twice that distance. We rounded an enormous mosque, its minarets standing alongside idle cranes. Unlit, at this time of day it gave the appearance of being abandoned.

And then for the first time I saw it, the single feature that makes Baghdad what it is: the Tigris River. I had stood on the banks of the Elbe in Germany and marvelled at its width and flow, and I had seen the short vicious rivers of New Guinea and Southeast Asia, hurtling down from the hills and blasting into the sea, but these lacked the gravitas of the world's great rivers, and there was no doubt about the might of the Tigris. This, I thought, is what Iraq is all about — water — but with people, oil, history, suffering and dirt thrown in.

We skimmed across the surface of the Tigris, nearly low enough to touch it, rose over a big water purification plant and US military barracks, then headed back south towards our destination. As we arced around, I could still make out the river through the Blackhawk's opposite side.

Thanks to the helicopter's noise and torrid slipstream, I could neither talk with colleagues nor read documents — flying, as I was to find out, was about the only time in Iraq when I stopped doing things.

I realised that although I had been in Iraq for a week, I was really only *arriving* this very instant. For the first time, I was filled with awe at where I was and what I was likely to do.

Of my own role, I still had only the vaguest idea. Only a few weeks earlier, I had been in Canberra commanding nothing more threatening than the Australian Defence Colleges. Now I was coming to take a key, but still unspecified, position in the world's most powerful army in its most critical and violent challenge. Although my knowledge of the Land of Two Rivers was shallow, I was reasonably well informed about Iraq's recent history: the 'Shock and Awe' invasion, the fall of Saddam, the transformation of the conflict into a protracted 'war among the people'. I came to Iraq believing that the war would shape global concepts of freedom, religion, human rights, democracy and the international order. I grasped the enormity of the stakes for the tens of millions of people directly implicated, and for billions of others who were more involved than they thought. I was firmly of the view that if this struggle was not resolved in Iraq, it would need to be resolved somewhere else.

Yet I also recognised that we had not managed to win the support of the people — either the Iraqis or our home populations. I was keenly aware that in little more than a year this conflict had given rise to new varieties of extremism, both religious and secular, and to the bitterest temper of anti-Americanism since Vietnam. I could only imagine how those who had stood with President George W. Bush on the deck of an aircraft carrier in 2003, under a banner proclaiming 'Mission Accomplished', might have regretted their presence.

When I arrived in Iraq, I did not see myself as an ideologue who had been mugged by reality. I did not believe that merely stating high-minded platitudes about freedom would be enough to convince a sceptical world. But nor was I in Iraq to join a debating society on the rights and wrongs of the original invasion. I was, and am, a practical man committed to solving problems, and was under no illusions about the size of the problem in Iraq in April 2004. The war's unpopularity had been fed by the now-established absence of weapons of mass destruction, dissolving one of the purported reasons for deposing Saddam, and by slowly mounting casualties. I did not need this war to teach me that without the active support of civilian populations, military conflicts are ultimately unwinnable. I knew that the international coalition was struggling to make progress in Iraqi cities using a 'bombs and bullets' approach; I knew it had been failing to coordinate the military, information, economic and political aspects of the struggle; I knew that the coalition had built up only a small Iraqi security force — just one infantry battalion was willing to fight with us in the current round of conflicts. Adding to these failures, faint whispers of the Abu Ghraib prison scandal, in which some American soldiers had humiliated their prisoners and themselves, were now being heard and would soon humiliate us all. Nations who had belonged to the original 'Coalition of the Willing' were under constant popular pressure to withdraw. Some left, some joined, and some others increased their commitment.

Whatever else I was doing in this uncomfortable aircraft seat, whatever the uncertainties swirling around me, I was sure of one thing: my presence here was a part of that commitment.

The two Blackhawks rose again, and I had the chance to look closely at the Tigris for the first time. It ran through the city roughly from north to south, making a few sweeping bends and then stretching straight for several kilometres, crossed regularly by bridges. It then swung abruptly to the west for about 4 kilometres and drooped down a bit before returning to its previous line. The peninsula formed by this loop was longer than it was wide, so I would soon be hearing it called, with male logic, the 'Donkey's Dick' or other phallic variations. In this area were the University of Baghdad and a prestigious housing estate that included the original Australian Embassy. The biggest power station and refinery within the city limits of Baghdad, called Daura, was just to the south of the Donkey's Dick. The bend where the river first headed to the west was a reverse 'L' that housed the Green Zone, our immediate destination.

The Tigris was sluggish along the edge of the Green Zone, but the way it formed eddies around the bridges' concrete pylons gave an impression of quiet strength. Alexander the Great had approached this river from both sides and taken his army across it several times. The city of Baghdad had expanded around the water. I could see bands of rushes, 3 or 4 metres wide, that fringed the river where there was no concrete bank. And I could still see a slight gleam of oil on the surface of the water, reflecting what little light was left of the day and the night lights of the city as they came on.

Where I crossed the Tigris, just to the south of an area called Adhamiya, the river was relatively narrow. This meant that for thousands of years, people had come to this place to cross. They had swum, boated or been ferried across until the bridges were built; these bridges had been spared by the coalition bombers during the April 2003 invasion.

As we crossed the river I looked through the Blackhawk's interior towards the south. Framed by my fellow travellers, I could see the Daura power station with its four smokestacks reaching high into the evening sky. Ominously, smoke issued from only one of the four.

Lights were now twinkling around Baghdad, a hint of normal life. At one or two points of the city I could see smoke rising into the sky — I wondered if it meant conflict or was just some mundane peaceful action. I looked out my side of the aircraft and saw what I soon learnt was Sadr City (later called Thawra), a Shi'ite neighbourhood of one million people that was to take much of our time and attention.

Below me, paralleling the river on both sides, ran what had once been pleasant wide boulevards. As we slowed down to land, I could see that these areas were now desolate and deserted, cut off from the rest of the city by concrete barricades and kilometres of barbed and razor wire. The park benches that must have allowed Baghdadis to contemplate their mighty river were now bare slabs. There was even a large playground with gaudily painted attractions; it looked sad without the children, and sadder for the neglect. Lamp-posts had been left where they had fallen, and there was a general air of foreboding about the place. The many cafés and businesses along the east side of the river were closed, shutters down.

Individual structures lay ruined by the war. Once we got close to the centre of the city, I was able to see that some major buildings had been destroyed. Often a side had been blasted out or the front had collapsed, or the building had a small hole in the top and one side blown out. Some buildings had been hit so often they were a pile of rubble under the metal skeleton that invariably seems to survive modern weaponry.

Over my headset I heard the pilots receive clearance from an air traffic controller with an Australian accent. She instructed us to approach the landing pad in the Green Zone, called Washington Pad. We were warned of other aircraft in the vicinity — I had seen several other helicopters during our flight from Camp Victory.

The Green Zone was right in the centre of Baghdad. Both legs of the reversed 'L' were about 3 kilometres long and perhaps 2 kilometres wide. The area had a high wall most of the way around it, studded by surveillance devices, and five heavily guarded entrances. The area had been the administrative centre of Saddam's Iraq. Now the coalition were the new tenants. By April 2004 it was the home of the Coalition Provisional Authority (CPA) — the civilian occupation government — led by US Ambassador L. Paul 'Jerry' Bremer III, the supreme civil authority in Iraq. It was also where the new Interim Iraqi Government would be accommodated. The zone was coded 'green' because it was (or was considered to be) a secure area. Other parts of Baghdad were referred to as 'red'. As soon as you left the Green Zone you entered the Red Zone, where anything was likely to happen and very often did.

Major Saddam-era palaces, the palace complex of one of his sons, the premium residential areas and the old embassy precinct all lay within the Green Zone. One of the biggest buildings was the former Ba'ath Party headquarters, now almost totally destroyed by bombing but with one of Iraq's more impressive bunker networks still intact in its bowels. On the western side of the Green Zone was the old Baghdad Zoo, now empty of those animals once notoriously 'nurtured' by Saddam's son Uday. The Tomb of the Unknown Soldier stood out because of the familiar statue of crossed swords often seen on Saddam-era video footage. Straddling the Green Zone's north wall were a number of multi-storey hotels and government buildings.

Washington Pad was the only helicopter landing area within the Green Zone, although helicopters could and did land in many other open places. The key to flying and moving safely around Baghdad was always to be unpredictable. Within the wall that surrounded the Green Zone, Washington Pad had its own even higher wall to protect helicopters from rockets or mortars, which were regularly fired in from surrounding suburbs. Washington Pad was big, able to take six to eight Blackhawks or Apache gunships at the one time or several of the bigger, twin-rotor Chinooks.

The Blackwater security company's helicopter operation was also at Washington Pad, and several of their Little Bird helicopters were parked next to a big maintenance hangar. These helicopters were a constant feature of life in Baghdad, particularly in the Green Zone. Highly manoeuvrable and fast, they were favoured by the US Special Forces. Blackwater imitated Special Forces techniques by having 'shooters' sitting in the door areas of helicopters with rifles. The Little Birds were the top of the fleet: aerial escorts for Ambassador Bremer and successive ambassadors, among other activities. I found out later that security for Bremer for the last six months of his time in Iraq cost something in the order of US$15 million. I was also to learn that the radio call sign for these aircraft was, for some bizarre reason, 'Arse Monkey'.

But what really caught my eye as we hovered towards the pad was Saddam's Republican Palace off to my left, nestled against the river. Even from a few hundred metres away it was impressive; I could understand why it was a symbol of Saddam's regime. The palace did not appear to be more than about a decade old. It was not a Western kind of palace, with turrets or crenellations; it was a vast administrative building that demonstrated the power of the regime. Its entrances were imposing, with a liberal use of columns, magnificent doorways, and tiled rotundas. One entrance area had a painting of a missile streaking up to the heavens, and when I arrived there were still pictures of Saddam himself painted on some walls — but they were covered up. The palace had reception areas that now housed operations centres and living areas with bathrooms and tawdry gold-painted fittings that were now offices. It was two and in some parts three storeys high, and at the highest points Saddam had placed giant busts of himself dressed in the garb of various Mesopotamian kings: Hammurabi and Nebuchadnezzar, for example. These had been removed and were now stored near a shooting range not far from the palace. Like the Tigris, and like everything else in Iraq, the palace was the colour of the desert, only relieved by a few sad palms trees in gardens that showed the effects of being driven over by numerous heavy armoured and tracked vehicles. Along with Saddam's al-Faw Palace back at Camp Victory, I was to become very familiar with the Republican Palace. It was to become, in its unique way, my new home.

CHAPTER 2

A soldier in a time of peace

My life before Iraq

A few weeks earlier, with the Canberra leaves turning and the heat of another Australian summer almost forgotten, I could never have imagined I would ever see the Tigris, let alone be flying over Baghdad during a time of war. But in retrospect, I can now see that everything in my military life had pointed me towards something like Iraq. Although Baghdad was a long way away and my experience as an Australian soldier had focused on our region, soldiers in even the most peaceful countries are constantly preparing themselves, consciously and unconsciously, for the possibility of conflict. By 2004 I had been tested in some unusual situations — as an infantry commander and trainer, staff officer, army helicopter pilot and military diplomat in Indonesia, interspersed with periods in our military schools and colleges — but I had always sensed deep down that before I finished being a soldier, I would face a test that would push me to my furthest limits.

War and soldiering had been part of my life for as long as I could remember; perhaps they were part of my DNA. I was born in 1950, at the end of the charnel house that was the first half of the twentieth century. My father was away almost continuously for the last four years of World War II. War separates and unsettles families, and I believe that my parents' desire to have many children — I have a brother and four sisters — was as much a product of war as of the supposed Catholic wish for bigger families.

Mine was an archetypal Australian Irish-Catholic family of that era, and my father had a lifelong chip on his shoulder about being a Catholic. Whenever he encountered a problem in his career or social life, he blamed it on his faith, even though, ironically, he did not seem especially devout.

Our mother, Noni Molan, certainly was; the family revolved around her. Mum imbued in us a pronounced work ethic — both a blessing and a curse! She understood the value of education and insisted that we all get the chance to go to university. She needed to insist because Dad believed that as soon as we had completed even part of our secondary education, we should go out to work.

My parents had different views on a lot of things, one of which seems to have been my name. I was baptised Andrew James Molan, Andrew being my father's first name. But I was always known as Jim because, the explanation went, the name Andrew was very common in our extended family. It might also have been because my second name came from my mother's father, James Harnetty. An educated member of the establishment in Victoria, he was head of the State public service through the 1920s and '30s. I recall black and white photographs of him looking sternly Victorian — in the other sense of the word. We children liked to look at his imperial decoration, the Commander of the British Empire, which we sometimes took out of its box in our mother's drawer.

Australia has a remarkable military history and perhaps, somehow, that history passed into my blood. Like most families, each year we celebrated the April 1915 landing and battles against the Turks on the Gallipoli Peninsula. In typically complicated

Australian fashion, our most powerful national day commemorates an event that was certainly no victory, except a victory of the human spirit. Costing us 8000 dead from a tiny, basically rural population of 4 million, 14 years after our Federation as a country, Gallipoli was our cruel blooding into nationhood. But Gallipoli was only the beginning of World War I's lasting trauma on Australian society. The new industrial warfare of the Western Front consumed 54,000 Australian lives, and over 100,000 returned with their wounds. My godfather had been badly gassed in France, and I have a childhood memory of uncharitably wanting to escape from the unpleasantness of visiting him with my mother at his dark, quiet house. That would have been in the early 1950s; I can only assume the poor man had been like this, virtually crippled and blind, for more than 30 years.

The trauma of the 'war to end all wars' did not dent Australia's willingness to flock to the colours to fight as part of the Commonwealth in 1939. Australia quickly raised four high-quality divisions with supporting troops, led by men with vast experience of combat in World War I; there were still many such leaders. The mass of the army was made up of young men raised in an egalitarian, well-educated, and healthy society who rose quickly to become excellent leaders as the battlefield took its toll. By the time we were directly threatened, after the Japanese attack on Pearl Harbor in December 1941 and the fall of Singapore, Australia was ready to commit totally to the war, a totality of commitment that is often forgotten today, even by Australians.

My father, Andrew Myles Molan, could not be held back from joining that effort. The odds were against his serving. Born in 1912, he was older than most enlistees and was, by 1939, a married man. To boot, he worked in a protected industry as a radio technician, having attended the very first radio course conducted in the Royal Melbourne Institute of Technology. He missed the first call-up but managed to serve from 1941 to 1945, reaching the rank of Warrant Officer Class One, the highest level for a non-commissioned officer.

In 1945, despite being offered a commission in the post-war army, he returned to civilian life. Radio was now only a hobby for him, and when I was born in 1950, Dad worked in the sales area of General Motors Holden, at that time the largest car manufacturer in Australia.

Growing up, I did all the 'normal' kid things: I played soldiers and wars and made models of military equipment in our 1940s house in the quiet Melbourne suburb of Ivanhoe. The end of World War II spelt by no means the end of war for Australians. Most of my father's military comrades returned, like him, to civilian life, but some missed the mateship and the adventure and, within a few years, rejoined the army to fight in Korea, where Australian forces were again among the first to deploy. The fighting in Korea was serious combat, and Australian forces performed brilliantly, staffed by many who had seen it all before. As tensions rose in Southeast Asia, Australia soon had forces in Malaya and, later, Vietnam.

Only a stone's throw from our house was one of the biggest veterans' hospitals in Australia. The Heidelberg Repatriation Hospital treated the long-term injured from both world wars and, as I grew up, from Korea, Malaya and Vietnam. My sister Elizabeth nursed there, my brother Maurice worked there as a young doctor, and my many uncles, most of whom were 'returned men', went in and out of there for treatment. Dad was treated there before he died in 1987 from a respiratory illness contracted during his military service.

The military exerted a pull on me from a young age. I attended the Christian Brothers College in East Melbourne — known as 'Parade' or the 'Bluestone Pile' — where students were usually able to join the military cadets in the fourth year of secondary school. But if you were willing to go into the band, you could join one year earlier. I was so eager that I signed up for the cadet band at the age of 13, in 1963. For my first 12 months in uniform, my main challenge was pretending to play the B-flat bugle.

When I left school I was 17 and, with the Vietnam War at its height, I was determined to join the army. The big battles over higher education had been settled by my three older sisters, all of whom went on to tertiary studies. My mother, essentially, had won the argument. By the time I finished school, my father would have agreed with her that education was the key to success in Australia.

Fortunately, there was a way of getting into the army that did not mean missing out on higher education. The Royal Military College (RMC), at Duntroon in Canberra, offered a four-year tertiary course — three years of a university degree and one year of military work. My application was successful and I entered Duntroon on 26 January 1968, Australia Day, the first of many public holidays that I was to miss in the military.

Although I was barely aware of it at the time, 1968 was a troubled year for Australia and the world. Not only were Australians fighting in Vietnam, but there were student riots in Paris, the Tet offensive occurred in Vietnam, the Cultural Revolution was raging in China, the Soviets invaded Czechoslovakia, and anti-war demonstrations took place across the US. Despite this ominous background, I left Melbourne for Duntroon with my parents' blessing. A photo staged by the local newspaper on my departure shows me as a tall, slim, fair-haired young man, slightly self-conscious. Strangely, I have an overnight bag in my hand, as if I am leaving my parents for nothing longer than a weekend.

Duntroon soon ironed out most of that callowness. In my first year, thanks to the emphasis on physical training, I grew taller and broader and more self-confident. The anti-Catholic discrimination which my parents had warned me against was never a feature of the army I joined — or of broader Australian society by that time. The only discrimination I ever experienced in the army was that which divides Australian society at all levels: football. The Australian Army is dominated by rugby union, and anyone with a predilection for Australian Rules football was forced with all the other Victorians, South Australians, Tasmanians and Western Australians into our own Saturday afternoon ghetto. But at least we were not as badly off as those who played soccer or, even worse, hockey!

I had only played Australian Rules seriously for a year before I joined the army, and that was at the insistence of our local parish priest, Kevin Toomey, who, having played for Collingwood, was a hero to us all. I was good at it because I was 6 foot 3 inches (1.9 metres) tall, and I became a better player as my body toughened up with army life. I will never forget the comradeship of my army teams, and as the military moved me around the country I managed to play at relatively high levels in Brisbane and Melbourne. I last pulled my boots on in 2003, at the age of 53. My knees told me afterwards that this was probably the most stupid thing I have ever done.

On joining the army I had expected to go to Vietnam, but the world changed rapidly during my four years at Duntroon. Every aspect of our life at RMC was dominated by Vietnam. Our force there was approximately 8000 strong: a three-battalion brigade with tanks, air and naval support. We Duntroon cadets had to memorise the newspaper descriptions of the battles and regurgitate the news to our cadet seniors at breakfast. This activity — which, I hasten to add, we performed with naive acceptance — was one of the least objectionable parts of the hazing, or 'bastardisation', which was then a central feature at Duntroon. When the Tet Offensive broke across Vietnam in my first few months in the army, I saw it as just another battle which, apparently, we won. But the true significance in terms of lives lost and bodies broken, as well as the impact on winning or losing a war, was well beyond me.

Due to the nature of the fighting in Vietnam, at RMC our training and thoughts focused on counterinsurgency. All our tactics were jungle tactics, and all our exercises were counterinsurgency exercises. Guest speakers spoke to us about Vietnam, and our military instructors were either posted to the college from tours in Vietnam or went from the RMC to Vietnam. I remember being tremendously impressed by one staff member, Captain Ivan Cahill, who was posted to Duntroon following a tour of duty with the US Marines in Khe Sanh, scene of a memorably long and vicious battle. Not only was he a hero, he was a local Ivanhoe boy!

Watching classes ahead of us graduate and go to Vietnam, we assumed we would do the same. We listened to tape-recorded radio nets from Vietnam where the previous year's graduates were in combat, and behind the clipped voices we could hear rocket-propelled grenades slamming into the turrets of the venerable Centurion tanks. On our exercises, we were hearing the very sounds of Vietnam, if not through the quirks of radio-wave propagation then at least in our imaginations.

In 1971, my last year at Duntroon, the war was slowing down for Australia. I received a posting notification to a battalion of the Royal Australian Regiment that would deploy to Vietnam in 1972. But US forces were pulling out, handing over to local Vietnamese forces, and our government started withdrawing Australian troops. Shortly before graduation, my posting was changed to the next most exciting option, the Pacific Islands Regiment in Papua New Guinea.

As a newly graduated lieutenant, I belonged to the first generation of Australian officers to spend a career preparing for war while rarely, if ever, being exposed to combat. Undoubtedly this is a triumph of diplomacy and good fortune for the nation but it presents a challenge for a professional military force. With few exceptions, the ADF spent many years without the experience of sustained close combat that was the central experience of Australian soldiers from World War I until the end of Vietnam. This has been a constant challenge of my professional life: armies are far better if they are used, but giving them experience can never be a rationale for using them.

My posting to the Pacific Islands Regiment in 1972 was the first of many to countries that were moving from a colonial or post-colonial past to something that approximated a democratic future. The culmination of this would be Iraq, and of course Iraq was the most difficult and the most dangerous. My boss in Iraq in 2004, General George Casey, once reported a conversation he'd had with Donald Rumsfeld, then the US Secretary of Defense. Rumsfeld had observed that since the 1950s, an average of one-and-a-half new countries per year had come into existence, most as democracies. In my life as a soldier, I have accompanied five of these countries down their road to democracy.

The first was Papua New Guinea, where at 21 years of age I was a platoon commander of 30 Melanesian soldiers in the 1st Battalion Pacific Island Regiment. My two classmates and I were the last Australian platoon commanders posted to the Pacific Island Regiment, which had been raised to fight the Japanese in 1942 and whose leadership was now being steadily localised.

In two-and-a-half years there, I spent much of my time on 'patrols' of four to six weeks walking through the mountains and jungles with weapons, ammunition and a heavy pack. We walked from village to village telling the local people that there was a country called Papua New Guinea, and they were it! This was nation-building at its most basic. It is not disparaging to say that many parts of Papua New Guinea had just emerged from the stone age. We would stop at a village overnight and put up the PNG flag, talk to the people and give small demonstrations of what soldiers did. We also offered basic medical treatment. It was an incredible experience but one I was almost incapable of appreciating: I was deeply frustrated at having missed out on going to war after four years of preparation.

Outside of combat, there could be few better preparations for a life of soldiering than a posting to Papua New Guinea. In Port Moresby, the police would call on us for riot control after Saturday afternoon football matches. Being considerably taller and whiter than my soldiers, I was a target for projectile-throwers, and I discovered that to survive as an officer, you must learn to duck. I started to develop some judgment and gain confidence in my physical strength and endurance. I also experienced the beginnings of a deep sense, an intuition possibly unique to military life, that perhaps I had some of the courage and quickness of mind needed to be a successful soldier.

PNG was a savage introduction to service life for my wife, Anne, who was then 21. We'd met during my second year at Duntroon and married when I graduated. To the yawns of our children I often tell the totally untrue story that having known Anne for three years I went to PNG and then wrote back to her in Canberra suggesting vaguely that we should think about getting married, only to be sent a copy of the engagement notice from the *Canberra Times* by return post. The truth was that I carried my new wife across the threshold of an awful apartment I'd found in a suburb of Port Moresby, and nearly dropped her because on the doorstep was a hairy spider the size of my fist that reared up and actually hissed at us. Welcome to the tropics! As a platoon commander, my separations from her were long and frequent, but she handled loneliness in a foreign country with her usual calm style. I still cannot believe how she did it.

Together we watched PNG achieve self-government and so peaceably take its first step on the road to democracy.

I left the Pacific Islands Regiment in late 1974, and Anne and I embarked on a travelling scholarship I had won as a cadet at

Duntroon. The scholarship, plus some accrued leave, enabled us to go on the road for six months.

We made up for our times of separation, travelling the world together on local transport. We started in PNG and went through Portuguese East Timor, westwards through Indonesia, up through Southeast Asia, across Burma, India and Pakistan, through Afghanistan and Iran and into Turkey to see Gallipoli, then on to Europe. At the time, such a trip was almost a rite of passage for young Australians.

We met the youth of the Western world on the 'hippie trail' to Europe. Since leaving school I had been in a conservative, disciplined institution and then in the jungle. We both found that the so-called hippies were mostly a fine group of people. We fell in with some Canadians in Bali, and travelled with them for much of the way to Europe. Their values may have been different from ours in some minor respects, but they were great people, we were young and seeing the world, and our differences didn't matter. On the way back from Europe I went to Vietnam just to say that I had seen it. For a week I was a tourist in a war zone.

In those six months of travel and three years of absence from Australia, we had passed through thousands of years of world history, and we returned with the knowledge, more hard-won than a mere slogan, that we lived in the best country in the world.

While I had merely felt frustrated at missing Vietnam, the war there had had a far more serious impact on the Australian Army, and on Australian society as a whole. In the 1970s, our society seemed to choose to forget that we even had an army. The army was going backwards in strength and capability. Meanwhile, I was going upwards in rank. Army life was interesting but seldom exciting. I spent some time with a Reserve unit and a year learning to speak Indonesian, but then I took a most unconventional detour for an infantry officer: I decided to fly helicopters in the Australian Army Aviation Corps.

The army consists of tribes, or 'corps', each of which regards the others with more than a little suspicion. It was not my intention to leave the Royal Australian Infantry Corps for good, only for this one posting as a pilot. For a soldier, modern infantry has a unique nobility: it is the ultimate combat force. But the Australian infantry post-Vietnam was in a poor state. It had not recovered from extensive manpower cuts, and (understandably, perhaps) its ideas were focused firmly on the war that had just consumed it.

The growing Aviation Corps, desperately short of pilots, was plundering other corps as well as recruiting people from outside the military. I was the first infantry officer to take such a path and the system was not used to it. My Infantry Corps personnel managers were very critical of this deviation, telling me in a thinly veiled threat that if I left Infantry Corps even for a few years, I would prejudice my career prospects and disadvantage myself when competing for future infantry command positions.

But in my search for something different, I took the risk — and spent three magnificent years flying light reconnaissance helicopters with the 1st Aviation Regiment. As a pilot I gained a broader understanding of all the army's interlocking and complex parts, and a love of aviation that exists to this day.

Just to prove they had a sense of humour, when I finished my flying, the Infantry Corps personnel managers posted me as second-in-command of an infantry company in South Australia, the exact position that had caused me to consider aviation in the first place. If you can't take a joke, don't join the infantry!

When I returned to the infantry, however, the army was three years further ahead in recovering from Vietnam. The honour of serving with the Third Battalion of the Royal Australian Regiment, with its unsurpassable history and traditions, restored my battered faith in the Infantry Corps.

I worked my way through the system during the late 1970s and early '80s. Rarely did I get the posting I wanted, but without fail my postings turned out to be great. One of the most rewarding was as the senior instructor for tactics at our Infantry Centre — the school where all modern Australian infantrymen of all ranks are trained in their combat skills — in the beautiful Hunter River Valley north of Sydney, with the rank of major. As a teacher, I had the opportunity to think deeply for the first time about the profession of soldiering, and now I had enough experience to make some sense of it all. I was also surrounded by Australian infantrymen who had served in Korea, Malaya and Vietnam, and just living with these men, and hearing about their extraordinary experiences, added to my knowledge and changed some of my attitudes.

Not only did I teach, I also studied. Over many years I completed a degree in economics from the University of Queensland to match the degree in history I had gained at Duntroon, and I kept up my Indonesian language skills and my flying skills in what passed for my leisure time. Despite my personnel manager's warnings when I went flying, I commanded an infantry rifle company of 100 soldiers in the 3rd Battalion in South Australia; I was selected to attend the year-long course that prepares certain officers for the middle period of their career (called Command and Staff College — a key gateway to senior rank); and I commanded a 600-man infantry battalion, the 6th Battalion of the Royal Australian Regiment in Brisbane, in the rank of lieutenant colonel. After I had spent two years commanding the 6th Battalion, the army surprised me again by creating the new position of army attaché in Indonesia at the rank of colonel and offering it to me.

By 1992, the roller-coaster relationship between Australia and its enormous northern neighbour was as bad as it has ever been. Australia and Indonesia are divided by racial, religious, economic, ideological and cultural differences; we are as unlike as any two countries on the face of this earth. Tensions regularly bubbled to the surface and Australians had fought Indonesians on the Malayan Peninsula and in Borneo. The often brutal Indonesian occupation of East Timor, across the Timor Sea from Darwin, kept our differences in Australians' minds. In 1986 the journalist David Jenkins had written an article in Australia's robust media that was openly critical of the Suharto family, and as a result almost every link between Australia and Indonesia was severed. It was in this climate of mutual suspicion that I was sent to Indonesia, with Anne and our four very young children in tow. Before going, I was briefed by the just-appointed Chief of Army, Lieutenant General John Grey, who said, 'Jim, I am not sure exactly what I want in the army-to-army relationship with Indonesia, but I want a lot of it.'

I obliged him over the next three years by setting up a relationship between the Indonesian and Australian armies that was more extensive than the Indonesians had with any army in the world. I perfected my language skills, and within three years I knew every significant figure in the Indonesian Army, a familiarity that later proved enormously useful.

At the end of 1994 I returned from Indonesia and was promoted to brigadier, commanding the army's 1st Brigade, a dispersed mechanised force of 3200 soldiers being centralised in one big modern base in Darwin. During this period I was subject to a seminal experience that was to repay me greatly in Iraq.

The command elements of the 1st Brigade were invited by the US to participate in the 'Warfighter' program, formally called the Battle Command Training Program. This was a key feature of the reinvigoration of the US Army after Vietnam and represented a true revolution in training for war. It culminated in two three-week exercises in the US, exposing me to a US military that Australian veterans of Vietnam would never have recognised. Since I had joined the army, almost every story I had heard from my superiors and every account that I had read concentrated on the deficiencies of our powerful friend. I believed that US soldiers were certainly brave but far from competent. This way of thinking was also part of Australian military folklore — we had always fought in coalition with more powerful friends who had led us into disaster. For the British at Gallipoli, substitute the Americans in Vietnam. We spoke of how the US lost the Vietnam War, not how 'we' lost the Vietnam War.

For me, these myths were upended by the 'Warfighter' program, in which I was able to 'fight' for an extended period against a 'live' enemy that was clever, unpredictable and much more experienced than me. I was now working with the best commanders in the world. The climax of the program was a period in Washington State with the US I Corps, working in a future Korean conflict scenario. We fought day in and day out with the most professional simulated enemy that this sophisticated system could produce.

I was provided with a senior mentor, known as a 'greybeard'. Dick Cavasos was a famous retired four-star general. He watched how I commanded, how I organised my staff, how I ran a battle, and he offered me advice from his extraordinary reserve of experience gained over 40 years and four or five wars. In fact, he enthusiastically shared his knowledge with almost every member of my staff. Most importantly, he knew how to mentor and did not try to take over. My commanders and I learnt an extraordinary amount just from his presence in the headquarters, walking and chatting and debriefing us on every big and little thing that we did. As a Korean War veteran, his most enduring piece of advice to me was only half in jest: 'If you get a choice,' he said during a pause in the battle, 'don't fight the North Koreans!'

This was the first time I had been exposed in detail to a Western military at a high level. As a captain I'd had a valuable posting to a British mechanised battalion in Germany, but I was now observing senior US command. I'd always joked that the army never posted me anywhere overseas where you could drink the water. Now in Washington State, under the shadow of the Cascade Mountains, I saw how rigorous and dynamic the Americans really were in their soldiering, having learnt from the trauma of Vietnam. Failure is without doubt the best teacher.

I could not avoid making comparisons with my own army and the battalions I commanded in the 1st Brigade during the mid-'90s. I concluded that at the lower levels, at what we in the military call 'units' (battalions of approximately 600 soldiers headed by lieutenant colonels), the Australian Army was certainly competent but dangerously underequipped and often undermanned. As we used to say at the Infantry Centre, our fathers in World War II would have felt quite at home 50 years later in our infantry battalions. And at the higher brigade and division levels, by the mid-'90s we were furiously trying to catch up with the mid-'50s.

Even at the time, I considered that these exercises 'made' me as an operational commander. Nearly a decade later, in Iraq, the lessons I learnt from this program would pay off many times over.

After I finished my two years as a brigade commander, to my surprise Indonesia beckoned again. The defence attaché was leaving, and I, having come home from Indonesia as the army attaché with language skills, great contacts and a credible track record, returned to Jakarta at one level higher.

As our eldest daughter, Sarah, was approaching the critical last two years of schooling, she remained in Australia at boarding school. Anne and I and our three youngest children, Erin, Felicity and Michael, left Australia two days after Christmas Day in 1997.

The Asian economic crisis had smashed Thailand a few months before, and we all wondered which fragile economy would be next. Would it get to Australia, and would it have military consequences? In the first week of January 1998, as my predecessor was briefing me,

Indonesia's economy suffered the first staggers in a series of collapses that over a few months would wipe out the savings of the nation and destroy the middle class. Since his ascent to power in a coup d'état in 1967, Suharto had established a compact with the people: as long as prosperity continued, the Indonesian people would sacrifice certain freedoms and tolerate dominance by Suharto, his family and his generals. But as the economy collapsed, the compact dissolved. Once Suharto fell — an event that led to Australia's involvement in East Timor — I found myself for the second time in a country going through the birth pains of democracy. What followed my appointment was two years of incredible events in the midst of an economy and society in freefall. Because of the Indonesian Army's power, my office's ability to maintain contacts with our friends and know what was going on was vital.

In May 1998, rioting erupted across Jakarta. The city seemed to be burning from one end to the other, and about 2000 Indonesians were killed. The army factionalised, loaded up with live ammunition and deployed onto the streets of the city.

Anne and the children were in the centre of this turmoil, living outside the relatively secure embassy precinct in the suburb of Kuningan Barat. As the violence increased, so did my workload, and the vagaries of Jakarta traffic meant that many of us in the embassy's defence section were sleeping on stretchers in our offices, not with our families. The sudden rioting and killing passed through the neighbourhood where Anne and the children were hunkered down before we knew what was happening or how to respond. Mobs roamed the roads between the embassy and our house, and I could only rely on what I heard over the phone from Anne, our intelligence sources, and my Indonesian Army friends. The rioting got so close to the house that I told Anne she had to leave right away and get to friends in a more secure part of Jakarta. With her great presence of mind, she hid the children under blankets in the back of the car, sat in the front with our family driver, and they drove through streets full of rioters and burning buildings to safety.

Within a few days, she and the children, along with almost all the 10,000 Australians in Jakarta who had not already left, were evacuated back to Australia. This was the first of three evacuations in the next two years. The first was the biggest; relatively few Australians outside the embassy stayed in Jakarta, and few returned before things really settled down. The subsequent two evacuations mainly concerned dependants and non-essential personnel in the embassy. After the first evacuation, we made the decision to leave the two girls with their elder sister at a boarding school in Canberra, and when things quietened down a little, Anne and our young son, Michael, returned, with the expectation that they would again be evacuated if there were signs of trouble — which happened.

A milestone for Indonesia's journey towards democracy was the first post-Suharto session of the Indonesian Parliament, held over several days and, ominously, due to end on Friday 13 November 1998. The interim president, B.J. Habibie, and the members of this once docile parliament were now to define the future political process, particularly the critical election laws. This became a focus for dissent, especially by student groups who suspected that the Suharto remnants would fight democracy and try to revive his power.

Many hundreds of thousands of protesters were on the streets of Jakarta every night, pressuring the parliamentary process with their aggressive presence. The students and others assembled at the centrally located Catholic University (where Anne used to teach English), closely watched by the security forces. The protesters would charge against the riot troops, who would rebuff them and counter-charge, firing tear gas. After a break, the cycle repeated itself.

I was following events closely and keeping Canberra informed. I located my staff either in hotel rooms overlooking critical parts of

the city or, as I was, unarmed and in civilian clothes on the streets
with the Indonesian troops. Our embassy political officers were
among the students and protesters. By talking to each other, we
could monitor both sides.

We Australians had the permission of Indonesian authorities to be
there, but a friend of mine who was head of Indonesian intelligence
had warned me, 'Pak Jim, you can put your people out, and I will tell
my officers on the spot not to arrest them, but if you do it, you must
understand that we cannot protect you.' My friend's priorities were
with his agents, who were constantly at risk. Early on 'Friday the
13th', one of his officers amid the protesting students at the Catholic
University had forgotten to turn off a hidden radio; someone heard
it crackle, his cover was blown, and he was beaten to death on the
spot. We became adept at ducking down alleys and hiding in
doorways, but what caught us out regularly was the tear gas.

On the night of the 13th, everything came to a crescendo. By our
estimates, the numbers of protesters swelled to at least half a million of
Jakarta's 12 million people. By 5pm the protesters had forced the riot
police to pull back as far as the Semanggi flyover, a choke point on
the highway to the parliament, and the scene was set for a showdown.

I was beside the Indonesian Army colonel who ran the 10,000
troops deployed around the parliament: there were heavy battalions,
in their Darth Vader gear, and more mobile light riot troops. It
surprised me to see a junior officer commanding such a critical
activity. The colonel handled the situation well, however. He
positioned himself at the front of his troops, watched by 500,000
protesters, and surrounded himself with a military police bodyguard
that faced all directions and shielded him from the missiles thrown
by the crowd. Close by him were his 'shooters', a small group of
riflemen that he could authorise rapidly to use live ammunition.
Between bouts of fighting, he rested his light and heavy troops on
the grassy verge of the flyover.

Jakarta's temperature varies only between 28°C at night and 35°C during the day, and every day approached 100 per cent humidity. These riots had been going on for weeks, and the troops were tired. There had been repeats of the 'mysterious killings' that characterised previous dissent, where elements in the Indonesian military were suspected of acting extrajudicially and assassinating dissidents: to this day, the 500 or so injured, and upwards of 20 student deaths that remain unsolved is an open wound. Powerful forces in the Indonesian military were not supporting the army's withdrawal from politics or the country's move to democracy. So there was much at stake for this colonel in terms of both how he controlled his troops and how he managed this extreme manifestation of the voice of the people. Understandably, there was little sympathy for the Indonesian military after 32 years of Suharto rule. The protesters seemed less interested in storming the parliament than in attacking the troops. It was noticeable that the colonel's superiors were staying away in droves.

The protesters became more daring, their attacks more effective. As the night went on, they started throwing molotov cocktails. The soldiers began losing patience. Normally they used only blank ammunition, fired to frighten the rioters, but some placed stolen live ammunition in their magazines. Now, when a push was over, there were dead or injured bodies lying in front of the troops. Ambulance sirens added to the wall of noise: the horrendous screaming and chanting, interspersed by the riot troops bashing their batons in cadence on their riot shields. To spread confusion, one feral faction within the Indonesian military were sniping indiscriminately from the tall office blocks, firing at both the protesters and the riot police, trying to create the utmost anarchy and so collapse the parliamentary process.

The colonel did not activate his shooters, although some of his soldiers illegally shot live rounds. He kept his head even when his troops were being shot at by their feral comrades. He brought in the water cannon vehicles at the right time, and pushed the protesters back a reasonable distance without overdoing it. He did not lose overall control, and he put a lot of effort into rotating his tired troops. He was a man caught between the old Suharto world and the new world of democracy. Later, many commentators, including some in the pro-democracy factions of the military, called for the colonel's blood. Whenever an opportunity arose, I told my Indonesian friends how well the colonel had done, despite the incompetence of their system and the appalling lack of discipline of some of his troops.

Midnight came and went, and word spread that the parliament, supported strongly by the younger progressives in the military faction, had passed the election laws in a form that favoured true democracy. After the students realised that democracy had won the day, the colonel went forwards with only a few members of his bodyguard and met with the student leaders. Within an hour, by the light of burning buildings and cars, the troops and the students were arm in arm on the highway that for most of the day had been a killing ground, singing a popular and beautiful Islamic hymn in the warm tropical night.

We reported this extraordinary sight to a disbelieving Canberra. After checking that all our people were accounted for, we set off to our homes to sleep. On foot, I passed students walking home interspersed with soldiers moving back to their barracks. A general who was a close friend of mine later confided with pride that two of his teenage children had been on the streets that night, with the protesters. Life was indeed strange in Jakarta, and the people would ultimately triumph over authoritarianism and violence.

But there was one more significant impediment for Indonesia on its road to democracy — East Timor.

East Timor had been a major focus for the Australian Embassy in Jakarta for years, and I had visited many times, normally with my Indonesian Army contacts. When President Habibie offered the East

Timorese a plebiscite in 1999, we were as surprised as the Indonesian Army, who were absolutely astounded. Nothing since the fall of Suharto had so emphasised the military's loss of power. None of us could predict what would happen.

My main focus was still on evacuation. As the plebiscite approached, we evacuated the military families and some of the political officers' families from the embassy in Jakarta. It didn't look good but we had no choice: if things went bad, as we feared they might, the military and political officers in the embassy would not be able to look after their own families.

On my recommendation, Australia deployed five attaché staff to East Timor ready to evacuate the thousand or so Australian citizens and other foreign nationals if necessary. The army attaché, Colonel Ken Brownrigg, took the team to Dili initially, did the reconnaissance and planned the evacuation. I went to Australia and rehearsed evacuation plans with commanders there, then flew to Dili. The Australian Defence Force had positioned aircraft at airfields around Darwin and the navy had ships in the area.

Once again we had the permission of Indonesian Intelligence and the army to move freely in East Timor. As in Jakarta during the downfall of Suharto, the main players in Dili were people we had known for years, and who trusted us. From memory, there were roughly 30,000 Indonesian troops and police in East Timor. They were assisted by paramilitary groups referred to as 'militia', who were Timorese supporters of the Indonesian cause, armed by the Indonesian military. The Indonesian security forces made efforts to appear neutral because of the UN presence in the country, but the militias opposed independence. We knew they were willing to use violence, which is why we had prepared evacuation plans, but we did not know how it would manifest itself, or when. As the tension increased to alarming levels, we refined and rehearsed our evacuation plans. Dressed in our own distinctive and unthreatening office uniforms or sometimes in civilian clothes, we would wander Dili and East Timor — once again, unarmed.

The East Timorese voted in the face of significant intimidation, the votes were counted over a few ominously quiet days, and the result was announced by the UN from New York: the East Timorese had chosen independence. Then the violence really began. The militias set up roadblocks in the city looking for independence supporters, and their 'justice' was swift. It was mayhem in Dili: there was murder, arson and random shooting across the city. The homemade pipeguns that had until now been the main armament of the militias were suddenly replaced by modern military rifles and pistols, and some started to fire at the consulate building. Discipline in the Timorese battalions, never high, now failed.

Ken Brownrigg and the others were everywhere: seeing, talking and then reporting to Canberra. After weeks in Dili, we all knew our way around, even at night with the street lights gone. Finally, we began the evacuation. Each of the five of us drove a civilian SUV vehicle to designated houses and picked up Australians or foreigners wishing to be evacuated, to take them to our C-130 aircraft. It was a very personal, door-to-door style of evacuation.

At one stage, we were speeding in convoy through the burning Dili suburbs towards the airport, each car loaded with its cargo of evacuees. I had six or seven Philippine nuns, some of the toughest and most impressive women I will ever have the honour to know. Only a few days before, they had given the ambassador and me a cool drink in their living room, but now the violence was out of control and we were returning the favour by getting them out.

I drove the last vehicle in the convoy of five. Ken Brownrigg was leading. In an environment where the rule of law had gone out the window, I was sensitive to anyone following us. The roads were crowded, but I soon noticed a lone Indonesian policeman following us on a motorbike, his rifle slung across his back, obviously trying to catch us. I told Ken and kept an eye on him. At this stage I had one eye on the road, one eye on the rear-vision mirror, one hand on the wheel and one hand on the radio.

The policeman was gaining on us, riding full pelt. He tried to get his rifle off his back and over his head, for what reason we will never know. Dili was full of traumatised people, and normal behaviour no longer applied. Suddenly a truck packed with refugees pulled into the traffic and caused our five vehicles to come to a screeching halt. The motorcycle policeman was unable to stop, and as I jammed my brakes on, he hit my fender, flew off his bike and came through my rear window. He ended up lodged over the nuns' baggage, his head on the contorted kind of angle that meant his neck was broken.

I noticed that, 50 metres away, the guards at the police headquarters had seen what had happened. All I could think of to say to the nuns was, 'Is everyone okay?'

Wide-eyed, they made no answer.

I launched backwards out of my seat and, lying horizontally over the nuns' heads, I pushed the dead policeman out through the smashed rear window. By this stage the road had cleared and police were approaching from their headquarters. Having to make a split-second choice — stay and explain what had happened, or keep going? — I decided that to get embroiled with the police would be madness. Our convoy drove off, leaving the unfortunate young policeman on the road to be looked after by his comrades.

We made it safely to the airport, delivered our nuns and went back to get the next load. We tried to cover the hole in the rear window but thought it might be incriminating, so we knocked the whole window out. Luckily, the next trips were comparatively uneventful. That day, we evacuated hundreds.

Once the nuns arrived in Darwin, they must have recounted this incident during their debriefings with Australian officials. That night

I received a concerned call from a Foreign Affairs officer in Canberra who suggested that I turn myself in to the Indonesian Police. I filled him in quickly on the anarchy in Dili and the probable consequences of me turning up at police headquarters admitting I had been involved in an accident in which one of their own was killed. My answer to him was direct — I did not yell, because that is always the worst thing to do when reporting back to any headquarters, especially a civilian headquarters in a Canberra suburb — but I was forceful with my language. I knew that this officer lived in a different world and was totally incapable of understanding mine. Later I would encounter this a few times from Iraq — sometimes you need to get a little authority into your voice so that people in distant operations rooms understand that things on the ground are not what they imagine.

We evacuated almost all the Australians and other foreign nationals from Dili, but the UN were still present, in force, and doing a fine job. When our consular staff said it had become too dangerous for them and decided to leave, it took me by surprise. I had forgotten that violence is relative; we in the military had come to expect it, but our civilian comrades were not as sanguine. The exit of the consular staff reminded me that we soldiers have a different mindset. My world as a soldier is a violent world, and violence in all its forms is ugly. In our society we can generally control the extremes of violence, but that is not the case in some of the societies I have worked in. The five of us in Dili were able to help Australian citizens because we could put violence in perspective and accept certain risks without being cavalier. If an Australian soldier were traumatised into either inaction or rashness by the level of violence in Dili in 1999, what could our country expect from us in a serious killing war? What did Australia expect of our fathers and grandfathers?

*

The UN asked us to evacuate their personnel and those East Timorese who had supported them: two to three thousand people. The first Australian C-130 aircraft were to begin landing in Dili on 6 September 1999 and in Timor's second-biggest town, Bacau, the next day. The five of us spent all night working with the Indonesians to keep the militias away from the evacuation route. It was difficult, to say the least. The presence of Australian troops on Indonesian soil created high tension, and Ken Brownrigg and Captain Noel Henderson had to be all over the place, keeping the Indonesians calm. We had invited the top Indonesian general in Dili, Major General Damiri, to be at the airport to give his imprimatur to what was happening, but he declined.

In Dili, the evacuation began according to plan, but our air force, quite reasonably, were reluctant to come into Bacau without an Australian military presence on the ground. I flew to Bacau with some UN officers in two UN Puma helicopter to receive these aircraft, expecting a fairly routine pick-up. When I arrived, there were about six truckloads of militia, with their families and their worldly goods, by the terminal. They were due to be evacuated by an Indonesian C-130 to Kupang in West Timor. These were 'old militia' — organised, disciplined and more a part of the Indonesian Army than the rabble in Dili. They were local residents, and their lives were about to change forever. They were led by a local 'sergeant' whom Ken knew well. I had met him before, and when I went to the office of the Bacau airbase commander, dressed in my unthreatening office uniform, he was in the commander's office, drinking coffee.

There had been some very ugly incidents in the town of Bacau the previous night, of which I was not yet aware. UN officers and local Timorese employed by the UN had been hounded by militia trying to kill them. The UN and their local employees and their families had sheltered in a church all night, and now wanted to get out.

While we were drinking coffee in the commander's office, the UN expatriate staff began arriving at the airport in their white vehicles — there were 20 vehicles, and all were going to be abandoned. Then, to my surprise, the Timorese UN staff and their families were escorted onto the tarmac. This was a red rag to a bull for the local militia, who saw their fellow countrymen as traitors deserving the harshest retribution. Nine members of the Catholic church — a priest, nuns and a driver — would be murdered the next day in a riverbed outside Bacau.

As the only uniformed Indonesian-speaking person who knew some of the militia, I tried to sort out the mess on the tarmac. The UN quite bravely refused to leave unless the safety of the locals could be guaranteed. Groups of terrified locals sat in a big block of humanity on the tarmac, with the UN workers surrounding them. Meanwhile, the militia were getting more and more worked up.

I proposed a number of options to the militia sergeant, such as sending the Timorese and their families on a C-130 to Dili, not to Darwin. He refused, suspecting that I would have them flown directly to Australia. As he spoke, he became more and more anxious, concerned by what his Indonesian Army boss would want him to do and by the fact that his life in East Timor was over. These people, from his point of view, were the easiest to blame.

For most of the day we negotiated over each group of local refugees. As I spoke with the sergeant, he nervously drew and re-holstered his pistol. This worried me, both because it may have been a signal of his intent and because it definitely was a safety issue. The tension kept building. The Australian security detachments arriving with the two aircraft had no weapons visible but were ready for action, standing on the C-130s' ramps watching.

I convinced the militia sergeant to allow the children to go to Dili in the UN Puma helicopter. Knowing a helicopter could not fly to Australia, he rang his contacts in Dili to check that I was not duping him. I thought that if the worst happened, at least I could get the children out. But the idea of being separated from their children was increasing the anxieties of the parents who remained on the tarmac. They were terrified about what might happen to the kids or, now that they were isolated, to themselves. The Australian security personnel commented later that they would never forget the East Timorese being bullied by militia: cowering, hunched over, wide-eyed, some sobbing and crying, shaking uncontrollably with fear.

Eventually, the Pumas were packed with about 40 children and adults — a record in helicopter-loading, I suspect — and sent to Dili. I told the Puma pilot that when he arrived, he was to get the children onto an Australian C-130 and out to Darwin.

Now that we had moved some Timorese off the airport, the logjam was broken and the sergeant agreed that the rest could go in the C-130s. I felt I was finally making some progress, but as the militia commander and I were walking back towards the remaining group of Timorese, we noticed that among them was the religious leader of East Timor, the vehemently anti-Indonesian Bishop Carlos Belo, dressed in civilian clothes. Belo had been awarded the Nobel Peace Prize in 1996 — with José Ramos-Horta, then the voice of his people overseas — for advocating non-violent resistance to Indonesian rule. Now here he was, sitting on the tarmac at Bacau surrounded by other refugees. Early on, Belo had been threatened by the Dili militia in a pamphlet that read, 'For now your robe is white. But it will soon be covered in the colour of your own blood.' He had fled Dili the day before when his residence had been attacked and burnt. Having this world figure among the refugees might change everything.

I greeted the bishop and asked him where he wanted to go. 'I want to go to Rome,' came the reply.

'I can't get you that far. Perhaps Darwin might be a first step?'

Conscious of how much danger Belo was in, I told the militia sergeant that the bishop should be allowed to go to Australia. Allowing such a prominent global figure to be killed would be unforgivable, even to Jakarta. I remember stumbling, in my fatigue, for an appropriate local translation for 'Nobel Peace Prize winner'.

The sergeant seemed confused as he weighed up whether to permit Belo to leave the country. His pistol went in and out of its holster at an even faster rate. The C-130s were parked behind us, partially loaded with the UN personnel and waiting to go. He accused me of having known Belo was among the refugees.

To get him away from Belo, I invited him to walk over with me to check out the parked aircraft so he could see I was not trying to trick him. It was a meaningless activity but it gave us something to do as he unsuccessfully tried to contact his boss by mobile phone, and it slowed the pistol down. It was almost a Monty Python moment when we looked into the dark interior of the C-130 to see the security people trying to look anything but armed.

The militia leader, still unable to reach his boss, finally agreed to let Belo and his assistants climb aboard.

Just as I was breathing a sigh of relief, with the first C-130 lumbering to the top of the runway, he changed his mind and demanded that Belo be removed.

'It's too late, I have no communications with the aircraft,' I told him, trying to ignore the several military radios hanging around my neck. He became agitated again, and ordered a truck to block the runway. This was done with much shouting and waving of rifles.

Having run out of ideas, I again suggested that we walk out to the aircraft and the truck. On the walk, I continued to assure him that getting Belo out of the way would be the best result for everyone.

The sergeant finally called his truckload of troops back and permitted the C-130 to take off. After the second Hercules followed, I left the militia commander to his uncertain future.

After a long day at the office, we flew low in UN Pumas along the coast back to Dili. As we rounded the headland on which Suharto had built an enormous statue of Jesus for the Catholic East Timorese, I was greeted by the extraordinary sight of a city in flames. Dili was burning from one end to the other. That night, on my routine call to Foreign Affairs in Canberra, I forgot even to mention Belo. John Dauth, the senior Foreign Affairs official in charge of the East Timor situation, came on the line and conveyed the Prime Minister's satisfaction that I had been able to rescue Belo. I was amazed at how quickly it had moved to the back of my mind as we had bounced from one drama to the next. It was just another day in East Timor.

I oversaw more evacuations. On a beach near Bacau — from where an Indonesian battalion and a Timorese battalion were leaving at the same time — I chatted with several junior officers from the Indonesian battalion who had recently been to Australia on a course. The situation was bizarre in a way, but I felt my 20-year involvement with Indonesia had paid off handsomely for Australia. From the beach, I looked back towards the mountains, and on the edge of some rice paddies stood 40 or 50 armed East Timorese guerrilla fighters, casually observing the Indonesians leaving their country after 28 years of brutal occupation.

From Indonesia, I was posted to Brisbane at the end of 1999 to follow Peter Cosgrove in command of the 1st Division, and was promoted from brigadier to major general. The Australian Army has two divisions: the 1st Division is almost entirely full-time soldiers and the 2nd Division is a part-time reserve formation. The 1st Division was 15,000 strong and consisted of five brigades, some at a high state of readiness. Once again I was going to be a commander of combat troops, and once again the possibility of adventure arose. Perhaps during this posting I would have more than my office uniform shirt to protect me.

We were called on to assist another neighbour's transition to democracy in mid-2000, when ethnic rivalry in Honiara, the capital city of the Solomon Islands, triggered an evacuation of Australian citizens and the possibility of Australian troops going there to restore security. As rival forces in Honiara fought each other and threatened residents, we deployed to Townsville and prepared an evacuation force.

Organising at lightning speed, within a few days we had a balanced and rehearsed force standing by in Townsville, ships at sea with helicopters and troops, a parachute commando force on standby, and the ability to insert special forces for a hostage release. In the end, there were peaceful evacuations and, rather than sending in troops, the government organised a very clever police-led operation a year or two later. The Solomons has tripped a few more times on its journey to democracy, and Australian troops and police have been back in, but I remain hopeful that some form of democratic government will be sustained there.

The next three-and-a-half years involved less adventure, but offered me a variety of experiences. As the commander of the 1st Division, I refreshed my association with the American military, commanding an international 'exercise enemy force' for a US 7th Fleet exercise off the Queensland coast. For the first time I commanded a truly joint force of conventional Australian and nuclear US submarines, Australian, US and Canadian ships, strike, reconnaissance and fighter aircraft from Australia and the US, and about a brigade of Australian and US Marine land troops.

During 2002 and 2003, I moved out of the field army to take command of the Australian Defence Colleges: one undergraduate university (the Australian Defence Force Academy), one staff college for mid-level officers (the Australian Command and Staff College), and a year-long course for civilians and officers of colonel equivalent rank (the Australian Defence and Strategic Studies Centre). My main focus was to balance the combat or warrior focus in senior officer education with the necessary bureaucratic and diplomatic skills. I was determined to do what I could to increase the alignment of Australia's joint forces of army, navy and air force: improving our joint training and preparing our senior colonels to be field commanders as well as bureaucrats and diplomats. In all of these ambitions I was drawing together what I'd learnt of our strengths and weaknesses during what was then a 35-year career.

While I was in this job, the US led the 2003 invasion of Iraq. Peter Cosgrove, now Chief of the Defence Force, wanted to improve our command at the strategic level and asked me to join the Strategic Command Group — Australia's highest level of military planning and management — for the invasion phase of the war, to study all that was said and done in relation to Australia's contribution, and to report to him on whether it was effective. My review found that we had effective commanders, but that they had to overcome a system that was too bureaucratic. Of course a commander like Peter Cosgrove could work around it, but command systems are there to help commanders, not hinder them. My review was the first step in a process that would produce the current system of command for operations that Defence now uses.

By 2004 I had reached a stage in life where my ideas about conflict and military operations had been tested. I had personal confidence in my intuition and physical courage. I'd led groups both large and small through demanding and sometimes extreme challenges. I knew I could make decisions fast, often relatively correctly, and I would always surround myself with talented people who would point out to me when I was wrong.

As I pondered my future at the end of a hot but peaceful summer in Canberra, it struck me what a different person I was from the young man pictured leaving home to join the army in 1968 with his overnight bag. As a member of the first graduating class from Duntroon that did not send graduates to another war, I had entered an army surrounded by bemedalled combat veterans. Many of the graduates of 1971 carried a professional inferiority complex that lasted at least ten years. But now I felt that was well and truly behind me. I had become as competent as a peacetime soldier can be, and that was a much greater achievement than I'd ever thought.

In March 2004, Peter Cosgrove, who was then Chief of the Defence Force, asked me to come and see him in his office. He got straight to business.

'Jim,' he said, 'I want you to go to Iraq. The US has accepted an offer that we made earlier this year to provide a two-star officer to be the chief of operations. You will be replacing an American officer and you will go to Iraq for a year, which is the normal posting period for US officers. What do you think? Will you be in it?'

I told Cos that of course I would be in it, but first I'd need to talk to Anne. I expressed surprise that the Americans would give the chief of operations job to any foreigner. Cos agreed that the details were unclear but suggested that I remain flexible. He quipped that I should prepare to be 'assistant to the deputy or the deputy to the assistant'. Not wanting to appear ungrateful about an opportunity to get into the biggest war on the planet, I did not press for details which Cos obviously didn't have. Whatever job the Americans gave me, I would make something of it. The most important thing was that it was operations rather than training. Operations are what combat officers live for.

I am not given to giggly fits of exuberance but I did indulge myself with one minute of excitement before trying to look steely-eyed about it. This would be serious business; slaughter was occurring every day in Iraq. This was not something to trivialise or speak of in terms of 'What's in it for me?' While it would probably be the culmination of my soldiering life, I only had to look at the evening TV news to know that it could also be the culmination of my mortal life.

As soon as I left Cos's office I called Anne. She realised how important this was to me and backed me up without hesitation. A day or two later, I spoke with Cos. He told me to keep the posting confidential until Defence Minister Robert Hill and Prime Minister John Howard made the announcement.

I had only a few weeks to prepare. Oddly enough, my biggest worry was having one of my front teeth replaced. Five years earlier, when I was a brigade commander, I had hit my face on the troop hatch of an armoured personnel carrier. I'd survived with a temporary tooth, putting off the series of appallingly uncomfortable surgical procedures and gum build-up until what I thought would be a quiet period in my life. When Cos told me I was going to Iraq, I was halfway through this awful process. I had a clumsy false tooth in the middle of my mouth, my gums had been cut open, implants had been sewn in, and I was waiting for six more months of gum growth before the permanent tooth could go in. I feared that what little credibility I might have as a general in Iraq would be diminished by having a gaping hole where my front tooth should be, emitting a whistle every time I rallied the troops! Reluctantly the orthodontist agreed to open up my gum again and insert a replacement tooth prematurely, on the condition that I signed a paper saying that anything that happened was all my fault. I completed my preparations for war with a bloody, stitched-up hole in my mouth and an aching face, wondering if a passable smile was essential to success as a general in Iraq.

General Cosgrove gave me a written directive only a few days before I flew out. After reading it I still had no real idea what I was getting into. I don't think Cos had either. The directive told me the title of the job, who I would answer to in Australia and in Iraq, and cautioned me not to do anything illegal.

Public statements from the Prime Minister and Defence Minister provided me with more of the picture. In parliament, Prime Minister Howard said that I would be 'responsible for planning such missions as finding and destroying terrorist cells, patrolling areas where anti-aircraft missiles could be fired and, in general, providing protection to the Iraqi and coalition community'. The reference to anti-aircraft missiles seemed incongruous, but recently a civilian cargo jet leaving Baghdad had been hit by a missile. Obviously this had caught the attention of the PM's speech writer. The Defence Minister's press release went further, accurately describing the yet-to-be-raised headquarters in which I would work as being 'responsible for security and anti-insurgency operations in Iraq'.

The Prime Minister also gave me what I would call 'attitudinal' guidance. He said in his public statement that my appointment demonstrated several things: the high regard in which allies like the United States held ADF personnel; the Australian government's continued determination to be an active partner with the new Iraq; a sign of his government's and the nation's continuing intention to see through our responsibilities in Iraq until the job was done; a reinforcement of the importance of remaining united with nations who were working to build a new Iraq; and not to give comfort or solace to those who would want otherwise. It was now up to me to work in with these requirements.

Between my directive and the words of my political leaders, I had been told to do many things, but not much that was specific. As we normally do in the military, I set about constructing for myself a simple guidance statement. I typed it out, edited it and re-typed it. When I was happy with it, it told me the following:

I am to perform the duties of deputy chief of staff for operations within HQ MNF-I [Multi-National Force — Iraq], in accordance with the counterinsurgency functions of HQ MNF-I and abiding by the current Op Catalyst [name of Australian participation in the Iraq War] rules of engagement and Australian laws of armed conflict. The details of my duties are to be as directed by CG [Commanding General] MNF-I but, based on PM's and Defence Minister's public statements, I should expect that my duties would include: planning missions; finding terrorist cells; destroying terrorist cells; protecting the Iraqi people and coalition security; and other duties as directed by CG MNF-I. I should carry out these duties in a way which reinforces the high regard in which ADF personnel are held, that shows Australia unified with other nations in the coalition, and as an active, responsible and committed partner to Iraq. My actions are not to give comfort or solace to those who are working against the new Iraq.

This turned out to be a fairly accurate description of what I would do in Iraq for the next 12 months.

Having taken the 'Queen's shilling' for many years, I was obligated to obey a legal order from the government of the day. But I also had a responsibility to consider the morality of my participation in the war and to satisfy myself that this was a just war. If I could not do that, then I could not participate. For any soldier, an order to participate in an unjust war is an illegal order.

Still based at the Defence College, I had access to all the readings on the just war concept and on the Laws of Armed Conflict. I had followed the legal debate closely during the invasion, so I was not starting from scratch. In the military, we live and breathe legal issues, and increasingly senior commanders conduct modern war with a lawyer by their side. I reviewed the principles and discussed them with one of our operational lawyers. The principles would guide me only so far, and I would have to make final judgments based on the actual situation that faced me in Iraq and my part in it. There would be much more to this than following theory and, of course, I would be personally accountable for what I did.

What I could say to myself at this stage was that the initial invasion, founded in the chain of UN Security Council Resolutions going back to the first Gulf War, had a debatable but still defensible legal basis, even though it may have been unpopular. But I was not invading Iraq. That war had finished a year earlier. I was being asked to participate in the conflict that followed the invasion.

Unlike some observers who think war is something they can simply wish away, as a soldier I was acutely aware that what the laws of armed conflict cannot do is prohibit violence. It was important, then, to separate the legality of the ongoing war from the emotion surrounding the 2003 invasion. I also had to separate the way the war was being run, institutionally, from isolated excesses. There had been recent media reports of ugly incidents in Iraq such as the bombing of a wedding party near the Jordan border, but errors or transgressions by individuals were not the issue. Every indication I could find was that the war was being run in accordance with the laws of armed conflict, and that institutionally, military actions were proportional, humane, discriminating and necessary, as required by those laws. This was also a fair conclusion to reach from my knowledge of US commanders and how they worked.

Like most of life's big decisions, this was complicated, and clouded by how much I had to rely on second-hand reports, and the lack of detail on exactly what I would be doing. As a result, I had little context in which to situate my judgment. I could certainly conclude to my satisfaction that the war as it stood in 2004 met the requirements of a just war. It was also reasonable for me to conclude that US commanders, under the glare of the media and in a coalition of 28 countries, had been following the laws of armed conflict. I concluded that there was nothing, legally or morally, that should stop me going to Iraq, but once in Iraq and with specific responsibilities, I would have an ongoing responsibility to assess the legality of all my actions, and the way the war was being run. Just as I had in East Timor, I wanted to ensure that, in some small way, Iraq would be a better place for my having been there.

We Australians are well remunerated for fighting in Iraq. A few times in the weeks prior to my departure, even though my replacement tooth was hardly up to it, my family and I went out to restaurants, an uncommon activity for us. The family started irreverently calling these outings a 'Saddam Shout', trivialising the issue to cover our unease with what lay ahead. But we knew that Saddam had left enormous debts unpaid. (We didn't know it then, but our last 'Saddam Shout' would be in December 2006, the day after the dictator was executed.)

On the night I left Australia, we had an early evening farewell dinner at home with my family and Anne's parents. This was a year-long separation, and I was going to a seriously dangerous place. I said a few words at the end of the meal, feeling keenly the inadequacy of anything I could say. Anne and I then slipped out of our house and made our final farewells in the Canberra airport lounge.

CHAPTER 3

Assistant to the deputy or deputy to the assistant

First impressions of Iraq, April 2004

After a 17-hour flight from Sydney, I arrived in Dubai on 14 April 2004. My instructions were to go to the Gulf State of Qatar to visit the US headquarters, then fly to Kuwait for a day prior to entering Iraq.

No Australian in the Middle East had any better idea than Canberra of what I was likely to be doing in Iraq, so I was well and truly in uncharted waters. In Qatar, I visited the forward headquarters of US Central Command (known as CENTCOM), responsible for military interests from Pakistan to the Horn of Africa. CENTCOM was running two wars, one in Afghanistan and one in Iraq, while trying to prevent a couple more in places like Somalia and Eritrea. I met the top American officer in the region, General John Abizaid, an extraordinary soldier, as I discovered when I came to know him better.

CENTCOM's main headquarters was in Tampa, Florida, but because of the level of US operations in the Middle East this forward headquarters had been set up in Qatar. The US had a technique for setting up its bases in the Middle East. It built warehouse-like structures that stretched for miles, then put big containers inside the warehouses with specialist functions already built into each container. For example, each warehouse might have ten or so containers, each of which was fitted out for power, water and the specialist needs of its function. Headquarters might have tables, chairs, lights, air conditioning and computers. Other containers might be shower or toilet facilities, for sleeping or eating, or for food preparation. The big warehouse structure kept the worst of the heat out, and the arrangement of the containers on the inside could be changed to satisfy multiple functions. Depending on the threat, blast walls protected the warehouses and sometimes also the inner containers. Most US bases throughout the Middle East had a similar layout, which, in the most charitable sense, I would describe as 'utilitarian'.

In one of these 'office containers' I met Major General John Sattler, who was responsible for all CENTCOM's operations across a vast expanse of the earth's surface. He welcomed me and generously gave me more than an hour of his time to update me on operations in Iraq. John gave me a verbal tour of his responsibilities, and I was reminded of how extraordinary these times were. It was almost a year to the day since the invasion of Iraq had ended as a brilliant military success. The strategic sense behind the post-invasion occupation was already being questioned by commentators, but this was not something we discussed above the hum of the ubiquitous air conditioner — we were practical men and had today's problems to solve.

After the invasion — in March and April 2003 — there had been a period of looting as the people claimed back some of the riches of their country, long denied to them by Saddam. The looting had mostly finished by midyear 2003 but left extensive damage. As the looting ended, an insurgency among the minority Sunnis emerged as they rejected the post-Saddam era. Sunnis comprised no more than

20 per cent of Iraq's population, but dominated the central portion of the country, with the Kurds in the north (who are Sunnis but not Arabs) representing another 20 per cent and Shias in the south being the majority with 60 per cent of the population. Saddam Hussein, himself a Sunni, had run his regime using the Sunnis, as had the British during colonial times. Sunnis had benefited in all respects, at the expense of the Shias and Kurds. Many members of elite units in Saddam's security forces were Sunnis, and despite the defeat of the Iraqi Army, they still had weapons, ammunition and organisation.

By August 2003 coalition forces had been drawn into a series of battles in the Sunni centre of the country, called the Sunni Triangle, which included Baghdad. There were also signs that some of the Shia Muslim majority, unhappy with the occupation, were intent on enforcing their rights. In the anarchy that followed the invasion and the looting, al Qaeda terrorist groups were able to establish themselves among the Sunni community, bolstered by Muslim extremists from all over the Islamic world. The scale of the looting and disruption was so great up until about August 2003 that the coalition's subsequent attempts to deliver essential services to the people of Iraq, so important in a counterinsurgency campaign, and to re-create some form of army and police (at one stage referred to as '30,000 in 30 days'), were clumsy at best and generally ineffective.

My limited intelligence briefings at home had been detailed on threats to Australians, but had not covered how the larger war was going. As most of my knowledge had come from media reports, briefings such as this were invaluable.

John told me that in the previous month, March 2004, insurgents had killed 20 American soldiers. It seemed bad, but 20 would turn out to be the smallest monthly number in all of 2004. As I sat in his air-conditioned container in Qatar, US forces were fighting in a small Sunni town a little to the west of Baghdad, in what we would come to call the 'first battle of Fallujah'. But it wasn't restricted to

Fallujah, or even to the Sunni Triangle. In no time, fighting had spread to the southern Shi'ite towns and in Shi'ite parts of Baghdad, especially Sadr City.

John had a good feel for the detail of the war, especially when it came to the US Marines, of which he was one. He would soon be promoted to lieutenant general and command all Marine units in the western Iraq province of Anbar, fighting the very war that he was now explaining to me. The US 82nd Airborne Division was handing over responsibility for Anbar province to the US Marines, and the town of Fallujah — on the eastern edge of the province — would be a very large part of John's life during 2004, as it would be a large part of mine. We would talk often during the next 12 months.

As was the case for most of Iraq, he explained, war for Fallujah had been a way of life. Following the invasion, Fallujah had been occupied by various units, including the 82nd Airborne Division, who would be remembered in Fallujah for an incident when troops returned fire from a crowd and killed 18 demonstrators. Fallujans probably suspected early that for them the occupation was going to be tough.

Days earlier, one of the worst incidents so far had taken place in Fallujah. If it had not been for the desire of some contractors from the Blackwater private security company to get home from work early on the last day of March 2004, Fallujah might not have achieved its notoriety. Blackwater was essentially a private army under contract to the US government. Four contractors returning in two vehicles from western Anbar province decided to cross the main bridge in Fallujah and take Highway 10 through the city to get to Baghdad. Normally they would have skirted the city, but they were either in a rush or lost. John described how they were ambushed in their unarmoured vehicles and killed, their bodies mutilated and burnt. Some young Fallujans compounded the indignity by dancing on the bodies in front of television cameras. Two of the US contractors' almost unrecognisable corpses were hung from the northern of Fallujah's two bridges, known among the coalition as 'The Brooklyn Bridge'.

This was a front-page story for the media, resulting in a demand by those in authority on our side for action against the guilty in Fallujah. John said it was highly likely that the killings and desecration of the bodies was carried out by former regime elements (often Saddam's Fedayeen militia, Special Republican Guard or Iraqi Special Forces), assisted by the citizens of Fallujah, and although he was circumspect at the time, I later discovered that the demand for action from Ambassador Bremer and Washington was met with marked reluctance by the US Marines in Anbar province and higher commanders in Baghdad. I could sense already the diverging priorities between experienced soldiers on the ground and their political masters.

The Marines, John explained, elected not to storm into the city immediately but to persist in a more temperate strategy. The bodies of the contractors had been returned, but the Qatar-based al Jazeera television network played and replayed footage of the grisly scenes around the world. Inevitably, parallels were drawn with the helicopter crewman's body that was dragged through the streets of Mogadishu in 1993, significantly contributing to the US withdrawal from Somalia.

As the US command chain debated what could be done, events in the holy city of Najaf, south of Baghdad, were taking a course of their own. John pointed out these places on his wall map, and I committed as much as I could to memory. In the past few days, the Mehdi Militia, an armed Shi'ite group allied to a fiery young imam called Moqtada al Sadr, attacked Iraqi and coalition soldiers and police across southern Iraq and in Baghdad, responding initially to an attempt to arrest Moqtada for the murder of a fellow imam and to close down his newspaper. But the violence had built a momentum of its own. On 4 April 2004, as the images of bodies swinging from the Brooklyn Bridge continued to ripple around the world, Mehdi Militia elements attacked a US and El Salvadorean base known as Camp Golf/Baker on the edge of Najaf. They posed as patients, occupied a five-storey hospital, and from there attacked the base. Two weeks later when I was in Najaf, I was to find out that the 'El Sals' distinguished themselves by recapturing the hospital. While these fights were still raging, on 6 April the Mehdi Militia struck and occupied al Kut, a town on the Tigris.

With all this going on across southern Iraq, John explained, Ambassador Bremer and other authorities perceived that the coalition was being challenged in a most serious way that could not be tolerated. As a result, the Marines had been directed to commence operations in Fallujah on 5 April. They protested, but their view was rejected. The Marines put their heels together and did as they were told, calling the operation 'Vigilant Resolve'. Heavy combat in Fallujah went for five violent days before a ceasefire was declared on 9 April, but Operation Vigilant Resolve would continue until the end of the month.

John was a gifted storyteller. As he described the fighting, I could almost taste the dust and the dirt and feel the command tension. The assault by the Marines had all the characteristics of a typical urban fight. It was nasty, dirty and vicious. Most homes in Fallujah, a city of 300,000 people, were armed with at least one rifle, and many had access to more. The people of Fallujah opposed the Marines at each turn, fighting not only with their own rifles but also with the ubiquitous rocket-propelled grenades, mortars and roadside bombs. Faced with such opposition, the Marines were forced to kill not only large numbers of armed Fallujans but also skilled and fanatical members of the former regime who were resident in the town, and terrorists who were attracted by the fight.

As the casualties mounted on 5, 6 and 7 April, the resolve of those in the CPA who had ordered the attack melted away. The Iraqi

Governing Council — an Iraqi body appointed by Ambassador Bremer to represent Iraqis, and which included Sunnis — threatened to resign. The global media were critical of the casualty numbers, and the British within the coalition expressed a deep unease with the tactics. When the Marines declared the ceasefire on 9 April, its public justification was to advance some so-called peace initiatives.

John couldn't even estimate the number of civilians killed: many Fallujans had taken up arms and enthusiastically attacked the Marines, and in so doing had shed the protection of international law as civilians. Nevertheless, John said, enemy propaganda played up 'civilian deaths' to the maximum throughout the United States, Britain, Europe and in the Arab street. It is likely that hundreds died.

It became clear, as I listened to John, that I was walking into a crisis of bewildering complexity and escalating violence. Between 10 and 12 April, the fighting with the Shia militias across the south had kicked up a notch. Saboteurs destroyed five or six of the big flyovers on highways used to resupply the coalition from Kuwait, known as the 'Main Supply Route Tampa', and alternate supply routes. They simply parked large car bombs underneath the flyovers and blew them up. The Marines, still fighting in Fallujah — the enemy constantly broke the ceasefire — felt their vulnerability.

In response, a series of offensive operations was commenced across the south of Iraq. They were given the names 'Valiant Sabre' and 'Iron Sabre'. The US always chooses such names for its operations: our presence in Iraq was Operation 'Iraqi Freedom' and Afghanistan was Operation 'Enduring Freedom'. It was a different practice from my own military, but as a member of my staff commented, 'I would rather die for "Iraqi Freedom" than some of the Australian names — "Operation Plumbob", for example!'

The US 1st Armoured Division, 15,000 to 20,000 strong, had only just been replaced by the 1st Infantry Division in the provinces north of Baghdad. After a year in Iraq, the 1st Armoured was moving to Kuwait to go home; but because of the worsening situation, Secretary of Defense Rumsfeld recalled it. The first group of troops was actually in Kuwait with their equipment loaded on ships ready to depart when they were recalled and allocated an area of operations south of Baghdad. Their recall was a stark indication of the size of the fight the coalition was in.

John described the meetings the CPA was holding that very day with the Iraqi Governing Council to regain its support. The situation seemed to become more chaotic the closer I was to entering Iraq. Surely, I thought to myself, it will all be solved by the time I arrive.

After leaving John, I was given an extensive intelligence briefing from the Director of Intelligence, Brigadier General John Custer. Most importantly for me, everyone I met in Central Command assumed that I was going to be chief of operations in Iraq — so far so good, I thought, and a big improvement on the vague communications I'd got from Australia.

Having come from a military at peace, I never thought I would see Australian C-130 pilots wearing body armour and Kevlar helmets, but here it was. In Kuwait I boarded an Australian C-130, or Hercules, to fly to Baghdad. Carrying the pistol, ammunition, body armour and helmet I had been issued in the Australian logistics unit in Kuwait, I settled down into the bench seat behind the pilots to see what the trip would bring.

I should be used to the fact that distances outside Australia are short and most countries are close together, but I was surprised that as the C-130 climbed over Kuwait, I could easily identify Bubiyan Island and the al Faw peninsula between Iraq and Iran. Almost before the aircraft crossed into Iraq, I could see as far as Basrah and the Shatt al-Arab waterway from the Northern Arabian Gulf stretching up to Iraq's only port, Umm Qasr. It was a clear and relatively cool

April day, and I felt as if I could see forever. We tracked over Basrah airport and turned northwest for Baghdad. I worked the one-to-a-million scale aeronautical map I'd borrowed from the pilots, trying to get travel times and distances into my head and to identify places.

Looking over the pilots' shoulders and out the side window of the C-130, I could see at least one significant fire among the oilfields west of Basrah. I didn't know, and couldn't tell, if it was the result of an attack or just normal flaring off of excess gas from wells. Once we left Basrah, visibility was reduced. I had heard a bit about the marsh Arabs, and assumed that there would be some body of water north of Basrah, but the marshes had been drained by Saddam and I had trouble even seeing the Tigris or the Euphrates. I could identify only a very long and straight canal, then desert, then the holy city of Najaf that John Sattler had told me so much about.

I had yet to appreciate the significance of these cities, which are holy for the Shia; they were likely to be the real beneficiaries of Saddam's fall. Even though I had lived for five years in the largest (Sunni) Muslim country in the world, Indonesia, I had no idea that the split between Sunni and Shia was so deep and acrimonious. The first Iraqi I would come to know, the Director General of Health, Dr Shakir, would explain to me that the split was like the Catholic–Protestant schism at its very worst, and chided me, 'You Christians have been killing each other for centuries!'

Looking back, I cannot believe how much I did not know. However, it was not the first situation I had gone into where I would need to climb a steep learning curve. Sitting behind the pilots at 30,000 feet, I was building on an accelerated education that had started in Qatar.

We continued northwest and I was lost again in featureless desert crossed by roads and dotted with small towns that were difficult to see because they were the same colour as the land. We headed towards the international airport at the southeastern edge of

Baghdad. I had been briefed that as we approached Baghdad we would conduct certain energetic evasive manoeuvres to avoid missiles, then quickly approach the runway and land.

The manoeuvres were certainly energetic, but we arrived without incident. I was given a bed in the headquarters of the Australian contingent at the big military base next to the airport, called Camp Victory, and prepared myself for whatever was to occur. Drew and Whitey, the first two members of my SAS bodyguard, whom I had met briefly in Australia, were soon protectively by my side.

In the first year of the war, military matters in Iraq were being run from a headquarters called Combined Joint Task Force Seven, or CJTF-7. When I arrived, this headquarters was based on the US Army's Headquarters V Corps ('V' as in Roman numeral 'five', but also linked since World War II to 'V' for victory), which was normally located in Germany. Designed to command about three divisions, each of about 15,000 troops, plus supporting organisations, Headquarters V Corps had now morphed as CJTF-7 into a multinational headquarters commanding army, navy and air forces men and women from 28 nations.

On my arrival, CJTF-7 was commanded by US Lieutenant General Ric Sanchez, the most senior Latino officer in the US Army. A second corps headquarters, Headquarters III Corps, commanded by Lieutenant General Tom Metz, was moving into Iraq to assist him. Sanchez was running the equivalent of seven divisions, each numbering 8000 to 20,000 personnel, as well as detention operations, the search for weapons of mass destruction, coordinating with the CPA, liaising with the emerging Iraqi authorities and, of course, working daily with the US government in Washington. As well, there was a new Iraqi Army and Police Force to create, and essential services to deliver to the people. CJTF-7 was being asked to command much more than would normally be expected, in an environment that was far more politically complex than such a headquarters could ever handle. It was a credit to Sanchez that it was functioning at all, let alone achieving results.

The seven divisions were in discrete geographical areas. Four were commanded by US generals, one by a Polish, one by a British and one by a Korean. Each of the seven areas was referred to by its location relative to Baghdad. For example, the Polish division, south of Baghdad but still in the centre of the country, was called Multi National Division–Centre South, or MND-CS. The British, in the Basrah area, were called Multi National Division–South East, or MND-SE. The US Marines owned Anbar province, the area to the west of Baghdad; a US Army division was centred on Tikrit, to the north of Baghdad; and a smaller US force was located in the north of the country, around Mosul. In the Kurdish north there were several thousand Koreans, close to Irbil — a very stable area, controlled effectively by the Kurds. Finally, and most critically, a US Army division was in Baghdad itself.

The need to rationalise the command structure and form a purpose-built headquarters to replace CJTF-7 had brought me to Iraq. It was Australia's impression that when the new headquarters was formed, I would hold one of the key appointments, the chief of operations. The quickest command solution had been tried in Iraq — take an existing tactical headquarters, add to it in an ad hoc manner, and give it a different name. But this structure, and this headquarters, had now reached its limits and the decision had been made to assemble a new headquarters in Baghdad in April.

When this plan was made, of course, the level of violence was much lower than it was in April 2004. April might have seemed a good month to make the change, but our enemies had decided that April was also a good month to increase their attacks dramatically. With the tempo of combat thus increased, there was no way Sanchez was going to make radical changes to the command structure.

Forming a new headquarters and transferring command in the middle of a war is like changing the tyre on a car as it speeds down the highway.

So when I walked in, although it was agreed that change certainly had to occur, there was no chance it was going to happen right then.

Initially I lived in 'Camp Victory', named after the one-word motto of the V Corps. After a day or so with the Australian headquarters, I headed up to the CJTF-7 headquarters.

Camp Victory was an enormous military complex, probably housing 10,000 to 20,000 soldiers and masses of equipment and stores. It was about 5 kilometres square on the southwest corner of Baghdad, set on featureless flat land between the Saddam International Airport (renamed Baghdad International Airport, or BIAP) and Baghdad's suburbs. When I arrived, accommodation in Camp Victory was a mixture of tents and cabin-type containers. Its only redeeming feature was the sumptuous architecture of the al-Faw Palace complex, named after the peninsula at the southern edge of Iraq through which most of Iraq's oil leaves the country, and over which some horrendous battles were fought against the Iranians in the 1980s.

The palace complex looked no more than a decade or so old. It was built around a set of artificial lakes, reflecting Iraqis' love of the water. It was another manifestation of Saddam's power, but also of his arrogance, as he lavished the people's money on himself and his family. Al-Faw had administrative 'palaces' and accommodation 'palaces', only some of which had been bombed. Internally, there were heavy drapes, gold-painted taps and impractically big rooms. The electrical wiring was terrifyingly primitive, and fires were not uncommon. The dirt removed to make the artificial lakes was piled up to make the only hill for about 200 kilometres in any direction; it was now festooned with US aerials and satellite dishes. The lakes

Command Structure of Coalition Forces in Iraq 2004–05

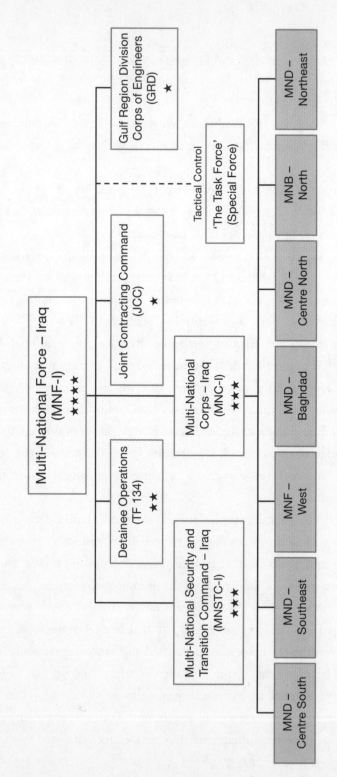

★ = seniority of general (number of stars)

HQ MNF-I Structure August 2004

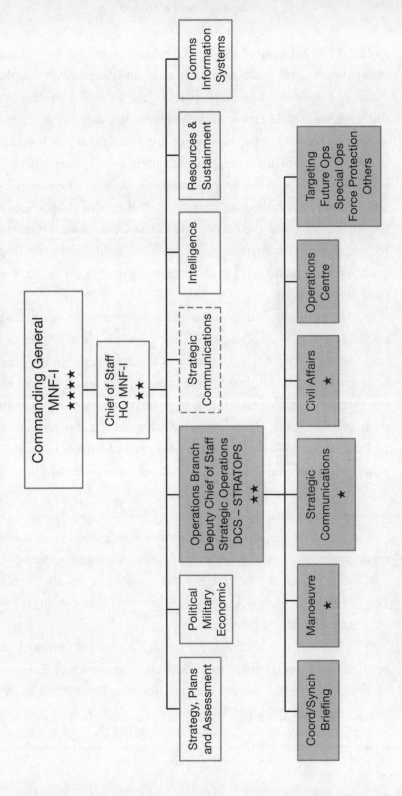

looked beautiful against the desert colouring of the buildings for about one hour at dusk, when the soft light disguised the stagnant water and the dead fish. Some parts of the extensive gardens were still struggling on, but most of the greenery had died from neglect.

My arrival was hardly the most exciting thing that was happening in Iraq. It was difficult to get anyone's attention for more than a few minutes, particularly the generals running the war. The one person who did see me immediately was the chief of staff, Major General Joe Weber, who had the office next to the Commanding General's. Joe had arrived recently too, but as Sanchez's right-hand man for just about everything, he was already deeply engaged in the military and political activity.

Sitting at his small desk in the far corner of what was probably once a large palace meeting room, Joe gave me a whole new set of information. Like John Sattler, Joe was also a Marine. He was solidly built, fast thinking but slow talking, with a Texas drawl. He had time for everyone, and a way of making you feel welcome no matter what your position. His working hours were appallingly long, and he handled some of the more mundane tasks in the war, as well as issues of great importance. He had an infectious laugh that I depended on more and more as time went on and we all became more and more tired.

He explained that the Marines were still in Fallujah, and that the most urgent issue was solving the stalemate. After their protests were rejected, the Marines had fought their way courageously into the city, but they were now sitting ducks for the insurgent attacks that constantly breached the ceasefire.

The Marines weren't the only ones fighting. Army units had been fighting solidly in Baghdad and in the cities to the south. Polish and Ukrainian units had taken casualties, and the British had been in heavy combat in Basrah and Amarah.

Joe made me aware of the impact of the attacks on our road

supply lines from Kuwait. Where the flyovers had been brought down by car bombs, engineers were furiously making repairs and bypasses were being constructed. In the meantime, fuel was being rationed, certain types of ammunition (particularly artillery ammunition, which was being used at a greater rate than ever imagined) was being flown in directly from Germany, and we were all issued with rations rather than the fresh food that had previously been shipped in daily. I began to realise that I was in the middle of a serious war. Joe concluded this initial talk by saying that he would arrange a meeting with General Sanchez as soon as possible, and by welcoming me once again.

My first meeting with General Sanchez came sooner than I expected, only a day or so after meeting with Joe. Sanchez was a hard-driving general, as tough on himself as on his staff. His office, next to Joe's, was strictly functional. Like most offices in this part of the palace, it had a conference table and a TV tuned to cable news stations. Its tall windows opened onto an internal courtyard. The outer office was occupied by the staff who closely guarded the Commanding General at all times. General Sanchez welcomed me to Iraq and got to the point.

'What do you think you can contribute?' he asked.

I told him as much as I knew. I was in Iraq after General Abizaid's request for a chief of operations in the successor headquarters to CJTF-7. Until it was formed, I was happy to do any job.

He pointed out firmly that there were two jobs that would be very hard for a coalition officer in Iraq: chief of operations and chief of intelligence. Both required high-level access to US intelligence. When I told him I expected access to the highest-level US computer system, known as SIPRNET, under current US-Australian agreements, he seemed surprised. But I realised that there were bigger issues at play here than me, and I had no intention of wasting any of this very busy man's time, so I did not push the point.

Sanchez was very polite and correct, but finding me an interim job was not his priority. He concluded the meeting by suggesting I make contact with the current chief of operations, Major General Tom Miller, and learn as much as I could.

I knew it wouldn't be easy to break into a situation like this. Although Sanchez's superior, General Abizaid, had made the request to Australia for the chief of operations, it was evident that either this fact had not been passed to Sanchez or he was ignoring it.

Not a great start, but I was determined not to become a problem. Pompous generals go down like a lead balloon with real soldiers fighting real wars. I returned to my sleeping space a little disappointed, but I knew I could not walk in and run someone else's war for them. They did not know me. They had no idea if I was competent or not. They had a team in place and Sanchez depended on that team in life-and-death situations. I fell asleep that night determined to make the best of the situation I was in.

The next day I linked up with Tom Miller, the US Special Forces officer who had been Sanchez's chief of operations for nearly a year. Theoretically, US generals were doing 12-month tours in Iraq, but I do not think I met one who only did one year. Most did much longer. Tom Miller was one of two senior staff who worked intimately with Sanchez. The other was the chief of intelligence in Iraq, Brigadier General Barbara Fast, the equivalent in this headquarters of Brigadier General Custer in CENTCOM. Someone told me that during his year in Iraq, Tom Miller had only left the country for a few days, to attend his father's funeral back in the US, and had not even taken the midyear break that all soldiers were entitled to.

Tom was a wiry man who, on behalf of the CG, as Sanchez was known, was the master of operational detail. There was nothing Tom hadn't seen in Iraq, and no idea he hadn't tried. His most common advice to his staff when they had an idea that did not pass muster was, 'If I'd had that idea, I'da gone outside, and sat under a shady tree somewhere till it passed. Then I'da come back in.'

Following such a busy man around and learning from him was challenging. Tom was an incredibly hard-working man, always tired but on top of all the detail, bearing the weight of the operational world on his shoulders. He had no time for pleasantries or idle chatter. The last thing he wanted was to be lumbered with a coalition general he had not asked for. The coalition was over-supplied with foreign generals who were there to show their countries' interest in the war but little else. They could contribute little to operations because they were not authorised to access US intelligence. In Tom's eyes, understandably, I was just another.

I had assumed that the pace of work would be fast, but I had never guessed how gruelling it would be. I'd always prided myself on my physical endurance, which had been tested for long periods in East Timor and Indonesia. I had extended myself on exercises as a battalion, brigade and division commander and as commander of the emergency evacuation of Australians from the Solomon Islands in 2000. But after the first few weeks in Iraq I was very tired just from accompanying Tom on his daily rounds, and he had been doing this job for a year!

Tom and his staff coordinated all coalition operations in Iraq. He had to know not only what his combat units were doing to defeat the insurgency, but also about logistic sustainment, the processing of reinforcements, the inflow of new units and outflow of old units, force communications, protection of the leadership and anything else that pertained to operations. Tom absorbed all the operational information coming in on behalf of General Sanchez, assessed it and delegated tasks, as well as ensuring that Sanchez was kept up to date. He knew the technical characteristics of every unit and the weapons they used, and their commanders. Tom was awake and fully engaged for 20 hours of each day. Every now and again, if the tempo of fighting spiked or a major crisis arose unexpectedly, he would lose even those precious four hours' sleep. If there is one thing that underpins every word that I write about Iraq, it is tiredness. I am loath to use the word 'exhausted', because if an officer admits that he is exhausted, he should remove himself from responsibility because he is dangerous. But stress and fatigue infused every action and every relationship that existed in Iraq, and as a soldier, you had to learn to manage it, and not let it get to a stage where you could be a danger to yourself or your comrades.

While I understudied Tom, I continued learning place names and distances, titles of the US and coalition units and their commanders, what equipment they had and what they could do. I looked at the road structure of Iraq and 101 other essentials. I covered sheets of paper with maps, diagrams and names and gave myself memory tests. I sat through conferences and meetings. Tom encouraged me to travel around Iraq — a somewhat transparent tactic, I suspected, to get me out of his hair. But I thrived on the travel. I could put names to faces and form relationships with commanders and their staffs. I steadily built up a picture of what we call 'the battlespace'.

One of my first opportunities to go outside Baghdad on official business, rather than as a military tourist, was to accompany Sanchez and Miller to a conference at the Marines' field headquarters outside Fallujah. Obviously the war had not stopped as I tried to find honourable work in Baghdad. The stalemate and the one-sided ceasefire was continuing, and the CPA had explored every opportunity but failed to find a political solution.

What eventually broke the stalemate was a Marine initiative born out of frustration. The Marines had not wanted to go so hard into Fallujah, but when told to, they did, and paid in blood. Their masters, surprised at the bloodshed, then demanded that they stop fighting. The Marines were reluctant to withdraw from the city they had bought with their soldiers' lives, yet they were now not allowed to finish the job by securing all of the city. I could see the Marines' point of view. If nothing else was going to work without excessive casualties on all sides, and if decisive military action was not permitted, then Fallujah should be handed over to an Iraqi force. In theory, this force would then discover and hand over the killers of the Blackwater contractors, and the coalition's authority in Iraq would be restored. No-one liked the idea much and everyone could see the problems. Few in the coalition had any confidence that an Iraqi force could hold the town. But with the Iraqi Governing Council strongly opposing further forceful action, no-one had a better idea.

On 25 April 2004, senior Marine commanders, one step ahead of their political masters, met with former Iraqi generals to talk about forming an Iraqi force to police Fallujah. These meetings resulted in an agreement to pull out the Marines and form a 3000-strong Iraqi 'Fallujah Brigade'. The fighting in Fallujah had died down. In many ways it was a good result, but the Americans still had to cope with the people of Fallujah celebrating, with great enthusiasm, their 'victory' over the US Marines.

I flew out to the Marines' headquarters in General Sanchez's personal Blackhawk. When he travelled, Sanchez was always accompanied by about 12 bodyguards in two or three Blackhawks protected by several Apache attack helicopters. Because he travelled a lot and needed to be able to stay in contact, his aircraft was impressively fitted out with communications gear, including Blue Force Tracker, a computer depiction of where all our forces were in almost real time.

Still gaining a feel for travel times, I was surprised at how short the trip was: 20 minutes. The closeness of Fallujah to Baghdad underscored its strategic importance.

The all-day meeting was to discuss the current situation and work out a way ahead. It was held in what had probably been a government building or school on the edge of Camp Fallujah, the headquarters of the 30,000 Marines in Anbar province. Camp Fallujah was only about 5 kilometres from Fallujah itself. We were close to the front line here and facilities were simple, as one would expect. The complex was a one-storey affair that had long ago been painted white, with a series of rooms around a central courtyard. It was heavily guarded with armoured vehicles and barriers, and there were guards on every roof.

What struck me about this planning session, my first serious operational conference, was the maturity of people's behaviour. The last two weeks had been a very unsatisfying combat experience in Fallujah for the Marines, who had had many killed and wounded, yet I heard from their commander in Anbar province, Lieutenant General Jim Conway, and his subordinate Jim Mattis, a professional, moral and level-headed assessment of the situation and all options. It spanned the big picture and the situation on the ground. There were no stereotypes. The Marine leadership was thoughtful and tactically clever, continually aware of the rights of non-combatants and the impact of the Marines' actions on the political landscape. There was no whiff of panic, even though the coalition had logistical problems and was fighting across most of southern Iraq. Fuel and electricity were not being delivered to the cities, and even I could see that we were eating into our reserves of certain types of ammunition and fuel. There was no outright anger, although the Marines had grounds to be deeply critical of the direction they had been given, and their righteous indignation was evident but well controlled. It was indeed sober and responsible operational generalship, I thought, as we flew back to Baghdad late in the day.

I was only just beginning to understand the complexity of the insurgency. Exactly who was fighting us? It is hard to argue against the logic that 'if you shoot at us you must be our enemy', but I could see that the Marine leaders and General Sanchez were uncomfortable with that view because allegiances change. They understood that even though you fought us today, you could be our friend tomorrow. This was the start of the hard part of this war. As in most wars, you learn by doing, and I could see that this coalition force was both doing and learning.

Although my analysis was simplistic at this early stage, there were at least four groups that opposed us in Iraq. The first group was the Sunni Arabs, who had lost the privileges they enjoyed under the old regime, and who we referred to as insurgents. The second group was the Islamic extremists, who were also Sunni but supplemented by foreign fighters from many countries. This group, which we referred to as terrorists, was led by a Jordanian named Zarqawi and later merged with al Qaeda. They hated the US second only to the Shia; they were few in number but extremely violent. The third group was referred to as the militias: armed groups from various Shia factions, such as the Mehdi Militia or the Badr Brigade, who fought each other as often as they fought the coalition. They were motivated by a hate for the occupier, based on their Islamic beliefs and their nationalism. The last group were the criminals, who were as well armed and organised as any other group and made alliances of convenience with any group, especially in crimes such as kidnapping.

The fighting in April 2004 was the most significant upsurge in bloodshed so far. We measured just about everything in Iraq. In April, the headquarters graph of the war's intensity spiked off its vertical scale. Amazingly, at the same time there was yet another serious call from parts of the US administration to reduce the number of troops in Iraq, even though an effective Iraqi Army and Police Force were years away.

On top of all this, the scandal of Abu Ghraib prison became public at the end of April, consuming the attention of the US military and political leadership — and of the public across the world. This scandal gave all of us, but especially the Americans, a deep sense of shame and disappointment when we saw the photos of the excesses of unsupervised prison guards. As I followed Tom around the headquarters, Abu Ghraib gave me cause to ponder how much personal responsibility a real-world general must take. If a nation takes a conscious decision to reduce the size of its military, and as a result critical functions such as detention operations and military policing become the responsibility of inexperienced reservists, how do we apportion blame when things go wrong? This was no theoretical staff college game that I was watching, this was the real thing, and it was going to have an impact on this war for years to come. Before Iraq I used to make jokes about being the first general to command any war — it's a bad career move, because invariably the first is the one whose mistakes the later ones learn from. 'Always be the second commanding general,' I used to say, half in jest.

Despite the intensity of the war, General Sanchez was recalled to Washington in May to account to a congressional committee for his role in Abu Ghraib. In Iraq, we watched the hearing on television. He came out of it well on the day, but many colleagues were saying it would hurt him in the long run. A commanding general has an awesome responsibility: he or she is still the only single person who can actually lose a war for a country. Abu Ghraib was indeed a disaster for the coalition effort in Iraq and the actions of those involved were shameful and handed a powerful weapon to our enemies. The detention of people by an occupying power in a country where the legal system has broken down is probably the most difficult of all occupation duties. On an infinitesimally small scale, Australia had its problems in East Timor, and the US is still struggling to put a moral framework around detention and interrogation that is acceptable to its society. The criticism of Sanchez both at the time and subsequently has annoyed me, particularly when made from a comfortable, knowledge-free and remote vantage point. I envy those who can make such confident pronouncements in the absence, despite many inquiries, of any proof of leadership involvement. But at the same time, we stand for the rule of law or we stand for nothing, and generals must be accountable.

During this understudy period I gained great insight into US operational command. I had attended large-scale US field exercises, but this was a real war, run not from tents in a German or US field but in one of Saddam Hussein's major palace complexes, amid a living and breathing society, against a brutal enemy, by soldiers who bled and died.

Saddam had misused his people's money to build the al-Faw complex, but the palace came in useful now. During the invasion, the Americans had spared most of it, with a view to the occupation. When I arrived, there was still rubble where a pair of US bombs had hit, searching for one of the dictator's sons. The bombed area was now being cleared and stairs were being put in for a second storey, where my office was to be. This newly fitted-out storey was made into one of the highest security areas in the building. The chief of intelligence as well as the chief of operations would work there.

The operations centre in the palace was the known universe for a lot of people during their time in Iraq. It was a marvel to behold — the 'Battlestar Galactica' of the Iraq War. It consisted of about 150 computer positions in tiers around a very big room with three enormous screens at the front. In the centre of the tiers was a line of positions where commanders sat. The operations room was manned 24 hours a day by two shifts. Tom Miller, as chief of operations for CJTF-7, owned the operations centre and was in it for most of each long day with his large staff, who made things happen at an ever-finer level of detail.

General Sanchez would come into the operations room for the morning Battle Update Assessment, or BUA (prononunced 'boo-ah'), and for the evening discussion with his commanders across Iraq. The evening session was known as the TACSAT because it was run through a tactical satellite communication system. Sanchez might come into the operations room through the day if there was a significant action on, but Tom Miller or the combat divisions out in the field handled the detail.

I got to know people initially in the operations centre. At the end of each evening TACSAT, Sanchez would offer a summary of events, give his direction for the following day and dismiss us all with a prayer. At this moment, everyone would stand up, salute General Sanchez and call out 'Victory!' I was somewhat surprised the first time I saw this. Although I stood and saluted as a courtesy, I refrained from calling out 'Victory!' It was an American thing. I respected it but, like the war itself, it was not Australian. Likewise, each and every sheet of official paper in the headquarters had on the top and bottom: 'We will not falter — We will not fail'. They were fighting soldiers from a particular culture, and it worked for them. The US was at war in a way that we in Australia were not, and have not been for a long time. I had to figure out my way of maintaining my identity. I was a part of the coalition team, but I did not want to fall into the trap of becoming a pseudo-American.

After the April spike the war plateaued at a new, higher intensity. I watched it all through the operations centre, spending as much time there as I could and learning by osmosis. I watched the most used measure of combat intensity — attacks on the coalition — go from about 150 per week to about 250. This set the pattern for my time in Iraq. We would be at a certain level of combat tempo that we seemed to be managing, then a spike in activity would occur, and when the tempo settled down after the spike, it was always at a higher level. By the start of 2005, in election week, the attack number reached 800 per week, of which 260 were on election day itself. This was extreme intensity by any measure.

By mid-May, I was still following Tom Miller around. And, with a group of first-class US Army colonels whose studies at staff college had been cut short so that they could come to Iraq, we began to plan the new headquarters, conducting task analyses in painstaking detail.

The new headquarters was to be called Headquarters Multi-National Force–Iraq, or HQ MNF-I. Its staff of 999 would carry out planning, operations, intelligence, logistics, personnel and communications functions. What made this headquarters different was a very strong planning staff of about 80, and, unusually, no other part of the headquarters was supposed to have planners. The operations staff that I would eventually take over from Tom Miller was big: 315 people. As well, a group in the headquarters would assess how we were going in this war. This was the first time I had ever seen assessment attempted on such a rigorous, scientific scale.

As for location, the colonels and I were unanimous that HQ MNF-I should move from Camp Victory to the Green Zone, where the political power was located. With at least an outline of what the headquarters should look like, all we needed was the order to form it.

But I was still looking for work. Tom Miller, in his tireless efforts to keep me occupied somewhere he was not, suggested I become chairman of the Improvised Explosive Device (IED) Working Group, involved in combating the roadside bombing campaign. Bombs were the biggest killers of soldiers in Iraq even at this early stage of the insurgency, and they remain the biggest killers today. The insurgents had no supply problems. Iraq was just one big munitions dump, and explosives were everywhere in abandoned military bases. What was unique here was our enemy's adaptability. A type of bomb or detonation mechanism would be used, we would find a counter to it, and the enemy would quickly make a new type, which we would, in turn, try to counter. The working group was a clearing house for information and a means for coordinating 'counter-bombing'. The Brits were great contributors because of their experience in Northen Ireland. One of them observed that the insurgents in Iraq were adapting at roughly ten times the speed of the IRA.

In the IED Working Group, I was quickly into statistics. At that stage, early in 2004, about one-third of all attacks on the coalition used IEDs. On any one day, we had about 50 IED incidents. Of those 50 bombs, we found about half before they exploded. Two or three exploded accidentally as they were being emplaced, either because we were using electronic countermeasures or because of a lack of skill on the bombers' part. This left an average of 20 bombs each day that were exploded against us: one coalition soldier was being killed every two days. Apart from the deaths, the injuries were appalling.

We conducted operations specifically against the bombers, and as we killed the ones with experience, novice bomb-makers stepped up, which meant the rate of premature explosions increased. We put a lot of effort into making the troops 'bomb-smart': we produced pamphlets, pocket cards, videos and newsletters, and we made training compulsory. But it was really the natural cunning and ability of the soldiers that kept casualties relatively low — experience and training told soldiers where not to go and what discarded garbage might be hiding a bomb. The coalition relied a lot on luck and on electronic technology, but experience and training accounted for most of our successes, which were satisfying but never enough to protect all our soldiers, and never enough for our critics in the media.

★

General Abizaid decided to postpone raising HQ MNF-I until he and General Sanchez had responded to the war's new intensity. Sanchez extended Tom Miller's term as chief of operations past the one-year mark: understandably, he did not want to change horses. A further complication for my aspiration to find an honest job was that I still didn't have access to the highest level of US intelligence.

In May, I decided it was time to make a move. I was not about to be given the job I was sent to Iraq to do. Nor was I going to learn much more by following Tom around. I had to find something worthwhile, or I might as well go home.

As I looked around I became aware of the assaults on the energy infrastructure — oil and electricity — and on the rail lines. A problem since the invasion, these attacks were escalating along with the overall intensification. Insurgents and criminals targeted the energy infrastructure for two reasons. The first was plain theft — there was big money to be had from high-tension electrical cables and from oil, or from stealing the cargo on trains. The second reason was that the insurgency wanted to demonstrate the ineffectiveness of the government and the occupying authorities by depriving the people of power and the government of oil exports.

It had been a source of wonder to me that our military strategy appeared to stay so detached from this problem. At our morning briefings, we reviewed the situation on the oil and electricity lines and reserves of fuel across the country, but we seemed incapable of taking effective action; the task was simply too big. Troops would bravely secure local infrastructure in their area of responsibility: bridges, power stations and water facilities. But what was the point in a military unit protecting local facilities if the towers that supported hundreds of kilometres of high-tension lines, somewhere out in the desert, lay on their sides? We didn't have enough troops, and hadn't yet trained up Iraqi contingents, to protect these vital links in the chain.

There was also a conceptual blind spot. The coalition military saw its job as fighting insurgents; it was someone else's job to rebuild Iraq and look after the people. In our plans and strategies we could see that the two tasks were intertwined, but we were not capable of intertwining them on the ground. The insurgents were strangling the cities, and after a year of occupation the Iraqi people were rapidly losing faith in the benefits of the post-Saddam era. This, in turn, fed the insurgency.

I discussed this with Joe Weber. He saw the merit in my taking responsibility for 'strategic infrastructure security' and raising a new organisation to protect the oil, rail and electricity lines, or coordinating the bodies that already existed. This appointment was perhaps as much about getting me a job as anything else, but I appreciated that someone at least was interested. I checked back with Peter Cosgrove, who also saw the benefits. We did not want to create an inconsistency with the Prime Minister's statements in parliament that I was going to Iraq to 'plan, find, destroy and protect'. In fact I would be doing all of this in my new job, just not in the way we'd expected.

After five weeks or so in Iraq, I was still living in Camp Victory with my bodyguard and my executive officer. I needed to move closer to the Iraqi oil, electricity and transport ministries and the CPA. A change would be as good as a holiday, so we moved to the Green Zone. We Australians were allocated a little bungalow within the Green Zone near the old Jordanian embassy, between the destroyed Ba'ath Party headquarters and the Tigris. It was a strange little three-room place consisting of one bedroom (mine), the living room (my bodyguards' bedroom, where they slept on cots) and a kitchen. My executive officer gained a bit of privacy by sleeping on a stretcher in the stairwell, which was also used as our armoury. The house was surrounded by gardens and a big decorative pool, neither of which looked healthy, with big fish floating belly-up. Across the

Tigris was the start of the Red Zone and the Donkey's Dick peninsula. Every shot fired in the Red Zone was audible, and often the clashes would go on all night. But still, we were not sorry to move from our cramped quarters at Camp Victory.

My new title was Deputy Chief of Staff for Operations (Civil Military). As far as my US superiors cared, I could have called myself Father Christmas as long as I did something about getting energy to the cities.

CHAPTER 4

Keeping some of the lights on, some of the time

Protecting the infrastructure, 2004–05

The first crisis in my new role was not long coming. To my surprise, the insurgent attack was not on my infrastructure responsibilities — oil, electricity and rail — but on the distribution of benzene into Baghdad.

Benzene is called petrol in Australia and gas in the US. Iraqi refineries had produced vast quantities for many years. But the refineries around Baghdad were now out of commission, damaged by past wars or present attacks, or unable to move what they did produce because the pipeline system had been destroyed. A modern Western refinery can take a barrel of crude oil straight out of the ground and turn almost 100 per cent of it into petrol. The Iraqi refineries that were working used ancient technology, and could only convert about 50 per cent of each barrel when they were at peak efficiency. The other 50 per cent was burned as fuel oil in electricity power stations.

Saddam's government had sold benzene at literally a few cents a litre at the bowser. It was so cheap that there was little incentive for anyone, Iraqis or foreigners, to invest in modernising Iraq's refineries. Because of war damage and inefficient technology, oil-rich Iraq had only produced a small percentage of its own vehicle fuel. The rest was purchased by the Iraqi government at commercial rates in neighbouring countries such as Kuwait, Jordan or Turkey, and trucked in over dangerous roads by contract drivers, often Jordanians or Turks. The benzene that survived these journeys was dumped into two big storage depots, one north and one south of Baghdad then, regardless of what it had cost, it was still sold to Iraqis at grossly subsidised prices, in reality almost given away.

It did not take the insurgents long to recognise the vulnerability of the benzene tankers and the fact that they could bring Baghdad to its knees by attacking them. These attacks had started during the looting period after the invasion and increased once the insurgency became really active in August 2003. There was no central control over the trucks and no-one provided any security for them — they just 'free-ran' on routes that the drivers chose using their local knowledge. The smoke from burning benzene tankers smudged the desert sky but had no initial impact on the coalition forces themselves, because their fuel came in military-protected road convoys mainly from Kuwait. The people who felt its effects were the Iraqi population.

When I was moving offices from Camp Victory to the Green Zone, the attacks on the road tankers increased. Very soon after we had settled into our new quarters, the contracted Turkish and Jordanian truck drivers had had enough and went on strike. It was not only the insurgents who realised the importance of the benzene trucks in keeping Baghdad running. The drivers began to realise it, and even though they were paid comparatively well, they wanted more, and they wanted some protection. When the fuel stopped flowing into the two fuel depots, the lines at the bowsers in Baghdad grew even longer, and extortion and violence at petrol stations increased.

Little boys on the roadside selling from cans at fifty times the official price were doing a roaring trade. But the black market postponed only by a few days the inevitable shortages, and poorer Iraqis could not pay the black market prices anyway. Slowly but surely, with no transport, what passed for the Iraqi economy ground to a halt. The CPA knew what was happening because it had US civilian 'advisers' who worked intimately with the Oil Minister. I too had military representatives in the Oil Ministry, but at a more junior level, and they passed their warnings to me immediately.

Major General Peter Chiarelli, commander of the 1st Cavalry Division, which had responsibility for security in Baghdad, did not leave me wondering either. He and his 20,000-strong division had arrived in Baghdad very soon before I did, and he had been involved in very serious fighting straight away, particularly in Sadr City. Many of his staff had been in Iraq during previous fuel crises, so he knew what to expect. At a conference where my appointment was announced, he came up and suggested that I keep an eye on a problem he saw developing across Baghdad. In the previous year, when fuel for civilian transport had been in short supply in Baghdad, insurgents had extorted money from the lines of cars waiting for fuel. To bring order to the ensuing chaos, US soldiers had to be physically stationed at each gas station to keep the insurgents away, because there were no civilian police to keep order. As Peter said, he could not look after gas stations and fight the war at the same time.

'Jim, you gotta figure this one out without coming to me for lots of troops,' he said. 'We have got to keep the economy in the city moving. If the people don't have an income, they'll turn to the bad guys and my soldiers'll die.'

Despite my having been in this job for a full five minutes, the entire crisis was somehow my fault (as I had privately predicted). Everyone at the strategic level turned to me to solve the problem, but I was an unknown quantity. I anticipated that I would have a very short period of time to produce a solution, and if my plan didn't work, I would be steamrolled and people would look for their own solutions in their own way.

That day of my appointment, General Sanchez summoned me to his Green Zone office. Unlike in Camp Victory, where General Sanchez was the centre of power, his office in the Green Zone was a long way from the seat of civilian power: Ambassador Bremer's office. I heard later that this isolation was one of many issues that made their working relationship so difficult. Sanchez was the senior military commander in Iraq and ran a force of 150,000 soldiers fighting a major war. Yet Bremer was said to have refused him an office in his central complex. The general had his main office at Camp Victory but he needed (and should have been given) an office in the centre of the Green Zone, as he spent part of each day there. Sanchez's Green Zone office was so humble that several months later, when a new ambassador and a new general finally worked together in adjoining offices and I was chief of operations, General Sanchez's office became mine!

Sanchez's military assistant, a particularly aggressive US colonel, took me in from the anteroom and stayed in the office while I told the general what I knew about the fuel crisis. After a few minutes, Sanchez put the inevitable question: 'Well, what can we do about it?'

My only answer could be: 'Sir, give me a day and I will get back to you with a plan.'

Before I could say more, the colonel interjected from behind me. In that tone reserved for working around non-US coalition officers who are never to be taken seriously, he said to Sanchez: 'Sir, I will call the Corps Headquarters and get them to work it.'

Clearly he thought I was part of the price the Americans had to pay to get other nations' flags into the Iraq War, and could not be trusted to perform a tough task.

I realised that this was a defining moment for my time in Iraq. If I let this thinly veiled professional insult pass, I would be retreating into the category of 'useless coalition officer', of which, to pay the colonel his due, there were many in the headquarters. But I wouldn't let a colonel walk over me in front of Sanchez. Knowing that my status and credibility would be gone forever if I remained silent or acquiesced, I turned on him. 'No, you will not,' I said emphatically, in the way a general should speak to a presumptuous colonel from any army. I turned back to Sanchez and said, 'Sir, you gave me this job, and I'll solve it. As I said, give me a day and I will have a plan.'

'Good,' said Sanchez. 'Brief me tomorrow on the plan. Ambassador Bremer is concerned, and whatever you come up with has to work. I have the legal power to take over all the fuel tankers in this country and to put US drivers in them, and I will do it if I have to so that I can keep the fuel flowing. Speak to the lawyers about what I can legally do in the extreme, but give me a plan tomorrow.'

I walked out knowing I'd made an enemy of the influential gate-keeping colonel but, at least until my first failure, I was still in the game.

There was a slightly bigger problem, though: I had no idea how I was going to develop a plan, much less actually supply five-and-a-half million people in Baghdad with the fuel they needed for their cars, trucks and buses.

I needed some luck. As I came out of the long corridor from Sanchez's office to the palace rotunda, wondering how I was going to get myself out of this one, a US captain, dressed in the khaki camouflage uniform but with 'US Navy' on his breast, approached me.

'Sir,' he said, 'I believe you might need some help in getting some fuel into this country.'

Here was my lucky shot. The navy captain, Brad Bellis, headed a very small group of energy specialists in a unit called the Defense

Energy Support Centre–Iraq. Brad had hundreds of millions of dollars from various funds to purchase benzene. His unit normally operated in the Pacific but had been sent to Iraq to work their magic. He had access to US military contracting officers in four of the six countries around Iraq, among other places. He and his unit had been underutilised and ignored, and, like almost every other US serviceman or woman I met in Iraq, he just wanted to be part of an effective team. 'Come with me, captain,' I said. 'Let's talk.'

By the end of the day we had worked out a plan. We quickly dismissed the idea of taking over the civilian fuel trucks. US military lawyers confirmed that although General Sanchez did indeed have the legal power, it would be very bad policy and quite impracticable. This was because (as I was soon to realise) we were going to need 800 benzene tankers per day to supply the capital. To take over so many trucks, man them with US drivers and maintain them was beyond the ability of even the US military. And if we did take them over, and even if we paid full compensation to the owners, every foreign privately owned truck would be too scared to enter Iraq ever again, and we would be stuck with the problem forever.

Our plan proposed that within two weeks, Brad's unit would have let or renewed contracts in neighbouring countries for 800 civilian tankers to deliver benzene into Iraq daily. Most importantly, my new best naval buddy had millions of dollars to pay for them. If my plan had depended on seeking funds from either the bureaucratic CPA or the Iraqi Governing Council, I would not have got a single fuel truck into Baghdad within six months.

As an agent of the occupying force, I had the power to take benzene supply and distribution out of the Oil Ministry's hands and set up a new import system, which is what I did. This would have been very bad policy, had it gone for any length of time, because it does not develop local capability. But the ministry, having just suffered de-Ba'athification and so lost a large proportion of its competent staff, was incapable of implementing much at all. I justified my actions by telling myself that taking over was not the arrogance of the occupier but pure practicality. The foreign drivers' strike had made everyone appreciate how important the truck drivers were, which was something I could build on. I was prepared to increase what we paid the drivers fivefold to get them to accept the risk of being killed by insurgents on Iraq's roads. I also planned to use the crisis to secure extra coalition protection for them. Indeed, I planned for US helicopter gunships to escort tanker convoys, rather than leaving truck drivers to run the gauntlet of bombs and RPGs individually and without protection. But I did not control the helicopters, so I had to figure out some way of getting commitments from those who did. We also planned to build the drivers some protected overnight truckstops where there would be food and a safe place to sleep, and to control truck movements from point to point so they would no longer wander into ambushes.

But 800 trucks per day was a very large number, almost beyond my comprehension, and I knew I could only protect a fraction of them.

Brad and I worked late into the night, and the next morning I was able to go back to Sanchez's office and present this plan. It went over well. He was reassured. Not only was I providing some hope of easing the Baghdadis' daily burden, but I might be able to get Ambassador Bremer off the general's back too. Sanchez authorised me to present the benzene plan to the wider leadership the next morning at the BUA.

The BUA linked all headquarters across Iraq and certain other places in the world. It began at 0630 and went for approximately an hour. From 0330, staff officers would prepare briefings from all parts of the force on what had happened the day before and what might happen in the coming day. The BUA aimed to update General

Strategic Oil Infrastructure, Iraq
Schematic: April 2004

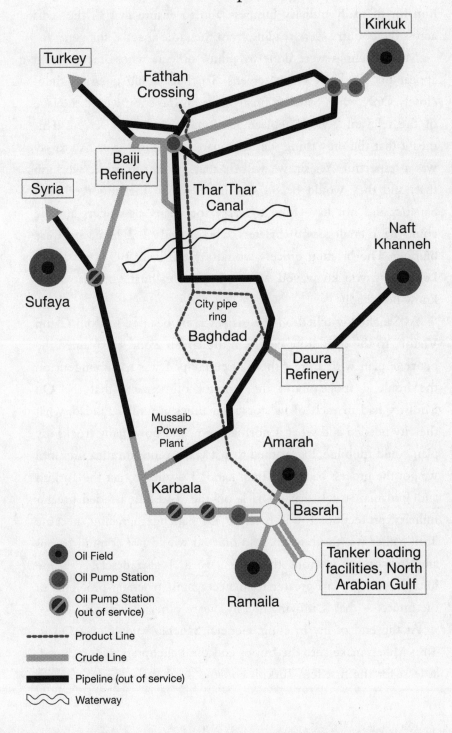

Kirkuk

Turkey

Fathah
Crossing

Baiji
Refinery

Syria

Thar Thar
Canal

Naft
Khanneh

Sufaya

City pipe
ring

Baghdad

Daura
Refinery

Mussaib
Power
Plant

Amarah

Karbala

Basrah

Tanker loading
facilities, North
Arabian Gulf

Ramaila

Oil Field

Oil Pump Station

Oil Pump Station
(out of service)

Product Line

Crude Line

Pipeline (out of service)

Waterway

Sanchez before he met with Ambassador Bremer at 0900, to prepare him for his daily military business, and to ensure that all the staffs across the country were reading from the same sheet as the general.

Most briefings were done by junior officers whose faces would appear on the giant video screens. Sanchez would question them closely. Only when Sanchez finally gave his direction would the face of the relevant general replace his junior officer on screen. This meant that the only thing the headquarters' generals ever had to say was a respectful, 'Yes sir, we will fix that,' or 'Yes sir, we're working that,' and they would be off scot-free. Not so the junior officers. Sanchez did not have time to carry too many passengers and he could be merciless with briefers who lacked confidence or were bluffing. The briefing officers would say the daily BUA was like a knife fight: you knew you were going to get hurt, you just didn't know how badly.

As Sanchez watched on the giant screen, beamed in from Camp Victory to the operations centre in the Green Zone, I explained the benzene plan with a great show of certainty. I was less confident on the inside. I spoke about the amount of benzene that the Oil Ministry had in each of its storage facilities around Baghdad, what the city needed and what it normally got, and how many trucks my plan could mobilise. I explained that it was an interim measure until we got the process back into Iraqi hands. I wanted to get the Turkish and Jordanian truck drivers back on the road, but needed greater military protection. I was banking on Sanchez agreeing, because Tom Miller was too busy to help me and would not commit troops and helicopters without the boss's word. I also described some initiatives to give us greater resilience against trucking problems in the future — that is, moving fuel by means other than roads.

At the end of my briefing, General Sanchez said: 'Good. Do it. Tom Miller, make sure the troops and the helicopters are produced, at least for the first few Turkish convoys, so that the drivers can see the support we give them. Jim, keep me updated on how it is going and go and brief Ambassador Bremer this morning.'

I had survived my first BUA without receiving any serious knife wounds. But I now had to deliver. Fortunately, Brad and his fuel experts were as good as their word, and in a few days we had contracts with drivers in three of the six surrounding countries; we had paid for them, plus sweeteners to make the risk worthwhile; and we had started to build protected overnight truck stops. On 31 May, we had the trucks moving again. Before long we would come close to reaching the target of 800 fuel trucks per day.

Of course the insurgents very quickly realised what we were doing. They had agents everywhere and worked out exactly how much fuel was flowing into the depots around Baghdad. In no time at all, despite the increased protection for the convoys, insurgents were blowing up or disabling ten trucks a day and killing their drivers. The tragic economic facts of life for Iraqis and their neighbours meant that, despite this, there was no shortage of drivers ready to try their luck at the rates we now offered.

I quickly discovered that it was all about persistence. The insurgents could not sustain this attack program indefinitely — they were not superhuman, and they too were governed by the laws of logistics. We killed some of them around the convoys. We provided security for the drivers each night. We re-routed convoys around the trouble spots as soon as we recognised them. Many drivers preferred to run the gauntlet by themselves rather than in convoys — if they knew the roads and the threat — believing they were safer this way because the presence of our units just attracted attention. So inadvertently we confused the insurgents, by sending trucks alone and in convoys, with and without escorts, at any time of day or night and on any route. In time, the frequency of attacks fell, and my other methods of providing benzene, mainly by repairing pipelines, also began to deliver fuel. Of course we still only provided a small percentage of what Baghdad really needed. Infrastructure security remained far less than perfect.

I reported daily to Sanchez and to Bremer on benzene levels and other energy issues. I began to go to a daily energy meeting that Ambassador Bremer attended as often as he could, sometimes held in his wood-panelled office off the palace rotunda. The most noticeable feature of his office was a carved sign on his desk that read, 'Success has a thousand fathers', indicating an admirable confidence by omitting the second part of the saying, 'But failure is an orphan.'

To Bremer, I would have been just another of the coalition generals who floated in and out of his panelled office. My personal view was that regardless of the torrent of criticism he has attracted, he was a most impressive man. He made things happen, and some of them were right. He made errors, but any of us would probably have made at least the same number. Getting things done is a trait I admire more than any other in a leader, and Bremer was a tough man. He was dealing with a diverse and complex group and caused things to occur by example and direction, as well as by bluff and anger. I can personally attest to this and was not so precious as to feel injured by it.

I became a regular briefer in the daily BUA, a reflection of the importance within any system of keeping your superiors fully updated. But the situation was always unpredictable and luck remained as important as ever. My petroleum people went out to the depots to physically check the amounts in the storage tanks, and to no-one's surprise, all was not as it seemed. Iraqi managers had been under-reporting their fuel holdings so they'd have some to sell on the black market. When we reported the real amounts of fuel on hand, I was seen as a winner already. I said to Brad that we were going to be blamed for a lot of things that we were not responsible for, so we should balance the scorecard up a bit in advance! But as soon as we notched up this 'win', insurgents or criminals attacked one of the fuel survey teams we sent out to verify the levels; this was probably a set-up by the managers to dissuade us from taking too close an interest in their scams. That was the nature of the fight in Iraq, but despite these setbacks, I was off and running.

As we started to execute the benzene plan, I paused to look at my wider responsibilities. I had been lucky to stumble across Brad Bellis, but now I had better begin to make my own luck. A number of international sports stars, including golfers Arnold Palmer and Gary Player and Australia's squash champion Geoff Hunt, have come up with a line to explain their apparent good luck: 'The more I practise, the luckier I get.'

Benzene was neither our only problem nor our biggest. The insurgents were tightening their stranglehold over the supply of energy in all forms. Most of us in the West take electrical power for granted. Without power, authorities cannot pump water through a modern city; the result is sickness and death. Without power, authorities cannot pump sewage; the result is effluent on the ground and more sickness. People surrounded by shit cannot be positive about the future. Streets without lights lower morale and facilitate crime. Homes without power rely on candles and fuel lamps for light and are without air conditioning, refrigeration or telecommunications. This means children cannot study. Hot weather, stinking streets, filthy water and fear create short tempers and resentment. Five-and-a-half million Baghdadis had never had more than 12 hours of electricity per day since the invasion, and normally had only three or four.

The public's attitude during a counterinsurgency campaign is critical. Infrastructure security came down to improving this attitude. The saying 'winning hearts and minds' has a bad smell about it from Vietnam, so in Iraq we said that 'the will of the people is the centre of gravity'. The insurgents knew this at least as well as the coalition did. Attacking the infrastructure eroded the people's confidence in the coalition and the new Iraq. No matter how good we were as soldiers, if we could not provide basic services, the people of Iraq would turn towards our enemies.

Ambassador Bremer's CPA and General Sanchez and his military commanders were deeply split over infrastructure security, and I found myself caught between them. My fellow generals argued that it was someone else's business to guard oil pipes, electricity lines, railways and civilian supply convoys between the different military areas, and pointed to the CPA's supposedly considerable resources. The CPA had created local Iraqi forces to guard rail, electricity and oil. However, these arrangements had serious problems because, for various reasons, there were not enough guards, they were not adequately armed and they would not go outside their bases. The CPA's plans were all based on flawed commercial contracts for security and repair, and assumed that security in Iraq would get better in time. Obviously, that wasn't happening.

Because of this buck-passing between military and civilian authorities, I was not receiving much help until Joe Weber, Sanchez's chief of staff, told me that I would be supported by about 100 US Army Reserve civil affairs soldiers from the 350th Civil Affairs Command under Brigadier General Sandy Davidson. Civil Affairs soldiers were part of the US Special Forces and handled the military's interaction with local civilians: in our case, the oil, electricity and transport ministries. I had never been exposed to such a unit before, but quickly found that they had expert teams in each ministry.

I was surprised at first by the warmth of Sandy's welcome. I soon realised why. Sandy's soldiers were undeservedly looked down on by some regular US soldiers. Mostly reservists, they were seen to have less of a combat role (this was often untrue), and on top of that they had responsibility for a function that was not going to be solved in the short term. So they tended to get a pretty hard time in the headquarters, and Ric Sanchez was a very demanding boss. I came to suspect that the main reason they welcomed a coalition general was that they hoped I would absorb a lot of the flak that had previously been directed at them! But I was very relieved that they were supporting me, so the pleasure was mutual.

I called together a planning group of the best of Sandy's young officers. To prepare, I studied countless more maps of Iraq. Some things were obvious. I saw Baghdad in the centre of the country: seat of government, five-and-a-half million people, very vulnerable but very important. We had to keep energy in all forms flowing into Baghdad, at least at a level that kept essential services running. I looked up north to the second-biggest city, Mosul: perhaps not as big a problem as Baghdad at this stage. But Mosul needed watching because of its size and because the oil city of Kirkuk was relatively close.

Kirkuk was not only an oil-producing site, it was also a flashpoint between the Kurds, traditional owners of the Kirkuk area and its oil, and the Arabs that Saddam had moved in. Oil from Kirkuk supplied the big refinery and power stations at Baiji, halfway between Baghdad and Mosul, and also crude oil for export to Turkey. But there was no oil being exported to Turkey because the pipe had been blown, and Iraq was losing US$170 million to US$240 million in desperately needed oil revenue every month. Rather naively, I assumed I could leverage this lost revenue to get resources for better security.

Crude oil from Kirkuk also flowed in pipes across the Tigris then south to Baghdad in an 'energy corridor'. This corridor consisted of about a dozen pipes that normally brought oil and petroleum products to Baghdad, plus the electrical lines from the power stations at Baiji that distributed power to the centre and the north of the country. I could see that this area was going to be important. Other electricity lines ran directly from Kirkuk to Baghdad across some pretty lawless country.

On my map I looked south from Baghdad to Basrah, which was surrounded by oilfields — the real source of Iraq's oil wealth. Basrah produced 90 per cent of Iraq's oil; only 10 per cent came from Kirkuk. A small percentage of the oil from Basrah was pumped north to Baghdad. Some was used to generate electricity, but the vast majority flowed south down the al Faw peninsula into a never-ending queue of thirsty tankers.

The oil pipelines around the country were of varying size and age. Some consisted of a single big pipe, such as the one that ran for hundreds of lonely kilometres from Basrah north to Najaf and Karbala and then to the major Baghdad power station south of the capital at Mussaib. After many years of attack, there were hardly any valves left in this enormous pipe system, so an explosion at any one point might mean that the contents of hundreds of kilometres of oil pipeline would flow out and burn on the desert sand. Until the pipe was emptied and the fires were out, no repairs could begin. Repair would have been a lengthy process even if the insurgents were not trying to kill you while you were doing it.

I now had sufficient background information for our planning session. The civil affairs captains, majors and lieutenant colonels were full of knowledge and energy, but were also very frustrated by working in the ministries. They knew we could achieve a great deal more than we were achieving. Somehow I had to harness this energy. I asked them a stream of questions, letting them guide me through the bizarre Iraqi world of oil, electricity and rail.

Soon I understood their frustration. Iraq's energy infrastructure, serving 27 million, was in a disastrous state. What had not been destroyed by the Iranians in the war from 1980 to 1988, bombed by the US in two wars or blown up by the insurgents, was old and falling to bits. I remembered that the Oil Minister had made a well-publicised estimate of how much it would cost to rehabilitate the Iraqi oil sector: US$25 billion. I did not have this amount in spare cash, so it was very important that I choose something doable.

My first question to these smart young people was about the human dimension. I asked them to draw me a picture of how oil and electricity were run in Iraq, and to tell me about the ministers themselves. While I had significant legal authority during the occupation to do pretty much what I wanted, it would end in a few months when power would pass to the Iraqis, and then I would have to work through the ministers and their bureaucrats.

Working on a whiteboard, they began with the dysfunctional oil system. It was split into three fiefdoms: the Northern Oil Company based in Kirkuk, the Southern Oil Company based in Basrah, and the central system in Baghdad. I was not surprised to hear that each fiefdom's director general only obeyed the minister in Baghdad if it suited them. The Oil Minister himself, an Iraqi engineer and bureaucrat called Thamir Ghadban, was a particularly prickly character, but from what everyone said and from my impressions when I came to know him, he was a true Iraqi patriot who had spent his career trying to make the oil system work. Ghadban had survived Saddam, was an expert in his field, and was thought to be an honest man. The civil affairs captain who worked with Ghadban predicted, quite accurately, that the first thing the minister would say to me when we met was that every coalition soldier in Iraq should be on the oil pipelines protecting them — no exceptions. 'He will also remind you constantly, sir, that Saddam had "thirteen divisions" protecting the oil infrastructure from sabotage, perhaps 100,000 troops. He sees us as amateurs in this game.'

The captain told us that Ghadban hated the security systems the CPA had set up, believing them — quite rightly — to be ineffective and ridiculously expensive. In fact, he refused to deal with the CPA's contractors.

The Electricity Minister was a different kind of man altogether. His name was Aiham al-Sammarae, and he was an Iraqi expatriate who had been living in Chicago for many years and had worked in the US electricity industry. To his everlasting credit, he had come back after the invasion to help the country of his birth. The civil affairs soldiers, however, felt uneasy about him. Like Ghadban, he knew what he was talking about in technical terms. I believe he had political ambitions in the upcoming elections and I heard later that he was charged with corruption, but that could have been for any number of reasons. When I met him, I would come to respect his genuine commitment, if not his overall strategic thinking. As we were hit by attack after attack, I wanted Minister al-Sammarae to reduce electrical power generation to conserve oil and build reserves so that, as a minimum, we could pump water and sewage in the cities and run hospitals during the crises. But he only ever wanted to maximise the power that he generated until the oil at the power stations was finished. In fairness, his attitude was a direct result of the CPA fascination with meeting electricity output targets to better the pre-war average megawattage. And, I suspected, perhaps it was the minister's awareness of his possible future electability. He would say in our heated conversations on this issue: 'General, this is not my fault. My job is to produce electricity. It is the Oil Minister's responsibility to keep the tanks at my power stations full. And general, it is your responsibility to protect everything.' He and Oil Minister Ghadban disliked each other profoundly, and would each ring me to complain about the other. My job would certainly be a lot harder when the occupation ended in July and I couldn't just tell them what to do.

I was briefed on the railways by an enthusiastic team who were more frustrated, if that was possible, than the others. They had very little access to the Minister for Transport. Using more colourful language, they said that the Iraqi railways 'are quite simply [not working]...!' The minister showed no interest in rail infrastructure, and the director-general was a good man but had been cowed by living under Saddam, they said. The CPA had given the minister a lot of money to set up a transport security system but the railways had seen none of it. Rumour had it that he was using the money to lease aircraft for Iraqi Air, his first and only transport love. As a result, his director-general could only hire 500 local guards to protect the entire Iraqi railway system. And this was not a small system. Centred on Baghdad, it ran to the north as far as Mosul, to the south as far as Basrah and west out to the Syrian border, each of these legs was about 400 isolated kilometres in length. Thanks to the isolation, by the time I took over, insurgents and criminals had shut it down.

My staff warned me that the minister would avoid me like the plague, and the director-general would agree with me on everything — and then do nothing. Both warnings turned out to be true. I could only imagine what these people had been through in Saddam's time, and I tried to be sensitive, but the director-general and his staff would happily make an appointment for me at the Central Station and then hide as I came into the building. I tried being more forceful, telling the minister and director-general that I would give them no security until they spent the money they had been given for hiring and training real guards — not just whistle-blowing station guards. Actually, I doubt they even blew their whistles, because there were no trains running in Iraq.

Having shown me the human side of the task, my briefers brought out some excellent detailed maps and diagrams, many produced by the CIA before the invasion and completed during the first year of occupation. We worked from the diagrams back to the whiteboard, building up a picture of great chaos, but I also sensed some potential. The challenge would have been chaotic enough with just the ministers and the bureaucracies to deal with. Oil for export or domestic use was only reliable where the British were protecting the main lines in the south, which ultimately took about one-third of their force. Pipes were blown, power stations and refineries were partially functional, rail lines were broken, and electrical lines were smashed. Hardly anyone was paying for electricity so there was no investment in the system apart from some big reconstruction projects which wouldn't deliver a watt of power for years. As a result, ordinary Iraqis' lives were unbearable. This worried me most, because the people's attitudes were going to decide this war.

'Then who is on our side?' I asked the briefers. 'What have we got to work with?'

They told me that there were forces out there, apart from the coalition, trying to do a good job. There were 14,400 Iraqi oil guards, 6000 electricity guards and the 500 rail guards, plus a fleet of vehicles, a few aircraft, and any number of contractors to repair pipes and build power stations. But no-one was sure who controlled them, and there were questions about their effectiveness. Still, the existence of this force was more than I expected — I just had to figure out how to get my hands on them. I certainly had the intense interest of Bremer's staff and the US government. The US intelligence community were also very interested in infrastructure security and oil. Maybe, I thought, this could work.

'But with such a force, why can't we achieve results?' I asked.

'Simple — the contracts don't work,' they fell over each other to tell me.

We were now getting to the crux of the problem. In the post-invasion optimism, the contracts for the security of the oil system and the repair of oil pipes had ignored the possibility of an insurgency.

Bremer's staff had contracted the 14,400-strong oil protection force to a British-based risk and security company, Erinys International. Erinys recruited foreign contractors to manage thousands of Iraqi security guards, whom they equipped with AK–47s. These contracted managers and their guards were distributed through the oil system — except, I was surprised to discover, for the most vulnerable part: the pipes.

Even as the contract was being signed for hundreds of millions of dollars in 2003, the security situation deteriorated well past what had been envisaged. The Erinys force was competent to guard the pumping stations and refineries because reliable foreign contractors managed the guards and fortified the facilities. And there were normally coalition quick reaction forces around the corner, if not on the spot. The insurgents had no real desire (or need) to attack these defended facilities when there were so many pipes sitting around unguarded, waiting to be blown up. On a few occasions when the Erinys guards went out bravely to defend the pipes, they were confronted by insurgents or criminal groups armed with rifles, machine guns, rocket-propelled grenades and unlimited explosives — they were more heavily armed and far more motivated than the oil guards. The Erinys personnel, clutching their AK–47s, retreated behind the barriers while insurgents blew up the pipes with impunity.

To pay them their due, the Erinys managers generally did a good job and met their contractual requirements. But the contract was at the very least, deeply inappropriate. Unbelievably, Erinys were not obliged to go out and protect the pipes if there was any threat! Erinys came cheap, but that was because they did not need armour-protected vehicles, extensive training or weapons heavier than AK–47s, and that was because their contract did not require them to do a large part of what needed doing in energy security in Iraq.

My briefers told me a similar story about a second contract. This was let by the CPA to a well-known US company to repair damaged pipes. This was a very expensive contract involving the latest technology in oil pipe repair. But like the Erinys contract, it made no allowance for anything other than a benign security situation. If there was any danger, the contractors did not have to go out and repair pipes, even if we provided them with military security. In short, the CPA got what they paid for, but again the contract was based on a naive assessment of the violence Iraq would face.

So this was the background: the CPA, having underestimated the insurgency, turned to the military to bolster infrastructure security. The military's reply was: Why should coalition soldiers die protecting oil pipes if the Iraqis and highly paid contractors are not prepared to take equivalent risks? I could see why my fellow generals were so glad to see me move across to the Green Zone as the 'general-in-residence' and become the whipping boy for the infrastructure protection dispute.

As I listened to the briefing, a plan began to coalesce in my mind. I decided to concentrate on the oil and electricity systems and ignore rail at this stage. I established two priorities. The first was to get some energy flowing into Baghdad, either electricity off the national grid or oil that could be turned into electricity in the city's power stations. The second priority was to keep oil flowing to export, from the north through Turkey and from the south through the Arabian Gulf. If there was a clash between energy into Baghdad and exports, Baghdad would take priority because Baghdad was where we would win public support and so win the war.

Our practical strategy was, as we called it, to 'protect the static and repair the linear'. We had to protect major installations and 'out-repair' the insurgents as they blew the lines up. We would also have to kill or capture insurgents who were concentrating on cutting the lines.

It would be the mother of all understatements to say that this strategy had a few problems. I had no illusions that I could achieve all of this, but I needed an aim to strive for. Everything I planned would put me on a collision course with just about everyone else in

Iraq: the ministries, who just wanted to pump oil and generate electricity willy-nilly; the military, who would not want to provide any more troops; the creators of the new Iraqi Army, who did not want to arm an infrastructure protection force; the contractors, who only wanted to service the contract they had signed; the Oil Minister, who resented paying for security in any form because he saw it as the coalition's and the Iraqi Army's responsibility; and last but not least, the CPA, who claimed that they had tried all this before, and so were not going to put any money into it again.

And of course, as soon as I failed to produce results, it would indeed all be my fault, and no-one would show the least interest until it had reached absolute crisis!

But there was no questioning the project's importance, both nationally and outside Iraq. The world's daily oil consumption in 2004 was about 80 million barrels. The US consumed 20 million, mostly imported. Iraq produced 2 million barrels per day, but had the potential to produce much more. In the months ahead, Ambassador John Negroponte would greet me jokingly at the daily update with, 'Well, Jim, what have you done to oil prices today?'

After the briefings and after settling in, I started to travel. I ranged from Kirkuk and Mosul to the power stations in and around Baghdad, the sweet oil wells on the Iranian border, the power stations and refineries in Basrah and the export facilities on the al Faw peninsula. I met oil officials and electricity officials and members of the oil security forces, the Iraqi Army and the tribal leaders (shayks) who had contracts to protect parts of the lines. I spoke to truck drivers and train drivers and mechanics in workshops that were armouring oil trains against rocket-propelled grenades. I visited pipe repair sites in the middle of the desert and at the edges of canals as Iraqi tradesmen and foreign contactors dug up the destroyed pipes, mopped up the oil, emptied the pipes, then fixed them.

At the Northern Oil Company headquarters, I saw first-hand the impact of the looting that had occurred as people took their revenge after years of repression. The building itself had been trashed and anything of value had been taken. As I was leaving our meeting, the local military interpreter came up quietly and said I should not believe that exports to Turkey had stopped: the Northern Oil Company was selling oil covertly. Once again in Iraq, nothing was as it seemed. The day after our meeting, the director-general of the Northern Oil Company was ambushed and killed as he drove home.

I felt as if I was boxing with shadows. The enemy had the initiative, so was I opposing a master planner somewhere out there with a centrally coordinated strategy? Sometimes I thought a strategy was there; at other times I was certain it was not. If it was centrally controlled, it veered between brilliance and total incompetence. What made me doubt that I was opposing a sophisticated centrally controlled campaign was that often, after a range of seemingly coordinated attacks across the country that had brought us to our knees, the insurgents failed to take the last step: to stop absolutely all energy supplies. What made me on other occasions think that there was a coordinating mind out there was the apparent simultaneity of the attacks, and a synchronised reaction to our tactics and strategy.

A consistent level of attacks, sometimes as many as ten or 12 per week, kept our energy reserves low but not exhausted. Was that their plan? Were the insurgents keeping us at this level so that whenever they conducted a bigger push against us, our energy resilience was low and they could then achieve maximum effect by a few actions in a short time? But if so, why didn't they go the whole way and cut off all energy? Sometimes an increased intensity in infrastructure attacks gave us the only warning that something, somewhere, was going to happen.

Whether or not there was an insurgent commander directing infrastructure sabotage, I was convinced that they had a unifying idea. It was simple. When the coalition was putting additional pressure on the insurgency or they suffered a setback, they would turn on the infrastructure. 'Let's blow up a pipe or a tower' did not require a sophisticated plan: it was a simple retaliatory plan that any cell in the insurgency could carry out.

One of my first tasks was dealing with the faulty Erinys and pipe-repair contracts. The Erinys people I dealt with were prepared to go that little bit further and try to protect the pipes if they were given better weapons. I tried to get them machine guns and rocket-propelled grenades. Unbelievably, until May 2004, even the new Iraqi military was not allowed to own anything heavier than AK-47s. This situation reflected an early US view that the new Iraq should have a paramilitary force but not a fighting army. This view had changed by the time I started my new job, but now every machine gun and rocket-propelled grenade launcher that was in storage in Iraq, captured from the insurgents, obtained through a 'buy back' program or found hidden in caches, was being sent directly to the new Iraqi Army. I was rebuffed when I asked for these weapons for my little oil protection force.

I approached Minister Ghadban for money to buy weapons. He was unhelpful, saying that it was 'the army's job'. In the end, I found an American contract manager who had discretionary funds for oil protection. Like many others in Iraq, we bought weapons on the streets. We obtained only a few poor-quality weapons, but at least we took some off the market. But for how long? I knew that a portion of everything I got for the oil guards would be sold directly back to the black market. I just hoped that a few would keep their weapons and protect some of the pipes. This was not a country where one expected perfection. It was a country of second-class, sub-optimal, compromised solutions that never got near even the traditionally acceptable '80 per cent solution'. At this stage, I was happy to be figuratively standing still, and ecstatic if I was not going backwards.

As for the pipe-repair contract, that was more simple. The contractors refused to repair the pipelines if there was danger, even after I offered them more money. Eventually, I suggested that their contract be terminated and we replaced them with the US military-led and Iraqi contractor-based Emergency Rapid Pipeline Repair Organization, which went under the wonderful acronym ERPRO. (As I was leaving Iraq in 2005, the US government and the original pipe-repair company were in legal dispute over the terminated contract. Many months after I left Iraq I ran into the in-country manager of the company on an airline transfer bus; he told me it had all been settled out of court.)

After my initial fact-finding, brainstorming sessions, settling into my office, travelling, and selling my 'protect the static and repair the linear' strategy, a strange thing happened. Individuals and groups began visiting me and saying, 'Sir, it's great to have you involved. Can we work for you?' This was mainly due to my exposure in the daily BUA. All the lost souls connected to infrastructure security gravitated towards me.

In the BUA I had cracked part of the code for how the system worked, even though I had no real authority and little influence over the staff. The staff would have been mad to jump to it if someone like me just walked into their office and asked them to do things. I was a one-man band supported by a bunch of civil affairs staff and an orphan petroleum organisation. But I had daily direct and visible access to the boss in a relatively public place, the BUA, where his directions had to be followed up.

Reputations were made and lost in the daily BUA. Everyone watched the BUA, and its results were accessed by people around the world, even as far as the Secretary of Defense's office in Washington.

So I used the BUA to draw Sanchez's interest, and then his commitment to action. He and the military leadership progressively bought into my version of infrastructure security because I could show the consequences of not doing so. When I wanted more resources, I could leverage Sanchez's interest. Everything was top priority in this war, but the real top priority was what the commanding general directed.

To capture and hold the interest of Sanchez, I simply exploited the 'power' of PowerPoint. I needed Sanchez and his subordinates to understand what I was up against and how the coalition could help me by assigning forces at critical times and places. I am the type of person who understands things best through pictures. Some people take notes; I draw diagrams and pictures. I got my staff to convert the hand drawing of the Iraqi energy system on our whiteboard into a clever PowerPoint slide. This simple picture of a complex system illustrated the flow of energy into Baghdad from all sources, the storage around Baghdad, and the location of the key facilities that, if blown up, would cut energy supplies.

The first morning I introduced this slide in my segment of the BUA, I had to explain what it was. This was a departure from the way the energy situation had been presented to Sanchez. Previously he had received information about the static state of the systems, the daily levels of each type of product or the amount of electricity being produced. What I was trying to do was to produce information about systems that displayed options, and the consequences for all courses of action and inaction. Sanchez seemed to understand what I was talking about.

On this day the slide showed that we had only two or three days' supply of energy in the form of oil within Baghdad. It also showed where insurgents had hit vulnerable areas. My guys had elected to depict our vulnerable areas with bomb symbols. When one of these points was hit, the bomb was replaced by a small explosion symbol, above which were two dates: the first for when the hit had occurred, the second for when we estimated that the pipe would be repaired.

From Camp Victory at the other end of the vidcon (videoconference), Sanchez listened to my explanation, interpreted the diagram himself, and said, 'So Jim, what you are telling us is that in four days we will have no power at all in Baghdad unless you can repair the pipe that comes up from the south into Mussaib power station. And that is not going to be any good to us unless we can keep the main electricity lines that bring the electricity up from Mussaib to the substation at the southeast corner of Baghdad, near Salman Pak. And your dates indicate that we may finish the pipe repairs in two days' time. If you can do that, how much power will Baghdad then have?'

Greatly relieved that the diagram was working, I replied, 'Sir, even if we repair the pipe in the time that is indicated, we still need two days to fill the pipe and to get the pressure up before any significant amount of oil flows in to the power station. We will then need one more day to get the generators running. We need to keep the pipe open for two weeks to fill the Mussaib storage to full capacity. And we have never been able to keep that pipe open for more than about five consecutive days since January. I have started to get the trucks to move residual oil from the Daura refinery to the Mussaib power station, but I need 40 trucks per day to make any impression at all. I am looking to get the 30 kilometres of rail track from Daura to Mussaib repaired because we have over 100 fuel rail cars that are not being used. So my priority for repair and for ground protection is the oil pipe; and for air surveillance and roving patrols, it is the last electricity line from Mussaib into the city. If we lose one of these we lose our ability to pump sewage and water in Baghdad. What I really need is as many troops as possible over about the next week until we have some oil stored or the trucks start to make an impact.'

This was how I got the holy grail: resources from the military. It would have been hard for Sanchez to resist my logic on this day, and each day was the same. We would watch the state of the reserves in each storage facility and the progress of the repairs, and move resources onto the lines and pipes as the situation changed. If things were going in our favour, we were able to supply a few hours of power to Baghdad. If things went very well, we reached six hours in a day. It was very unusual to ever reach 12 or 14. Six was the norm: Baghdadis would have two hours on, then six hours off, two hours of power and six off, and so on.

Our military leadership knew how important essential services were, and if we forgot, Ambassador Bremer and CPA officers would remind us. What I could do was show the role that infrastructure security played in the bigger battle. We would never harness the will of the people unless we kept power coming into Baghdad. The PowerPoint slide was titled, 'Keeping the Lights on in Baghdad', which was pretentious. It should have been 'Keeping Some Lights On, Some of the Time, in Parts of Baghdad'. As time went by we added a few extra slides, such as 'Keeping the Export Oil Flowing' and 'Benzene for Baghdad'.

I was using the BUA video conferences well, but nothing beats a good meeting. Getting people together in the same room had its risks in Iraq, but I held weekly meetings of what I called the Infrastructure Security Working Group. One meeting, the third that I held, was memorable and tragic. The British civilian adviser to the oil ministry and his driver were killed by a magnetic bomb placed under their vehicle in the ministry car park. It exploded on their way to the meeting. My British Army petroleum engineers were blown off Route Irish while driving in to the same meeting, and so arrived, as they joked, both shaken and stirred. And the newly appointed head of the Electricity Security Force, an Iraqi colonel, was arrested just before the meeting as an insurgent agent.

This was Iraq. We paused for a moment, adjusted the agenda and continued the war.

I worked from an operations room in Saddam's Palace in the Green Zone. My keen staff and I set up or refocused organisations to monitor, report, secure, repair, contract, liaise with ministries, and coordinate infrastructure security forces across Iraq. This may sound impressive and self-congratulatory, and I worked hard at giving the impression at the BUA of being on top of it all, but in reality what I had created was ad hoc and so inefficient that sometimes I could have wept. Our arrangements improved on what was in place before — which is not saying much. But that was how it was, and that was pretty much how it stayed.

It worked because of the quality and the dedication of the men and women behind me, mostly US reservists, with some British and some Australian full-time officers scattered about. I was the front man, committing us to do things we couldn't, and they continually saved my bacon by delivering. They were great people, especially the reservists, headed by US Lieutenant Colonel Mark McQueen and UK Colonel Gareth Derrick. Major Harry Callicotte lived and breathed oil and was never happier than when he was out on the road doing things, and never unhappier than when he was being ignored. Although I would never have admitted it at the time, Harry and I had a lot in common.

As oil pipes blew up and poured their riches into the sky, and electricity towers dropped to the ground in a flash and a cloud of dust, we would repair wherever we could, restrict the output of the power stations so that we did not run out too soon, and hold what few troops we had until we could see what the enemy was doing. I would pick the critical line or pipe and deploy to it every bit of protection that we had or could get at short notice. Then, while using what little oil reserves we had stored, we'd immediately start the trucks running. Having held one pipeline and one electricity line open, we would then repair pipes or lines in a set priority as fast as we could.

Iraqis have been repairing pipes for as long as they have had oil, so there were plenty of experienced repairers about, but mobilising them was a different matter. The experienced teams were controlled by the oil fiefdoms in Kirkuk, Baghdad and Basrah. Their priorities never seemed to be my priorities. And the Iraqi bureaucrats paid the repair team's salaries whether they repaired pipes or not, so they were in no hurry to get out and help us. The insurgents worsened matters further by threatening the repair specialists and their families.

I tried to direct these teams through the ministry, but received little help. After June, when the occupation legally ended, I lost even that power. The ministry teams worked at a comfortable pace. They only changed their work schedule when an insurgent threat surfaced, and then they would leave the worksite and seek shelter. They did not trust the coalition to protect them, not surprisingly, and believed, with some justification, that a coalition presence at their worksite only attracted insurgents. They went out by themselves or with local guards from the ministry, but one visit by armed men and they would be back in their depots. Once, just after we had equipped a ministry team with millions of dollars' worth of new specialist repair vehicles, bulldozers, low-loaders and tools, insurgents (no doubt informed by agents inside the oil ministry) stopped the team on the road going to their first job and relieved them of their new vehicles and equipment. The insurgents did not kill anyone, possibly confirming it as an inside job and reminding me that the ministry itself was part of the problem, rather than part of the solution. I tried to shame the ministry into getting back on the job, because oil production was the future of the new Iraq. But in the face of death threats to them and their families or the likelihood of being ambushed on their way to work, I was getting no assistance from the ministry teams.

Without any hope of changing the existing culture, I decided to set up teams that *we* controlled. They would be protected and would repair pipes that *we* determined it was necessary to repair, and do it when *we* wanted it done.

Through another chance encounter, I happened on the solution. As I have mentioned, the respected US pipe-repair company was not functioning because its contract did not provide for adequate protection for its crews, so they simply weren't going out to repair pipes. Company representatives and others in the CPA fed me a line that the problem was the behaviour of some US Army officers working with the company as contract administrators.

I found that this was a lie. The US Army officers concerned were very frustrated by the company's attitude. They saw the sacrifices made by their army mates across Iraq and knew the importance of keeping the oil flowing. The company was letting the US and its armed forces down. Once I understood that these officers were not to blame, they considered me their ally and came to me with a proposal to set up Iraqi pipe repair teams provided by Iraqi contractors that they knew, and to use some contract money not yet committed to the ineffectual US company. I could also chip in with other money from the CPA. Their proposal was an answer to my prayers. I authorised them to set up their own repair team and try it out on the next blown pipe.

We did not have long to wait. When a plume of black smoke climbing into the desert air signalled business, I deployed these officers and the Iraqi owner of the local engineering company by helicopter to the burning pipe and sent a local coalition unit to protect them. The Iraqi company vehicles, protected by another US combat unit, hit the road. The team was ready to start its repairs as soon as the pipe had stopped burning and the area had cooled down.

This was a significant improvement on being totally dependent on the Iraqis, and gave me a little hope that my strategy might work.

After the success of this trial run, we formed other teams and put one US officer in charge of each. We used them all the time from then on. We were in business! All of a sudden we had teams that could repair most pipes in one or two days, compared to weeks or even months. It was expensive, but not as expensive as the failed US company. The secret, for me, was getting the resources to pay for it. There was plenty of money in Iraq — I just had to find out who controlled it and how to get it.

Still, the job remained dangerous. The insurgents soon realised how successful our pipe repairers were and set trap after trap. They would blow a pipe and lace the area with roadside bombs which they would blow against our reconnaissance party, or try to bomb and ambush the soldiers or the road convoy. When we cleared sites for assessment and repair, the insurgents responded with hit-and-run mortar attacks.

Two of the US officers that I had most to do with were Captain Scott Davis and Lieutenant Colonel Tony Cusimano, known as the 'Roadside Bomb Twins': together they were the subject of 26 bomb attacks. They would come back with terrifying video shot by a camera attached to the dash of their vehicle. It showed a bomb exploding in the road in front of them, the vehicle rearing up with the blast and falling into the crater amid dust and debris. From memory, it was Scott who held the record for the most blown-up officer on the headquarters, having been the subject of something like 17 roadside bombs and numerous small-arms and mortar attacks. But they continued to go back out. These were people of the highest courage and I regret to this day that I did not intervene more effectively in the US system to have their achievements recognised.

One repair incident sticks in my mind. We were in a good operational rhythm, holding our own, when a pipe repair team went to a broken pipe after the oil had been cleared. They started working on the repair amid pools of spilt oil.

A US congressional party visiting Iraq had heard of our exploits. They asked if they could visit a repair site. We were unable to fit in a ground visit because VIP visitors were not allowed to stay in Iraq overnight — it was fly in, be briefed, and fly out. So on their way out of Iraq, I arranged for the party to fly over our latest repair site. The aircraft, a C-130, found the site and descended to take a look. Because he was flying low and may thus have been in danger of attack from shoulder-launched missiles, the pilot armed his countermeasures — these detect the flash of a missile and automatically launch decoy flares. What no-one had anticipated was that the pipe repair involved incandescent welding. The pilot's on-board computer interpreted the bright welding light as the flash of a missile and automatically fired off a raft of flares. The pipe repair crews, surrounded by a sea of spilt oil, cringed in horror as the flares floated down. Luckily, each flare landed harmlessly in the dry desert between pools of oil, and the team lived to repair another day.

We repaired so many pipes that we ran out of money from the dormant pipe repair contract, so I went to the US Embassy for more. Ambassador Jim Jeffrey, who had arrived just as I took over the infrastructure in May and learnt the ropes as a deputy to Jerry Bremer, was one of the most impressive people I met. Jim saw the connection immediately between the counterinsurgency battle and providing basic services. He wrestled the financial bureaucracy to the ground, and got us the money. Business was brisk. But bureaucracy is bureaucracy even in the midst of a war, and although the money was allocated, getting it paid to our contractor became harder and harder as the US Congress clamped down on perceived waste and corruption.

Through our struggles for resources, Jim and I forged a bond. He took an intense interest in my work, and we soon found ourselves collaborating on a dozen issues. He was about my age, maybe a few years older. Jim was a big man with a big mind, and when I spoke to him I was struck by how the US diplomats with whom I worked, as the representatives of the most powerful country in the history of the world, understood power in its rawest form. Having been a combat officer in Vietnam, Jim understood the military better than many others who surrounded Ambassador Bremer. When Bremer left in June, Jim became the acting US Ambassador to Iraq. It was always a delight to work with him.

While we were achieving some success, tragic setbacks were never far away. The luck of the Iraqi owner of our pipe-repair company finally ran out in late 2004, when he was murdered on his way home from work. Fortunately for us, his wife and brother took over his company and continued to fix pipes. It was to our shame that payment for such people remained a problem. They were working on my word that they would be paid, and while it came, it never came fast. Early in 2005, just before I left Iraq, the wife and brother had been to a coalition cash payments office at Camp Victory to pick up their money in US dollars: payment was late, as usual. They had concluded the torturous process and were on their way out of the compound when they were attacked and killed, and their money was stolen — by criminals set up by someone in the payments office, one must presume.

Murder and intimidation were the insurgency's favourite tactics. As we began to make progress on the battle for the infrastructure, the insurgents turned to widespread intimidation. We could protect workers at power stations and refineries, but not at home at night. Any worker deployed by us knew he was putting his family at risk. Power generation in Iraq depended ultimately on the bravery of individual Iraqi power plant managers, pipe-repairers, advisers and guards. We were rewarded magnificently by the commitment of ordinary Iraqis to doing their job in the face of appalling danger.

With each new day came a brand-new challenge. Following regular attacks on the towers that supported the high-tension electricity lines, we ran out of replacement towers. We could no longer just reconstruct one functional tower from parts of others that we would find each day lying smashed on their side or leaning drunkenly, two of their legs blown out during the night and now hanging from their wires.

As I was considering my options, Mark McQueen suggested matter-of-factly that we fly these monsters into Iraq using giant US aircraft, the C17s and C5s. I found a supplier in California, put in an order for towers, then ordered the aircraft. I then told the BUA what I had done — it was a 'done deal'. Sanchez's public concurrence made it harder for any bureaucrat to block the aircraft. Despite a good deal of friction, the towers started coming in, first from the US and later from Turkey.

Richer Baghdadis were able to buy generators and fuel on the black market. Even when we knew that the substations were not receiving any power at all, you could fly over the city and still see many lights. But the poor suffered in places such as Sadr City, and this was where our fight was taking place. Most people did not have the money to bribe substation managers to turn the power on in their area, so millions of Baghdadis sat in the dark and the heat, and thought about the value of the occupation to them and their families.

Within headquarters, the tension between individuals was high. I saw a fair bit of Pete Chiarelli, the commander of the 1st Cavalry Division in Baghdad, and we certainly had our moments, when in raised voices or heated emails we maligned each other's parentage and militaries. Peter was a passionate man of great personal courage and technical ability who wore his heart on his sleeve. He knew the importance of sewers, water, jobs and electricity, and at every conference he would call emotionally for those things that he and his soldiers' courage could not provide: money, construction, jobs, governance, energy and expertise. Those of us at the strategic level were a constant disappointment to him and I was a fair target because I was the one to blame for every infrastructure failure. His soldiers were dying every day in the streets of Baghdad. He knew better than many staff officers and bureaucrats that giving people sanitation, water, power and jobs could lower the level of violence in any area and save lives. I only wished I could have satisfied his demands.

I fought the battle on the infrastructure for the full year I was in Iraq, and it goes on in other hands to this day. The insurgents realise that they must deny the people of Iraq any material benefit that can be associated with the presence of the US, and they appear not to care whether or not a full generation of Iraqis is severely disadvantaged in the process.

Although the impact was felt most keenly where most Iraqis lived — in Baghdad — the fight was all over the country. Crucial oil pipelines in the energy corridor from Kirkuk were continually attacked where they crossed the Thar Thar canal north of Baghdad; this was a vulnerable spot because the pipes were exposed there. Most oil pipes were buried, but at this point, they either ran just above or just below the water's surface. It was very easy for the attackers to hit the pipes and get away quickly because they did not have to spend a long time digging the pipes up. Every time the canal crossing was hit, we repaired it. I had a watchtower built there, but the local staff manning it were intimidated and ran away. We did not have enough reliable troops to station them on the crossing, and even if we could, the attackers would have gone to another canal crossing and blown that up. I kept applying our main tactic of out-repairing the attackers, but that was always only a partial solution.

I sent some of my civil affairs soldiers to the nearest town with a pocket full of money to buy information about who was doing the attacking. The best information that we could get (and it was always suspect) was that the franchise to attack the Thar Thar canal pipes was held by the son of a local shayk. According to our informer, he was being paid good money by someone from Saddam's old home town, Tikrit, to blow the pipes, watch us repair them and blow them again.

The object of our suspicion received a quiet visit from us. We told him that we knew it was him and he was risking imprisonment. He denied everything, of course, and told us it could not be him attacking the lines because he held a locally issued contract from the Oil Ministry to protect the pipelines. In desperation, the ministry let contracts to protect the pipes to local tribal figures, really as a means of bribing them not to blow them up. This created two problems. In some places, those on our payroll still blew up the lines because the insurgents paid them as well. In others, those who had missed out on the legal protection contract, usually locals from other tribes, were blowing up the pipes to prove that they should have received the contracts in the first place. Have I mentioned that nothing is as it appears in Iraq?

So we set up covert sniping positions around the crossing. We had tried this before, with mixed results. It was always difficult to get sniper teams from local units because they could sit around for a long time without a target. The snipers, who were scarce, were then withdrawn by unit commanders who saw us as the boys who cried wolf. On this occasion we asked for the snipers to go in a few days after oil was flowing in the pipes following the last attack, and they immediately got a hit. The young men they killed fixing charges to the pipes were from the same tribe as our suspect. Once again my civil affairs soldiers paid him a visit and told him that we knew it was him, that it was his fault that his tribal members had been killed, and that if he was smart he would stop attacking the pipes and tell us who his contact was in Tikrit. We offered him a very large reward, and promised to increase his contract from the Northern Oil

Company if he took real responsibility for the pipes. As well, we would accelerate employment in his town and bring it some prosperity. He still denied everything, refusing to assist us, but for some time afterwards the attacks on the pipes slowed down.

When the snipers were withdrawn, the pipes were blown up again. Later we found out that the suspect tribal leader had been murdered. Perhaps he had tried to terminate his arrangements with the insurgents. Perhaps they thought he was compromised because we were watching him. Iraq is a tragically tough place.

Most of our fights were over the oil pipes, but the one fight for a power station during my tour illustrates the commitment of US troops to defending the energy infrastructure. The contest was for Mussaib, the biggest power station in Iraq — old, Russian-built, and located in North Babil, about 40 kilometres south of Baghdad. It took oil pumped hundreds of vulnerable kilometres from the southern oil fields, or trucked in from Baghdad, to run its four big generators. A battalion of US troops, first from the 10th Mountain Division and then from the Marines, occupied the Mussaib power station grounds.

Insurgents first tried to disable Mussaib with mortars and rockets in June 2004. Mussaib is surrounded by desert so there was little danger to local residents from our counter-battery fire from the power station or artillery fired from other bases. Radar detected incoming mortar rounds and rockets, so we could fire back quickly. Radar often saw mortars and rockets going from one meaningless place in the desert to another meaningless place. The insurgents seemed to be out there training and rehearsing.

The ability to fire back accurately and quickly did not stop the first salvo from hitting the power station, but it did stop the insurgents from following up, and may have killed and wounded a few mortarmen and rocketeers. The US battalion also patrolled the area and had a quick reaction force, but counter-battery fire, patrolling and sending out response forces could not stop the attacks completely.

Most of the insurgents' fire was inaccurate and ineffective, but twice during my tenure they hit the troops' accommodation lines, killing and wounding soldiers. The most calamitous event occurred shortly before the battalion was to return home, in July or August 2004. They had taken many casualties during a hard year, and just before they handed over to the Marines several mortar rounds fell among some tents. They lost several killed and 20 or so badly burnt after the tents caught fire.

I visited the site with the new commander in Iraq, General George Casey, a day or so after this terrible event. Our visit had its risks. Insurgent sympathisers employed at the power station advised comrades outside about the arrival of every helicopter. Typically, within an hour of landing, mortar rounds would begin falling. But it was worth the risk to show our support for people who had put everything on the line.

The railways were less important strategically than the oil or electricity infrastructure. Rail was only important to me as another means of moving oil. I began feeling guilty about my neglect of rail when my civil affairs liaison officers at the Transport Ministry begged me to help get the rail system up and running, but I had to stick to my priorities.

The coalition only wanted rail to move empty shipping containers back to the south after they had been trucked up from Kuwait, so there was no overriding military need to open the lines. But when we needed to get fuel by any means into Mussaib power station, the rail liaison officers saw their opportunity and came to me. 'Sir,' they said, 'rail has over one hundred fuel cars that could be used to move oil to Mussaib from out of the Daura refinery in Baghdad. The rail journey is only 30 kilometres. If we could make it work, we could get fuel into Mussaib and we could help the rail system get back on its feet.'

I told them to come up with a plan. What were the problems with the tracks? How much security would it take to get trains running? How long could we sustain train movement?

They came back with a proposal that sounded feasible — just. We would have to repair many blown culverts, assemble the oil cars and fill them at Mussaib, then coordinate the security of the train. We would have to repair and test the tracks and make sure that the oil upload and download points actually worked. And we would have to convince the train crews that they should run the gauntlet. But theoretically, all of these problems could be solved.

I visited the director-general of rail again. We talked about how he would find manpower to protect the trains and tracks. I assured him that as soon as he produced the Iraqi men, I would get him machine guns, rocket-propelled grenade (RPG) launchers and ammunition, and helicopters to cover a certain number of trains per day. I repeated the line I had given to his minister, that under no circumstances would I put coalition troops on the track or on the trains. If he wanted his trains to run again, he had to provide the protection.

He suggested that the trains be armoured. Like all Iraqis, he could remember having to do this type of thing during some other war or crisis. But the rail workshops only had soft steel for armour, and I could not supply any armour plate, as all of it was being used on our own vehicles. So soft steel it would be. The trains certainly looked the part — they reminded me of the *Mad Max* movies — but I knew that bullets fired from close up would penetrate the steel plate, and an RPG round would go through it like a hot knife through butter.

Repairing tracks and culverts, armouring trains and paying top dollar to persuade train crews to drive was only part of the solution.

The 'show-stopper' was one particular bridge. It was a bridge in name only: really it was a major culvert over a canal. It was just outside the big fuel depot at Latifiyah, in the centre of a particularly bad stretch of insurgent-dominated country, and after we had done a good deal of work on every other obstacle, it was the only thing that stood between us and trains running oil into the Mussaib power station.

The bridge had been blown so many times that the approaches were badly damaged. The insurgents did not try to interfere with the repair of the bridge: they knew they could wait until the job was done, then blow it up again at their leisure. So we guarded it lightly while it was being repaired, but insisted that the Iraqis protect it after it was open again.

The director-general had assembled some men, but they did not inspire confidence. He said they did not need training. They all had army experience, he assured me. I fulfilled my part of the bargain and supplied them with heavy weapons and plenty of ammunition. Once the bridge was repaired, the Iraqi guards took up their positions and things were looking good.

But not for long. The oil guards in the nearby Latifiyah fuel depot refused to go outside the depot, saying it was not in their contract, so the rail guards were on their own. Only a few hours after the bridge guards settled in, three cars arrived. Out climbed about ten heavily armed insurgents who spoke to our equally well-armed rail guards. The guards obviously took the advice of these hard men: they left the bridge and were last seen walking off into the distance. The insurgents then blew the bridge, got back in their cars and left.

This was an expected setback, and we rebuilt the bridge. I provided more heavy weapons. The director-general now tried the old trick that I had seen fail in so many other places: he employed local tribesmen to guard the bridge. Just to prove me wrong, it worked quite well. For reasons I could not understand, the insurgents were not able to intimidate this group. But there was a real cost to the local tribe: they were attacked by the insurgents, and many were killed. Finally, the tribal guards had had enough and they too left the bridge. The insurgents dropped around the next day and blew it up.

After we repaired it for the third time, I went against my word and put some US Marines on the bridge. I told the director-general that he had to get an Iraqi force from somewhere because I couldn't afford to keep the Marines on the bridge. He agreed and went off to do his business. The Marines were very innovative, as you would expect. A platoon of 20 defended the bridge by ambushing the approaches and fortifying a house about 100 metres away. They held the bridge for several days. We pushed trains through as often as we could, but initially we were still only achieving about one full train down and an empty one back up to Baghdad per day. The insurgents attacked almost every train and blew up rails. When a train was forced to stop, insurgents would pepper it with RPG fire.

We brought in helicopters, and Marine units shadowed trains by driving down parallel roads. If a track was blown ahead of the train, a team from the train itself would move forwards and repair the line. This could be done in an hour, and then the train would move to the next problem area.

The oil download point at the Mussaib power station looked good to a layman like me. When I asked the power station manager if it was serviceable, he gave me his assurance that it was. But the first train through proved otherwise. Downloading it took two full days rather than a few hours. During this time, two of the Marines holding the rail bridge were killed by a roadside bomb while they were out on patrol. I felt pressure to pull off the Marines, who had more important things to do than work as rail guards. We fixed the download points and ran trains through, but once again I had to take a risk with the bridge security by giving it back to the Iraqis.

The director-general put another group of guards on the bridge. Things seemed to be going well until he had a rush of blood to the head. Without telling me (I would have flown him safely down), he decided to show some leadership and drive down to see his train crews and bridge guards. Insurgents stopped him just outside the bridge, killed his driver, who was a relative of his, and shot him in both knees, leaving him alive to tell his story.

The defence of this bridge had now cost us 17 killed. We had killed only four insurgents. I kept asking myself, how long should I keep going? There had been sacrifice and substantial costs with poor returns. Even if I filled up the oil storage at Mussaib by trains going across the Latifiyah bridge, the Minister for Electricity would not thank us. He would try to use the hard-won oil as fast as possible and would then whinge about not having more. On the night I was told the director-general of rail had been maimed, I resolved to try the Iraqis one more time — but only one.

Yet another group of Iraqis went down to the bridge with yet another set of RPG launchers and machine guns. The Marines had conducted patrols to clear the area, then spent time with the Iraqis to check that they could at least fire the weapons we had given them. Then the Marines, having done their duty, left.

Within an hour, the Iraqi guards were gone. Almost immediately, the now legendary three cars arrived. With very little ceremony, the bridge was blown up yet again.

To say that I was angry is an understatement. I felt guilty that I had pushed and approved this operation in which so many had died without real gain. I stormed into the Ministry of Transport and said I would have nothing more to do with them until they were serious about helping themselves. As we drove back to the Green Zone from Baghdad Central Station, I told Steve Summersby that the rail staff were probably forever grateful. I had inadvertently — but manifestly — saved many lives by blowing my top. When I left Iraq in April 2005, the bridge at Latifiyah was still not rebuilt and no train had run south of Baghdad. And of course, the people of Baghdad were still only getting about six hours of power per day. The rail line between Baghdad and the south was not opened until December 2007.

The daily struggle on the pipes and wires was absorbing and exhausting. I travelled a lot, and when I was back in the Green Zone, the hours were very long indeed. We stretched our imagination and resources to the limit around the big oil and product storage depot near Latifiyah, an area so hostile that every pipe that we fixed was blown within days. We tried to ambush the sites after we left to catch those who were doing it, but they just moved 10 kilometres away and blew the line there.

At one stage I was desperate to keep a certain pipe open for four days at full pressure. I joked to my staff that I did not care what happened to it after those four days, and would blow it up myself to save the insurgents the trouble. To keep it open for the crucial four days, I decided to try some deception. Minister Ghadban had often lectured me on the deception that the old army used to protect the pipes in Saddam's time. Our plan was that once we'd repaired the pipe, we'd keep the repair team there for four more days, pretending the pipe was not fixed. We would burn the oil that was always lying around to give the impression that the pipe was still on fire. If we kept the deception running for the four days, I would achieve my aim. Ghadban agreed not to tell anyone in the ministry, so that the insurgents' spies would not know.

The deception went to plan until the team found that they could not actually get the oil to burn; they solved it by using a thermite bomb that was carried by their coalition protection team. The bomb certainly worked: the standing oil caught fire, and the fire spread to the nearest canal, which had oil floating on the water. The fire then raced down the canal until it hit the critical repaired — and furiously pumping — pipe. Predictably, the fire on the water caused the pressurised pipe to explode. The local media reported the black smoke as a new insurgent hit. So we certainly achieved a very realistic deception! It was the only time I ever saw Ghadban laugh.

I did not try deception on the pipes again, and it was only at the elections several months later that I felt confident enough to again try deception tactics at all.

Fortunately, our persistence was paying off in other areas. We stuck with our strategy, adjusted our tactics as we learnt, and repaired as much as we could in accordance with our priority list. Over time we killed or captured some of those insurgents who attacked the infrastructure. Killing someone is certainly a deterrent, but the deterrence was only ever local and short-term. We kept some lights on in Baghdad and a few hours of power for essential services, even through the worst times.

My appearances at the BUA were as frequent as ever, and although I gained something of a reputation for achieving results I was acutely aware of how much I was *not* achieving, and how it affected the people of Iraq. I travelled like a mendicant through the corridors of power trying to get money and troops to throw at the energy problem, and even when I was successful it was only for a short time: the resources were soon directed elsewhere, and we were back where we had started. I was learning about Iraq and how to be effective there. But it had been an expensive lesson for some.

We knew that in June 2004 the legal occupation of Iraq would finish and Bremer and the CPA would disappear. For me this would mean even less control over the ministries. As Ambassador Bremer prepared to hand over to the Iraqi Interim Government under Prime Minister Iyad Allawi on the last day of June, we all braced ourselves for an insurgent reaction on this date. As it turned out, Bremer handed over sovereignty a few days earlier and left Iraq immediately. I soon met Prime Minister Allawi and his ministers, and started to develop the necessary new relationships with the Oil, Electricity and Transport Ministers, the Prime Minister's security adviser and his two Deputy Prime Ministers.

The time of Ambassador Bremer, the CPA and General Ric Sanchez was over. The task of supporting the new Iraqi government and running the war was passing to the new US Ambassador, John Negroponte, and the new military chief, General George Casey. I was about to be swept up in these changing times and face the most difficult challenges of my military career.

CHAPTER 5

'Fight your way to the election'

Becoming Chief of Operations, June–September 2004

Multi-National Corps–Iraq ('The Corps') and the Multi-National Force–Iraq ('The Force') finally came into existence in a simple ceremony with lots of national flags in the rotunda of the Al Faw Palace on 15 May 2004, and CJTF-7 was consigned to history. I was one of three international generals standing on parade with Joe Weber at the activation ceremony.

Although it was simple, this was my first ceremonial parade for a very long time. We paraded in combat equipment — weapons, helmets and body armour in the summer heat — but I cheated and took the precaution of removing the heavy metal inserts from inside my body armour, which made my long motionless stand a little more comfortable.

With the war intensifying, we had still been unable to achieve the headquarters restructure we'd planned, so the activation ceremony marked little more than a name change. My frustration was so high at the time that I wondered if this parade might not be the most significant thing I did in the country in 12 months.

A picture taken of me by the local newspaper in January 1968 when I left home to join the army — with my overnight bag! I'm at the back door to my parents' house in the Melbourne suburb of Ivanhoe.

With Anne at the ceremony in which I graduated as a pilot in 1977. I had been told that by going flying I jeopardised my chance of being promoted.

Briefing the Chief of the Indonesian Army, General Edi Sudradjat, when he visited the 6th Battalion of the Royal Australian Regiment in Brisbane in 1991. I had learnt to speak Indonesian and was about to go to Indonesia as the first army attaché in the rank of colonel.

Dili airport, East Timor, 1999. When violence broke out following the UN-sponsored plebiscite, the Australian Defence Forces swung into action with our evacuation plans.

Lieutenant General Ric Sanchez was the coalition's military leader when I arrived in Iraq. Finding me an interim job was not on his priority list. 'What do you think you can contribute?' he asked.

The Tigris. This, I thought, is what Iraq is all about — water — but with people, oil, history, suffering and dirt thrown in.

Generally referred to as 'Saddam's Palace', the Republican Palace became the seat of power as the headquarters of the Coalition Provisional Authority. After the handover in July 2004, it was known as the US Embassy Annex. The centre of my universe, the operations centre, was in a former ballroom inside this building.

The Australian house — with sandbags and fishpond — where eight of us lived in the Green Zone. The Tigris is about 75 metres away.

The house behind the Australian house after a rocket clipped the front gate and hit the wall, killing two men. After this and another near miss, we decided to forego our view of the fishpond and sandbag our windows.

My Special Forces bodyguard, or PSD (personal security detachment), pictured on the back steps of the Australian house. We're getting ready for a normal trip to the office. Steve Summersby, my executive officer, is in the helmet.

In April 2004, I visited the hospital in Najaf which the El Salvadoreans had taken in heavy fighting with the Mehdi Militia. The lower levels were flooded, and bodies were everywhere. With me are US civilian Reserve surgeons from the Civil Affairs staff and, third from left, Dr Mohammed Shakir, Iraq's Director General of Health. Col. Chuck Betack (far left) did all the work.

ABOVE: With a group of Kurdish and Iraqi soldiers at a brigade headquarters in Baghdad.

THE LAST
STRAT OPS DCS?

LEFT: This was given to me in jest by the staff of my predecessor as chief of operations, Tom Miller, who said this was what I would look like after a year in the job.

RIGHT: A cartoon from the Iraqi *Ashiraa* newspaper, 10 July 2004. 'Unemployment', the word with the legs, is dragging Iraqis to the black 'Terrorist and Crime Swamp'.

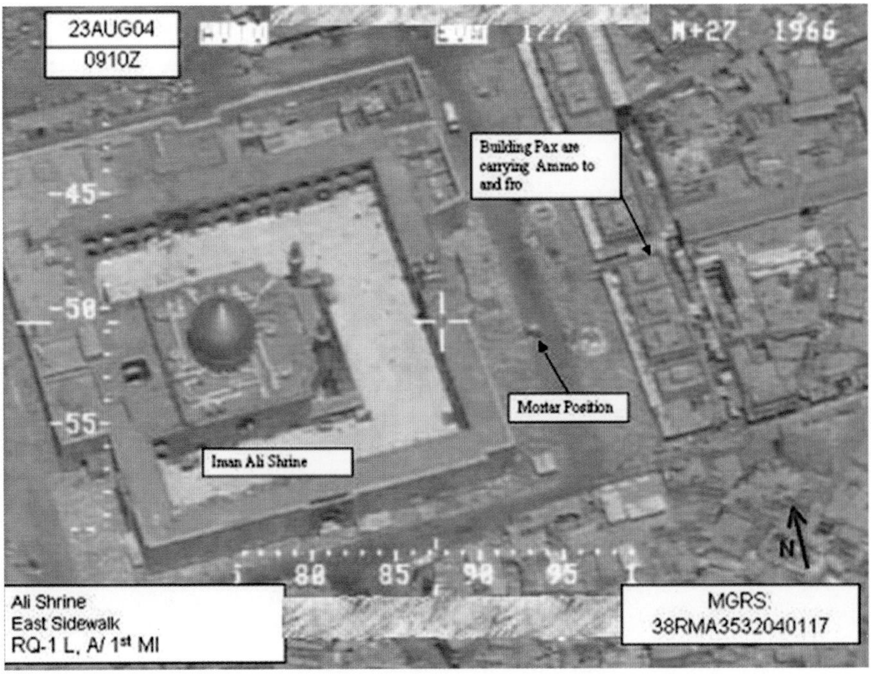
23AUG04
0910Z
Building Pax are carrying Ammo to and fro
Mortar Position
Iman Ali Shrine
Ali Shrine
East Sidewalk
RQ-1 L, A/ 1st MI
MGRS:
38RMA3532040117

A publicly used photograph from a drone aircraft showing the Imam Ali Shrine in Najaf during the heavy August 2004 fighting. Moqtada al Sadr and his fellow leaders of the Mehdi Militia escaped in a convoy of ambulances — yet another breach of the laws of armed conflict.

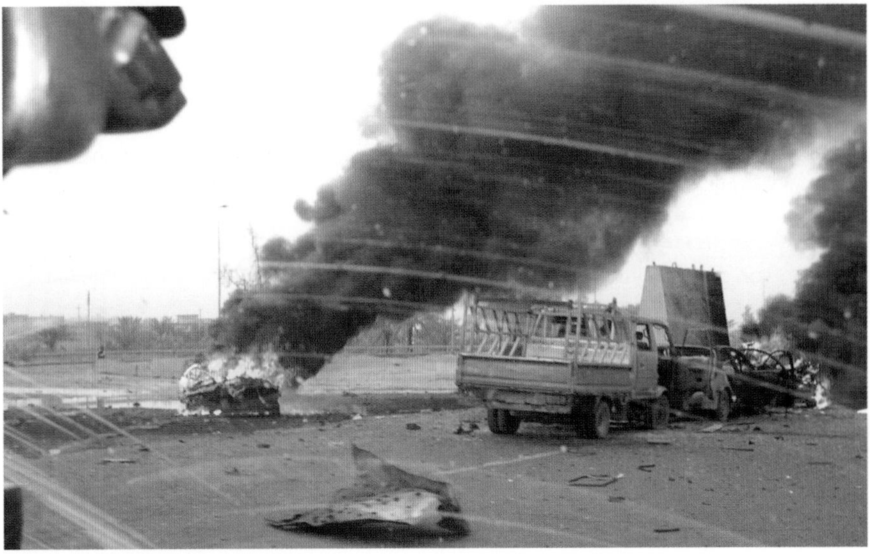

The aftermath of a car bomb which had just missed the convoy I was in. The bomber exploded his car in a line of civilian cars queuing to enter the airport.

These M2 Bradley armoured fighting vehicles were sent to Mosul which flared up while we were fighting in Fallujah. Their effect in Mosul was dramatic.

In Iraq there were 300 Stryker vehicles, powerful troop carriers whose strange bar armour could stop rocket-propelled grenades. This photo was taken in Mosul.

When General George Casey replaced General Sanchez in early July 2004, the headquarters began to take on the personality of its new commander. I first met Casey as he was doing the rounds of his staff. I had moved offices so often that I no longer cared where I worked, and now my office in the Green Zone was in the bowels of Saddam's Palace, on what might be called the lower-lower ground floor. It was close to an enormous vault, and as I walked past, if the door was open and people were working in there, I could see enormous pallets of US dollars.

At a pre-arranged time, Casey dropped into my subterranean office with Joe Weber. Casey seemed an excellent boss, asking for ideas and input from everyone he met. He was not a tall man, but he was built strongly and he exuded purposefulness. He was a very senior general in the US Army — a four-star general — whereas Ric Sanchez had been a lieutenant general, or three-star general, and a relatively junior one at that. Casey and I chatted for about an hour, about the infrastructure, the civil affairs staff, my relations with the US Embassy and what was going to happen in the future. I offered a few thoughts on the state of the insurgency and where I thought the campaign should go. Casey asked how long I was in Iraq, and Joe emphasised that I was committed to a year-long tour. I was the only coalition officer to do this. Casey seemed impressed by my performance so far and by the fact that I had come to Iraq for the same period as US officers. It was good to be noticed and to have the boss compliment the infrastructure security work. That night, at the last meeting of all the staff in the infrastructure game, I passed on General Casey's compliments. This was received with some vague interest from my jaded and cynical staff, but what really gained their attention was that Casey decided to put back the start time of the daily BUA from 0630 to 0730. With this decision alone he gained favour with every member of the staff, especially the many who were getting up at 0330 to prepare briefing material: an extra hour's sleep was priceless.

When the legal occupation ended, the Green Zone officially became the International Zone. But everyone still called it the Green Zone. Instead of working in the Coalition Provisional Authority, I, an Australian, was now a card-carrying member of the US Embassy. Saddam's Palace was now called the US Embassy Annex. The Iraqi Governing Council had become the Iraqi Interim Government under Prime Minister Allawi. Jim Jeffrey was the ambassador initially, until John Negroponte arrived.

I had very little to do with Negroponte at first, apart from a daily briefing on the energy situation. We exchanged pleasantries as we sat side by side during the BUA. I was not aware of his controversial past in Latin America — he was mentioned in the Iran-Contra scandal in the late 1980s — but I was greatly relieved to find him a more approachable man than Bremer. And he was prepared to work in an honest partnership with General Casey. I soon came to realise that the leadership combination of Casey and Negroponte was one of those rare convergences that are absolutely crucial to the flow of human events. The Casey–Negroponte combination started well, with a joint declaration of intentions, and then got better and better. As Casey would say, he and Negroponte were 'joined at the hip'. We had been fighting the war so far using a campaign plan that needed severe revision, and Casey and Negroponte revised it quickly and jointly.

They both asked to be flown over some of my infrastructure areas. Although I would have liked to take them together, their schedules and my risk assessment dictated that I take them a few days apart. We flew in Blackhawks with Apache escorts to each point of the compass, visiting power stations, well-heads, pumping stations and electrical substations. We landed at a pipe-repair activity and flew into Baghdad's biggest water purification plant on the Tigris. We saw the black smoke of a burning pipe and oil spread on the ground; I could illustrate the effect of not having valves. We flew low over the Latifiyah oil depot — I could hardly bring myself to look at the notorious bridge. We hovered in our Blackhawks next to a site where high-tension towers flown in from California were replacing one that had recently been blown over. I pointed out some scrubby country nearby where we had snipers watching the workers on the towers in case there was an attempt to intimidate or kill them.

As I briefed my two guests, I realised that I knew a good deal about this game after only a few months, and I was heartened by their curiosity. Ever the optimist, I wondered if I could expect more resources.

I had stopped thinking too much about the job that I had been sent to Iraq to do: chief of operations. As we bedded down our tactics to protect the infrastructure, we were achieving what I knew to be mediocre results but which many thought were miracles. I received congratulatory emails from organisations and individuals in the US and UK. Our team had developed a forceful demeanour and were considered local experts. We had credibility on the civil and military sides. I agreed that we deserved some good press, but I also told the team that we were 'only as good as our last pipe'.

July stretched out and General Casey had been in-country for a few weeks when I received a call from Joe Weber. Tom Miller, who was still the chief of operations, had been in Iraq for about 15 months and deserved to go home. Casey was thinking about offering me the job but wanted to know what the Australian government would think about it. I told Joe that the government had sent me to Iraq to be chief of operations and had publicly made statements to that effect. I would check back through Peter Cosgrove, but said I would be surprised if there had been any change. Some days later, after a routine conference at Camp Victory, Casey called me into his office and asked if I would be the next chief of operations after Miller left in August. In a nutshell I would be Casey's right-hand man for operations: putting into effect his operational plans across the entire country — running the war in Iraq.

I had now been in Iraq for about four months and was due some leave. It made sense to take it now and be fresh for the challenges ahead. General Casey agreed. So with very little time to think about it, I suddenly found myself flying home, prior to doing probably the most meaningful job an Australian soldier could ever expect to do in Iraq. Command is everything in the military. Command is what you prepare yourself for as a soldier. For 30-plus years, I had commanded at every level I could. Australia only had several hundred troops in Iraq, and all, at that stage, were in non-combat roles. The best non-command job was an operations job, and I was about to take over the top one in Iraq.

Of my nine days at home, I spent five meeting senior people in Canberra. Their focus was on making sure our troops didn't get hurt, which was understandable, but it didn't have much to do with me. I was asked routinely what I thought would happen for Australia in the war. I'd had almost nothing to do with the 411 Australians within a force of 160,000, so I could only answer in the context of the broader war, particularly the big milestone of the upcoming 2005 election. My questioners would listen politely, then ask again about the Australians. I did not feel that Australian Defence officials had any better appreciation of the big picture than when I'd left four months ago. Unfortunately for me, Peter Cosgrove was on a trip to Japan during this time. I would have liked to discuss Iraq with him and receive his guidance.

From Iraq in midsummer to Canberra in midwinter is a huge contrast. Anne and the children were living in a beautiful old house on the grounds of the military base at Duntroon, where I had started my military life all those years ago. It is the most delightful suburb in Canberra, and our house was surrounded by European trees whose leaves could still be seen on the ground. It was strange to think of where I had come from, what I had been doing, and what I was going back to. Anne and I spoke openly about what I had been and would be doing in Iraq, and then, for a couple of days, I switched off.

As my return to Iraq approached, my mind was flooded with questions about how I would tackle my new job. I looked again at the laws of armed conflict. With the knowledge I now had of Iraq, and a greater knowledge of what I was about to do, I spent some time with our operational lawyers.

I had already concluded that the war I faced in Iraq, that is the war in 2004 and 2005, satisfied all the classical requirements of a just war. We were in Iraq for a just cause, regardless of how we had come to be there. The war was being run by a recognised authority: it was a coalition led by the US but under the aegis of the United Nations. Now that we were in Iraq, my view was that there was no choice but to stay and fight — to leave now would probably have resulted in a terrible bloodbath. There was a more than reasonable chance of success. This was a war we could still win. And unlike our enemies, we were very attentive to minimising harm to civilians.

Having watched our operations at close quarters, and run a few small ones myself, I now had high confidence that as an institution, the coalition was effectively applying the laws of armed conflict. Where individuals on our side broke those laws, they were dealt with. My discussion with our Australian lawyers in Canberra, while instructive in relation to the principles and application of the laws, could not help me much in interpreting the specific rules of engagement that applied to the types of forces I would be using in Iraq. But in my new position, I would have 24-hour access to both US and Australian legal advice that was fully up to speed.

My month understudying Tom Miller had prepared me for running the fight for the infrastructure. I learnt things by doing them. When Casey had offered me the operations job, I was finally granted access to the top level of US intelligence, but had not yet had time to exercise that access. I was familiar with the battlespace in Iraq, with the civilians running the war, and with many senior Iraqi leaders and officials. I was coming to understand the scale of the violence. I saw the value of patience and persistence — this was a place where it was hard to get results quickly. Just as importantly, I had established a reputation of sorts and had come to know, respect, and be respected by my fellow generals.

I was also beginning to understand the diversity and complexity of this conflict. What motivated a terrorist from the Sudan to come to Iraq to conduct 'martyrdom operations' was vastly different from what motivated an out-of-work Iraqi Sunni who needed to support his family and did not want his country occupied by the Americans. Those who advocated a 'silver bullet' approach to this war — one act to solve it all, such as the call to 'close the borders' or 'withdraw all foreign troops' — were on a different planet. Borders, for example, might be important in some insurgencies, but we had no chance of closing off Iraq's borders, and anyhow, the country was already awash with weapons, and all the troops in the world were not going to stop small groups of insurgents being smuggled in. We had to integrate a number of approaches, and I already had a good understanding of how complicated it was going to be to pull them all together, particularly with limited resources. And we all knew it was unlikely that we were going to get many more troops.

But the operational detail was still beyond my grasp. I needed to know how intelligence was linked to actions, how intelligence reported the actions, and what intelligence really meant. Even the language of US intelligence in Iraq was still a black art to me. In particular, I did not understand how they were using intelligence for 'targeting', the word the military used for the process that focuses the political, information, military and economic tools of war. Hitting physical targets with bombs or missiles is certainly a part of targeting, but I had always believed that in a counterinsurgency campaign it should be a relatively small part. The idealism of that view was about to be tested.

When I returned to Baghdad at the end of August, my executive officer ('XO'), Steve Summersby, and my bodyguard had temporarily moved us back to the operations office at Camp Victory. Joe Weber scheduled five days for Tom Miller to hand over responsibility to me, but Tom was still moving at a million miles an hour and was as hard to pin down now as he had been in April.

An attack on energy going into Baghdad had my attention, but, when I could, I watched Tom like a hawk, absorbing the way he did his job. In August there was an uprising against the coalition by the Shi'ite Mehdi Militia across the south, particularly in Najaf. This uprising, by one of the most powerful of the Shia militias, was a manifestation of the complexity of the situation we faced in Iraq. Not only were we opposed by Sunni insurgents, by Muslim extremists such as al Qaeda and by a vast array of criminal elements, but the Shia majority were also factionalised and prepared to fight the coalition, the emerging Iraqi Army and Police and each other.

This was the US military in desperately serious combat against a very capable enemy. On the first night, the Mehdi Militia attacked all Najaf's police stations. We had to resort to throwing boxes of ammunition from low-flying helicopters to the beleaguered newly formed police units in their compounds. Once again, the fighting spread to other Shi'ite enclaves and generally across the south of Iraq. Over time, coalition and Iraqi units secured most areas and forced the Mehdi Militia back into a big mosque in Najaf, the Imam Ali Shrine. This was the first significant challenge to the new Iraq in the time of Casey and Negroponte.

The fighting was truly awful, particularly among the close-set mausoleums that make up a large part of Najaf. After many days, our troops forced the militia back into a ring around the shrine. Iraqi Army units, because they were Muslim, were set to enter the shrine area if that became necessary. For the first time, I saw a more sophisticated and integrated strategy being used. We were no less willing to use force when we had to be decisive, though, especially when we discovered a large concentration of militia just outside the shrine, fortified in a hotel normally used by pilgrims. After destroying the hotel, we were able to coordinate religious, economic and political intervention, and the fighting stopped literally in hours. It was just a shame that we decided to let the Mehdi leadership escape, which they did in a line of ambulances we had been watching for days: the Mehdi Militia continue to disrupt Iraq progress to this day. As I observed Tom working his magic, I kept thinking that very soon I would be doing this myself.

By the time I finally took over in early September 2004, the situation was a little calmer, but not much. I had to get up to speed on the headquarters restructure, but most of all I had to keep the fight going on the combat side, the information side and the civil affairs side. I would retain my infrastructure security responsibilities, but Sandy Davidson, the head of civil affairs, would handle the detail.

As soon as possible, I got a copy of the official document that told me what was expected of me as chief of operations. It contained some interesting new reading. I was to be known officially as Deputy Chief of Staff for *Strategic* Operations. The term 'strategic' meant I would be running the level of the war that interacted with the new Iraqi government, bringing the political, diplomatic, information, economic and reconstruction sectors into line with the military side. This was classic counterinsurgency theory, which requires a focus on the people by coordinating all aspects of power, not just military. Military purists would say that the true strategic level of the war lay in Washington, but our main ally was now the Iraqi government, so we referred to ourselves as 'strategic'.

My specific duties were laid down in this document as:

> Responsibilities. Strategic Operations is responsible to Commander MNF-I for the operations of all the US and Coalition forces assigned to the Iraqi area of operations. Responsible for implementation and execution of MNF-I assigned missions. Directs, manages and controls all activities under the command or support jurisdiction of the Iraqi Multinational Force. Serves as staff and advisor to the Force Commanding General.

These were catch-all responsibilities. As we read it, Steve Summersby quipped, 'Perhaps in your spare time you can find a cure for cancer!'

On paper my staff was 315 strong, but we never had anywhere near that number. By January 2005 we would still have only about 250 'hot bodies', mostly US reservists on short-term duty, plus a small cadre of US active duty officers and a handful of coalition officers. It was only as I was preparing to leave for good in April 2005 that we started to get staff who were actually trained for the job. This was symptomatic of the overall problem in Iraq: even the mighty US military can run out of trained people.

The Multi-National Force for which I was responsible, which included troops from about 30 countries, was enormous and bewilderingly complex. One part was dedicated to creating the Iraqi Security Forces, which was at that time planned to be 271,000 strong. The reconstruction organisation managed the billions of dollars being spent through contractors. A special forces task force hunted the al Qaeda leadership; its specific name was classified (it was referred to as 'the task force'). And a task force ran the detention centres, where at any one time we held about 10,000 prisoners. By the time of the election in January 2005, the MNF-I would consist of 175,000 troops supplemented by 125,000 trained and usable Iraqi Security Force members.

Each of the three major sections under me was headed by a US brigadier general, a 'one star' officer. The three sections were: manoeuvre operations, which looked after the manoeuvre of fighting units and their military support and this was headed up by Brigadier General Peter Palmer; strategic communications, a mixture of public affairs and a new military activity called 'information operations', was headed up by US Air Force Brigadier General Erv Lessel; civil military operations, now headed up by Brigadier General Steve Hashem, who had replaced Sandy Davidson, was the third. I was to coordinate these groups mainly through the 'targeting process'. If the operations branch lay at the centre of running the war, targeting was its engine room.

My targeting cell, responsible for the coordination of all these disparate elements, was headed by Colonel Brian Boyle, one of the group of smart colonels I'd worked with in April and May designing the headquarters. Running a war demands extraordinary amounts and degrees of coordination. If coordination is not tight, you find that one part of the organisation works against another, or opportunities are missed. My targeting responsibilities were laid down in my official duty statement. I was to run a 'force targeting board', and my duties included 'synchronising diplomatic, information, military, and economic elements of power, developing rules of engagement, developing targeting sections of plans and orders, executing time-sensitive targeting and managing attacks against high-value targets'. Technically I knew a little about each, but I had no real feel for how it all came together. I was to learn very fast.

I learnt most from my head of manoeuvre, Brigadier General Peter Palmer, who was in effect my deputy, and retired US General Gary Luck, who was in Iraq as a 'senior mentor'. Gary Luck provided the kind of measured and calm advice that was just not available from those who were running the war minute by minute. Gary's gift to us was his experience, but that would have been useless without his calm manner, his commonsense and his approachability. There is nothing magic about the US mentor system. It merely formalises the passage of knowledge and experience from one generation to another so that lessons are not lost over time. It relies on the mentors being up to date in modern operations while mentoring their past subordinates without wanting to take over. Both Luck and Cavasos could do this, and I owe them a great deal.

As I settled in, I found the routine of the headquarters unrelenting. Briefing followed briefing followed meeting followed meeting. To fit everything into one day, we worked out what we called the 'battle rhythm' of the headquarters. The battle rhythm started with the commanding general, George Casey. His staff would identify the major meetings for him to attend each day. For example, a major meeting held most days was the civil–military coordination meeting between General Casey and Ambassador Negroponte and their close staffs. This often took an hour. To prepare for this meeting General Casey needed to have attended the BUA, then a small group meeting where decisions requiring access to the highest classified intelligence were considered. Before either of these meetings, he needed to read the high-security intelligence 'take' that we prepared each day for him. So if the meeting with Negroponte was at 0900, Casey was normally delivered his intelligence 'read book' at 0430.

Once the battle rhythm was worked out for the commander, it flowed down. Everything would be worked out around the rhythm of the next level up. Although we hated having so many meetings, they were the only way to coordinate this extraordinarily complex activity. The aim of the staff was to relieve General Casey of the dull parts of military life. We handled the drudgery, so he could concentrate on leading and thinking and travelling and inspiring.

And when all that was done, perhaps there would be time left to sleep and eat!

My job title, Deputy Chief of Staff for Strategic Operations, was clumsy but had military logic under the American system. The logic was that the headquarters itself was run by a 'chief of staff' — a major general (referred to almost universally as a 'two-star general') and those that came under him in the headquarters were 'deputies', even though they were also two-star generals. Despite the title, I was referred to as the 'chief of operations' or just 'ops'. On other occasions, because some headquarters have numbered divisions within them and 'operations' is number three, I was referred to as 'The Three'. 'Ops, can you do this?' General Casey might say at video conferences. 'Three, are you there?' Or if he was tired and impatient, as war tends to make generals: 'Jim, do this please and don't make a career out of it.'

Staff work is all about detail. As chief of operations, I owned every operation that either had an agreed plan, was currently running as an operation, or would start in the near future. Original plans were prepared in a separate division, but when a plan was ready for execution, it would be passed to me. Getting the timing of this right was critical, because if the plan was passed too late or in an incomplete state, I did not have the manpower or time to do anything more than make minor adjustments on the run. This created many raised voices, not because I was right and others were wrong, but because the link between what has to be done in the future and those that have to do it is a point of maximum stress in any modern headquarters.

Everything demanded the most astounding level of coordination and synchronisation, which we were seldom able to achieve. Mostly, we had to accept the suboptimal, but that is a fact of life in most military operations. What we did achieve, however, would still belong in the top league of difficulty in large-scale human activities.

Unlike the infrastructure security job, which I essentially created, I was now in a known mainstream role. Senior people in Baghdad, Washington and elsewhere were falling over themselves to make sure I knew what I was doing and had the resources to do the job. This was a refreshing change, and as I settled in, even though the tiredness re-emerged quickly after my few days of leave, I began to relish the challenges ahead.

About the only handover activity that Tom Miller took me to was a video conference he attended three times a week where he represented General Casey. This was the CENTCOM Component Commander's Brief, or CCCB. (The military, in case you haven't guessed, is an acronym-rich environment.) The CCCB brought home to me just how much the war in Iraq was part of a global war.

General John Abizaid and CENTCOM, controlling the US's 225,000 personnel, were the frontline in this war. Abizaid also had an army headquarters in Kuwait and a navy headquarters in Bahrain. His air force and special forces also had forward headquarters in Qatar. He had a base in the Horn of Africa, and a Combined Forces Command in Afghanistan.

At my first CCCB video conference, I kept my mouth closed until I saw who was on the vidcon screen. The CCCB aimed to update General Abizaid on activities right across his command, and allowed him to talk directly to his commanders at least three times per week. Abizaid was a global general, and he attended the CCCB from Tampa, Qatar, Kuwait, Bahrain or Afghanistan. On occasions he sat next to me in Baghdad.

The CCCB was also a global information exchange. Staff from Afghanistan would describe how the high passes were closed, and produce images of the depth of snow, measured in metres, that stopped everything from working. A civilian-contracted aircraft had crashed in one of the highest mountains. I heard how rescue teams got into the site in the most appalling conditions and how bodies were recovered. I also listened to reports from the Maritime Interception Force in the waters around the Horn of Africa, including operations to protect the Iraqi oil export platforms and other Gulf State facilities. I saw how medical and veterinary teams were being sent into the Horn of Africa on humanitarian missions. US Army engineer teams were drilling water wells for villages while other teams were training local military forces to deter al Qaeda influence. The US also moved resources between theatres through the CCCB — when the satellites that link surveillance drones could not be used in Afghanistan for reasons of weather, Iraq operations borrowed them and linked more of our drones through them.

As I began to understand the CCCB and the role of Central Command, I also began to see the opportunities that this video conference gave us all. I had the biggest war so I would be given the longest time to get my points across. Every other US commander in this part of the world appeared religiously at this vidcon except my boss, General Casey. As his representative, I would take his points to the conference and report back to him. This would regularly test my judgment and communication skills.

Casey and Abizaid were close friends who often spoke by telephone, and Abizaid often visited Iraq. I became more conscious of this relationship a few weeks after taking over as chief of operations. We knew that Abizaid was in Iraq and were told that he would sit in at the evening's operations and intelligence briefing to Casey. Abizaid often attended the morning BUA, but it was a little unusual that he would attend our evening briefing as well. This was normally our time together as generals. We arrived to find Casey, but not yet Abizaid, in the conference room and began to give our brief as usual. Casey then announced that he had to take a call from Washington but General Abizaid would be coming. We should run the rest of the meeting in a normal manner and Casey would be back when he could. Casey then walked out one door and Abizaid walked in another. It seemed orchestrated.

Abizaid listened to the chief of intelligence, Brigadier General John Defreitas, and me finish off our briefs. Then he settled in for an unusually long discussion — he asked questions and we answered. Casey did not come back for the rest of the evening. I thought this was a bit strange. With the paranoia of a newcomer and a foreign officer, I got a strong impression that Abizaid was there either because he was worried about us or because Casey was worried about us as a staff. We all knew that many things could have been going better for the coalition in Iraq in September 2004. We were winning every battlefield challenge that the insurgents threw at us, but winning the battles while losing the war had been a common failing of militaries throughout the ages.

Abizaid was a most engaging man, but when there was a line of questioning he wanted to pursue he was like a dog with a bone. Having seen him so regularly at the CCCB, I knew he was asking questions to which he already knew the answers. He was giving Defreitas and me a polite but thorough grilling in those areas which were, or should have been, our fields of expertise. I was anxious because at this early stage I was having trouble with a new and inexperienced branch, and with many of our procedures, especially those relating to targeting. We were all new and clunky, and much of the past expertise had gone with Tom Miller. I had recently executed a number of strikes that were not as timely as they should have been, and there was friction between my responsibilities and those of the planners in the headquarters. So I was more than a little sensitive.

None of us on the staff discussed this grilling among ourselves because we rarely engaged in anything that resembled a social, non-work activity. Few of us in fact had any downtime at all. We performed our main jobs, ate at our desks or in vehicles, and every now and again slept a bit. John Defreitas and I sometimes exchanged pleasantries outside of the formal battle rhythm of the headquarters. We briefed each other regularly to figure out what was going on now and what was likely to happen soon. Importantly, we shared a similar sense of humour, joking about who had received the worst 'beating' from Casey. Intelligence traditionally briefs before operations and, like a child in school, John would blatantly steal points from my operations material to brief Casey on, and I would increase the slapstick by complaining in an exaggerated manner, or try to get in first. Casey would then apply a bit of adult supervision, and we would get back to work. A visitor from another world would have been convinced that we were mad, but this banter actually kept us sane. John was an ally because he and I seemed to be in the gun most of the time from Casey or, on this night, from Abizaid. But there was no horseplay at this briefing.

If Abizaid had come to Iraq that night to execute John or me, he must have decided that we had passed muster because we heard nothing more about it.

Since April, when I had arrived, the coalition had not initiated a single strategic-level operation. We had responded to every tactical challenge that the enemy served up, surviving the onslaughts of April and August 2004, but we were seriously on the back foot. We would fight at one place and win, then the enemy would attack us somewhere else and we would fight there and win. But as in all wars, victory would only be achieved when the enemy decided to give up the fight, and that would take much more than bombs and bullets. It was time for a new focus. The people of Iraq needed to remember that they had a stake in their country no matter what religious group they belonged to: they were also all Iraqis.

The first of our campaign plan milestones was the election on 30 January 2005, only five months away. A successful election was important for each member of our coalition, for our relationship with the United Nations, and for our own self-confidence. If we fell at this first hurdle to democracy, no-one knew what would happen. But how could the coalition hold an election in a country at war? In World War II at least one of the great democracies had cancelled their elections for the duration of hostilities. How could you hold an election in a country where every day there was death and mayhem?

Casey knew the election gave us the opportunity to go on the front foot. Cities were the key, because most Iraqis lived and would vote there, so we developed a '15 Cities Strategy' to prepare for the election. But every time we tried to focus on a particular city, we had to go and fight somewhere else. We fought every day in Baghdad, Mosul and Basrah. We all knew that the time would come when we would have to fight again in Fallujah. Would we have to drive the insurgents out of Fallujah before the election? Perhaps we could isolate Fallujah, then clear it after the election? How long would it take to secure a city? How many cities could we 'do' before the election, and would that be enough?

These thoughts were going around in our heads one night in September during a vidcon with General Casey not long after I took over from Tom Miller. The discussion was free-ranging, with the commanders and senior staff reviewing issues, looking for the key to success. We all knew counterinsurgency theory, which was to follow up battlefield success with political, diplomatic, information and economic 'weapons'. But the gap between theory and practice in this counterinsurgency was huge.

That night I was distracted. My mind was on the targets that we had been working on during the day and whether they would need my attention before midnight, when I'd try to get to bed. I doubted they would. Targets never presented themselves at civilised times, so I expected to be called back to the operations centre some time after I had gone to bed. This happened at least once, and sometimes twice, per night. That was the essence of targeting — when a high-value individual had been pinpointed by intelligence, you had to act. So my precious sleep time, from midnight to four or five in the morning, was frequently broken. Also, I rarely ate before about ten at night, so when my staff would bring me a complex target plan an hour before midnight after an 18-hour day, I felt I was brain-dead.

At some stage in the discussion that night someone said that regardless of anything else, it looked as if we would be fighting every second up to the election. On the video screen, acknowledging that I was planning our support for the election, Casey asked me, 'Jim, can we fight through to an election?'

'Yes we can, sir. It is possible.' I had just read a paper titled 'Elections in Violent Conditions' which had examined Colombia in 1998, El Salvador in 1982, Cambodia in 1998, Kosovo in 2001, and Nigeria in 2003. Others had done it. I continued, 'But I don't think it will be pretty. We probably won't have to fight across the whole country for the next five months, only in certain areas. But if we fight right up to election day, then the locals may not vote. Sir, you can run an election with violence but what you can't do is run an election without voters.'

I was glad Casey had asked this question, and not only because it shook me out of my distraction. The campaign to stage the election successfully was the embodiment of everything my staff needed to coordinate. It was my baby and would stay my baby. I was possessive about the campaign plan even at this early stage and would become even more possessive as time went on.

The discussion went on around the group. Finally, Casey tried to sum it all up as he prepared to leave. With his glasses pushed back on his greying hair, and bending down to adjust the bottom of his combat uniform pants into his boots as he did frequently, making him almost disappear from the video screen, he said, 'As the campaign plan says, what this fight is all about is politics. Whatever we need to do, we need to do it in relation to the election. The insurgency will focus on the election at much the same time as our subordinates do, so we at the Force headquarters need to move earlier and to stay ahead of that. So what we really must do, across all the lines of operations, is fight our way to the election. If you want to bring this down to a bumper sticker, that's it. "Fight your way to the election." Have a think about it. Any last questions or points?'

No questions, and he was off.

'Fight your way to the election.' Nothing could be clearer. Nothing could be more difficult. We all had this in our minds in one form or another, but Casey, in his own inimitable way, had brought it together. The sentiment was in the campaign plan in technical military jargon, but nowhere was it expressed so succinctly. Often, after that night, Casey would repeat it — 'Fight your way to the election' — and we knew what he meant. Everything we did must focus on achieving success in the election. It was not just fighting in a military sense, it was the struggle to bring our diplomatic, political, information, economic and reconstruction activities to fruition, manifested in a safe and well-attended election. That would be greater than any military victory over the insurgents.

I found Casey inspirational. I learnt a great deal about leadership, operational command and 21st-century warfare just from watching him. He was an intuitive leader, and came up with most of the really good ideas in the campaign himself. Like all the US commanders I got to know, he was highly principled, experienced at command, and very well educated. He was two years older than me and came from a military background. His father, George Casey Sr, served in World War II, the Korean War and Vietnam, and was the commanding general of the 1st Cavalry Division in Vietnam when he was killed in 1970 in the crash of his command helicopter. George Casey Jr served as a brigade commander in the 1st Cavalry Division and was then the commander of 1st Armoured Division. Immediately before moving to Iraq, he was the Vice Chief of Staff of the US Army, and it was obvious to me that he knew his way around Washington.

Casey was not traditional or stereotypical. He travelled extensively, and came back every night to brief us on what was going on in the real world. He drove us at a frantic pace and was continually trying to get ahead of the enemy. He was also ahead of us. While I would reach my physical and mental limit focusing on the current day's operations, General Casey was well into the next operation, leading the way both physically and intellectually. He understood the scale of the operations he was leading, and he had a great constructive and organising brain, but at the same time he was a realist. He often told us, 'We are an antibody in this society — they will never like us. The best we can ever get is consent to operate in their country.' This belief informed his view that we must hand the fight over to the Iraqis as soon as possible, and force them to take responsibility.

He continually advised all of us to read, sleep, exercise and think, and to fit a bit of each into every day. I rarely got to any of them: Casey observed this on a number of occasions and would drop into my office and encourage me to get out and exercise.

Every single activity and conversation was affected by how tired everyone was. In Casey, that manifested itself as a hatred of detail. Unfortunately, my life as chief of operations was all about detail. Now and again, I had to put some complex issues before him and try his patience, but it was not hard to see when you were approaching Casey's limits.

Once, appearing on the video screen from Camp Victory during a conference, he got stuck into me over something that had gone seriously wrong. Even though it was neither my fault nor my responsibility, I took the reprimand. The officer responsible sat quietly across the table from me. My annoyance must have been obvious to my comrades, because one of them must have rung

Casey after the conference. He flew across to the Green Zone and came into my office. Although he did not apologise (and I would not have expected it), he said how much he valued our personal relationship. That sort of considerate behaviour sustains all of us, regardless of rank.

The strong views of some of Casey's subordinate commanders brought a new dimension into my relationship with the boss. They sometimes used me to convey their view to him under the cloak of operations rather than have a confrontation with him themselves. If they were reluctant to put something to him, they would prime me to do it. Inevitably, Casey reacted. I would say to myself as I walked away from his office, 'Jim, you have obviously integrated extraordinarily well into this coalition, because Casey now beats you up just like a US officer.'

I would brief him at least twice a day and often more, but I could not get to him as much as I liked. Even when he came from Camp Victory to the Green Zone, which was almost daily, he was extraordinarily busy. I tried to resolve as much as I could at my level, but there were many things of a specifically US nature that I had no authority to decide.

For example, we needed to hold the extremely scarce US Special Forces soldiers in Iraq for even longer periods than foreseen to protect the Iraqi leadership against assassination, when everyone from the Secretary of Defense down knew that special forces were desperately needed elsewhere. This issue went on and on for months, with me as the meat in the sandwich. There were dozens of such issues I would have liked to spare Casey, but I couldn't, as they were political in nature and had specific consequences for Americans and no-one else. I always suspected he had a technique to handle the less important but difficult decisions for which there were no clever answers. I was regularly subjected to this technique, which was simple: put off making a decision with the knowledge, born of experience, that something would probably come up. This of course did not help me answer increasingly strident questions from CENTCOM or the Pentagon.

But on the big and important issues, Casey made good decisions in a timely fashion. He would serve in Iraq until 2007 and return to the US as head of the army. When this war is concluded, I hope George Casey will continue to be recognised as the great general he is.

CHAPTER 6

'We might let you fire a shot or two'

A year of living dangerously, 2004–2005

The lessons I had learnt in four months in Iraq only highlighted how much I still didn't know. Most of these lessons had been professional, but some were personal.

When I took over as chief of operations in September, my personal staff was running smoothly. My executive officer (XO), Major Steve Summersby, was performing excellently and life was manageable — just. My bodyguard, now from Australian Special Forces plus six to eight US soldiers, was filling me with as much confidence as you can ever have on the streets of Baghdad. My personal staff kept me sane, and they kept me alive. Actually, some might have disputed how sane I was, but I was definitely alive.

By my reckoning, more than half the coalition generals were the subject of at least one attack in Iraq. This was 'war among the people', and in order to fight it we had to move among the people, which made us vulnerable to a planned attack — and likely to be sometimes simply in the wrong place at the wrong time. My respect for the combat soldier requires me to make a disclaimer at this point.

The threat to me as a general in the headquarters, even one who travelled a good deal, was nothing compared with the continual threat to a US or Iraqi combat soldier on the streets. I never raised the issue of personal danger in front of my fellow generals. But it is worth mentioning in this account for Australians, to stress the importance of a general's personal staff. There is an old saying that nothing motivates soldiers as much as a few dead generals. I would like to think they can be similarly motivated by a live general who wins. The next time Australia sends a general to a serious fight 'among the people', we don't want to lose him.

When Peter Cosgrove asked me to go to Iraq, he assigned me one soldier from the Special Air Service Regiment as a bodyguard and a driver from our commando battalion. I was grateful, not having any idea that most generals who travelled in Iraq had six to 12 men for their personal security.

The job of my bodyguard was to get us out of any dangerous situation, by fighting if necessary. The job of my XO was to ensure that we did not get into a dangerous situation in the first place. Before I arrived in Iraq, General Cosgrove asked the Australian headquarters in Iraq to find me an XO from officers already in Baghdad. In the best military tradition, the only spare officer they could find was one who'd been moved out of his position because he'd been performing unsatisfactorily. I knew nothing of this officer's background and so had no initial reason to reject him. Rather naively, I would probably have given him a go even if I had known — a peacetime approach I should not have carried into a combat situation.

It did not take me long to realise I was working in a very unforgiving environment. I began to get a little concerned about my own security when I discovered how much travel both the infrastructure security and chief of operations positions required. The threat in Iraq was ubiquitous. A religiously inspired enemy who

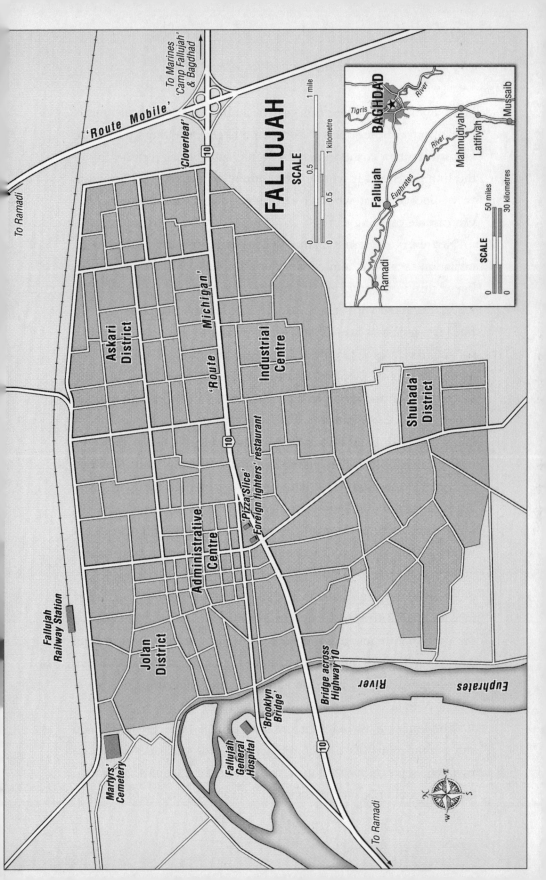

FALLUJAH

SCALE

1 mile
1 kilometre
0.5
0.5
1 kilometre
0
0

'Route Mobile'

To Ramadi

To Marines
'Camp Fallujah'
& Bagdhad

'Cloverleaf'

10

'Route Michigan'

Askari
District

Industrial
Centre

Shuhada'
District

Fallujah
Railway Station

Jolan
District

Administrative
Centre

'Pizza Slice'
'Foreign fighters' restaurant

10

Martyrs'
Cemetery

Fallujah
General
Hospital

'Brooklyn Bridge'

Bridge across
Highway 10

Euphrates River

10

To Ramadi

To Ramadi

BAGHDAD inset

BAGHDAD

Tigris River

Euphrates River

Fallujah

Ramadi

Mahmudiyah

Latifiyah

Mussaib

SCALE

50 miles
30 kilometres
0
0

N
S
E
W

hides among the people can wait in ambush every day and night. They can trawl the streets looking for a target or setting up traps. To kill or capture a coalition general would have been great theatre for the insurgents, but it would have entirely spoiled my day. So it was very important that whoever was organising my travel and security was capable of doing so.

Not everyone can function when every trip on a road is an invitation to a fight, and carries the possibility of death or injury. I knew this intuitively and it had been reinforced in East Timor, where I worked with superb people who understood the streets. In Iraq, everyone was armed and was expected to use their weapon if needed. As a combat officer, I had grown up with weapons and understood that I should always be prepared to fight. The XO who greeted me on my arrival in Iraq did not have that background; his expertise lay elsewhere. My SAS bodyguard was excellent and I knew that both would do their job, but they needed the XO to be on the ball, especially because initially I only had the two bodyguards and did not yet have my own armoured transport. I was dependent on the military equivalent of public transport, which, like much public transport, didn't run when I was ready and never went where I wanted to go. This stopped me from setting up essential meetings and visits.

I needed my own armoured vehicles and a larger bodyguard. My first XO had ordered two up-armoured SUVs, but had not pushed the order hard enough through the Australian headquarters in Iraq. The Australian staff bluffed him, and he would not stand up to them. If an organisation has no respect for your messenger, they will rarely go out of their way to assist you.

The longer I was without my own vehicles, a larger bodyguard and a competent XO, the more likely I was to be killed. After about two weeks, my poor XO was so exhausted he could hardly stay awake. I would not survive with this officer. By persisting with him,

I was making a laughing stock of myself and endangering us all. It came to a head when my bodyguard, then led by Drew, an extraordinarily experienced SAS corporal, quietly approached me and gave me his opinion. I relieved the XO of his duties and sent him back to Australia — exactly what the local Australian commander should have done when he first realised the officer couldn't perform in this environment.

After some time and a few more adventures, Major Steve Summersby arrived. My life improved markedly. Steve, an artillery officer, had commanded a parachute artillery battery of six guns and about 100 men when I commanded the 1st Division. He was overwhelmingly competent. Nothing fazed him. He was able to work with any nation and anyone of any rank. He was self-confident without being arrogant, and the bodyguard loved him. He was also tough. When I had to be even tougher on those who worked for me, Steve made things right by fixing things behind the scenes. Steve found me an interim solution to the car problem and even bolstered my bodyguard by hiring some excellent ex-soldiers, American and British, from the Blackwater security firm. Once again, I could concentrate on my job.

When things settled down and Australia recognised what I would need to function effectively, I was allocated a group of first-class people. My Australian bodyguard was increased to four and sometimes six. I had Steve as my XO, and a sergeant clerk who could operate a machine gun — at that time the machine gun was a technical requirement set by our headquarters for movement in the Red Zone. Finally I received two permanent 'hard cars', SUVs with about 3 tonnes of armour on them. When I became the chief of operations in September, I inherited another two armoured vehicles from my predecessor, one crewed by US Army reservists and the other by US Air Force personnel. From the middle of the year, my personal convoy always consisted of at least one armoured vehicle with a roof-mounted automatic weapon and the hard cars. Not only could we now fight back against an attack, but often we could combine with other convoys to present an even stronger deterrent. On Iraqi streets, it helped if everyone could see that you were ready to fight. Few insurgent groups would take on a strong convoy directly with small arms and RPGs, and sometimes they would even hold their bombs until a weaker target arrived. But our little group was still down the lower end of convoys in the deterrent stakes. This gave rise to some black humour, with someone suggesting we should hang a sign on our vehicles in large Arabic lettering saying 'MUCH WEAKER CONVOY FOLLOWING'!

During my 12 months in Iraq, my party and I experienced about 15 incidents — rocket attacks, mortar attacks and direct attacks with small arms or explosives. Most occurred in the first eight or nine months. The threat was higher when I was in the infrastructure job because I was travelling so much, but even working in Saddam's Palace — within the Green Zone, in the middle of a city of five-and-a-half million people, some of whom did not like us at all — rockets and mortars flew in almost daily. Once, as I was happily working in my lower ground floor office, a mortar shell hit the building directly above me, only a metre away, blowing off a large part of the building and causing us yet again to move down to the basement.

Rockets were more dangerous than any mortar, as they could be fired across a far greater distance and carried much more explosive. Most mortars used against us had a range of only a kilometre or so, and a few of the bigger ones went out to 5 kilometres, so you had a small chance of being able to pick the likely areas that they would be fired from and watch those areas closely. But some rockets could fly 15 kilometres, which meant that likely launch areas, called 'rocket boxes', were infinitely more numerous. It was not hard to tell the difference between a mortar attack and a rocket attack from the sound; experts could tell what kind of a weapon was used just from the crack at the receiving end. The only redeeming feature of rockets was that you could hear the faint whine of their engines. Or, to be more precise, you could hear the second rocket after the first had hit and exploded, because suddenly you were listening very keenly.

The Australian house in the Green Zone was about 20 metres from its neighbours, separated by gardens and a pond. One day a rocket hit Brigadier General Sandy Davidson's house, next door to ours, and two of its off-duty occupants (not Sandy) were injured. Another time, the house behind us was hit at night by a rocket which must have been travelling almost horizontally, because it hit the top of a gate post and then exploded against the front wall, killing one of two contractors who were living in the house while they renovated it. The glass in the windows across the back of our little house was shattered by another near miss, forcing us to replace the glass with ugly sandbags. As we arrived back at the house one night and were unlocking the door, a rocket or a mortar exploded close by and for the first time I heard the sound of shrapnel humming through the hot night air as we huddled in the doorway. We had assessed that the most solid part of our house was the short corridor outside my bedroom, and I remember the six or eight of us crouching in this dark corridor, all in night attire (or lack of it), as mortars or rockets fell around us. After 36 years in the military, I suddenly understood that the sound of a mortar or rocket arriving at its destination is far, far louder than the sound of it being fired on a training range.

One night I was in the Green Zone attending a video conference linked to the generals out at Camp Victory. General Casey, at Victory, was talking about his most recent trip to see his commanders. Without warning, a rocket exploded against the roof of our building with as loud a crash as I ever heard in Iraq, just above the vidcon room. Apparently the looks on our faces as the rocket hit, as seen by those at Camp Victory, provided great amusement. But it wasn't over. In the silence that followed the first hit, all of us at the Green Zone end of the vidcon heard the humming of a second rocket; abandoning all dignity, we generals, as one, hit the floor under the conference table. Fortunately, the rocket passed just over the building and exploded in the parking area, injuring no-one. This had our observers at Victory in absolute hysterics, seeing a room full of generals' backsides sticking up in the air.

The night before the 30 January 2005 election, we in the palace were not so lucky. In North Babil province, insurgents dashed out of some remote farmhouses and erected the metal frames from which they fired their rockets. In the Green Zone operations centre we saw them via an unmanned Predator drone flying high overhead. As the insurgents placed and aimed the rockets, we furiously tried to convert their location to a map grid reference to target them. In no time at all, their rockets streaked across the night sky and the perpetrators scampered back to hide in the farmhouses. Having finally pinpointed their launch site on our electronic map, I asked the operators what direction the rockets had taken: this information was not easily interpreted from the Predator data. Meanwhile, the two rockets flew through the night air, covering many kilometres from their launch site. Then both crashed through the roof of the palace building, hitting only metres from my operations centre, where a shift of 80 operators was running our part of the war. The exact impact point was a room containing another 40 people. Neither of the rockets exploded, but they physically hit a US soldier and a US State Department officer, a man and a woman, and killed them both. Had the rockets exploded, most people in the room would have died and the insurgents would have won a great propaganda victory on the night before the election.

The impact was so loud, I couldn't believe the rockets had not exploded. Their failure to explode could have been because of some operator error or because they had been stored underground for a long time and had deteriorated. Even though they did not explode, dust was still floating in the corridors the next morning.

This was one of a number of times when we worked in the operations room, in a fortified building in the Green Zone, wearing helmets and body armour. It was small compensation that within the hour we had our troops at the farmhouses and captured the rocketeers.

Compared with the Red Zone, life in the Green Zone was secure. I only travelled into the Red Zone when necessary, but that was often. My bodyguard counted how frequently we went up the 10-kilometre Route Irish, the shooting-gallery road linking Camp Victory with the Green Zone. The final count was about 120 times. When I was in charge of infrastructure security, we regularly visited the ministries of oil and electricity, the central railway station, where the director-general of rail worked, and the various power stations and substations around Baghdad. Outside Baghdad, I concentrated mainly on the power infrastructure, from Mosul in the north to Kirkuk in the northeast, to Naft Kanneh in the east and the al Faw peninsula in the south. For long distances, I would fly and then take vehicles provided by local military units.

The enemy wanted to make us afraid of moving among the people. Because an attack could occur at any time, routine travel was tense and had to be well orchestrated. Being stopped by heavy traffic in a Baghdad street focused your attention — this was always a likely time to die. Suicide car bombers and gunmen waited in even the most crowded streets. Civilian casualties apparently meant nothing to them. If we looked like being caught in traffic or slowed down to a dangerous level, we immediately switched to some pretty extreme avoidance techniques. We bluffed other vehicles out of the way, drove up the wrong side of the street against oncoming traffic or mounted the footpath and escaped that way. We ignored traffic lights or traffic policemen. To stop when asked to by a traffic policeman was to court attack. Of course this did not impress the honest burghers of Baghdad, whose life was already totally disrupted. I felt embarrassed the first few times we did it, but the alternative was worse.

A roadside bomb, a car bomb or an explosive rocket initiated most of the clashes on the roads. The car bomb might be a suicide bomber or it might be parked by the roadside, abandoned and then detonated by remote command as a target went by. A common device for triggering roadside bombs or parked car bombs was a commercial electronic garage door opener, but their range could sometimes be a bit short. Mobile phones were also used, but because the electronic signal went through a number of switches, the call had to be timed just right to get a moving vehicle.

If you were attacked, it was permissible to mention the attack to your fellow generals, but only in passing, and only to explain your late arrival at the meeting!

The first direct attack on my group was while we were returning from the Ministry of Oil, east of the Green Zone across the Tigris. Insurgent informers in the ministry had been telling their comrades that oil pipes had been repaired and could once again be blown up. A CIA agent in the headquarters told me the name and position of one high-level informer in the oil-flow control department of the ministry. This was just after the occupation had ended and we'd handed authority back to an Iraqi government. My authority over security issues in the ministries had been unchallenged for as long as the occupation lasted, but now, quite rightly, I had to convince Minister Ghadban to take action.

The attack occurred before I had either a full bodyguard or the best vehicles for venturing into the Red Zone. I was using an organisation called the 'Steel Dragons', a US artillery unit that had left its guns in the US and been re-task to act as an armoured and armed taxi service around Baghdad. If I wanted to go somewhere, the XO would book the Steel Dragons and their four armoured Hummers. (The High Mobility Multi-purpose Wheeled Vehicle — HMMWV, often called the 'Hum Vee' or Hummer — was to the Iraq War what the Wiley's Jeep was to World War II. It has a turret on the top in which the crew can mount various weapons and so fight back if attacked.)

A rule of thumb was never to stay anywhere for longer than an hour, and if you took the same route to come home as you took to go out, you were offering the insurgents a free kick. They might see you go out (or be told by informers), and quickly assemble to have a go at you as you returned.

We had gone to the ministry by the most direct route, straight out of the Green Zone, across a major bridge over the Tigris and down a main road. The ministry building was multi-storeyed, one of the few high buildings in Baghdad. At this stage it housed both the oil and the electricity ministries, so I was there often. It was one of the few government buildings protected from looting after the invasion. Its architectural style was east European, and like most Baghdad buildings, its lifts did not work. There was the usual abundance of young Iraqi security guards in the foyer, stern young men who would nevertheless break into a broad smile if you greeted them. I was very polite to all Iraqis, not only because it was the correct and civilised thing to do but, as I joked with my bodyguard, they might be standing behind me in a hostage video at some stage!

My meeting with Minister Ghadban went longer than we would have liked, and my XO and bodyguard grew anxious. The minister was, as always, reluctant to act on our intelligence and needed some convincing. He was not easy to deal with: I always visited him with one request, and came away with several new ones from him.

Usually I felt obliged to act on anything we agreed upon. Ghadban would say yes to anything once he tired of my presence and advocacy, but then he rarely acted.

Because the meeting had taken so long, we decided to make a big change to our route back to the Green Zone. This new route went through a long underpass, almost a tunnel. It was a choke point, and no-one liked it. But the decision was made and we headed off.

I often slept in vehicles, but this was only a short trip, 10–15 minutes. My Hummer was the second of four vehicles in the convoy. I sat in the back without a headset. My bodyguard, Drew, was beside me, plugged into the convoy's tactical radio net. My XO was in the car behind with the other bodyguard.

Everything went well as we swung north, then west towards the underpass. I was fatalistic about road travel. There was nothing I could do, so I pretended there was little point worrying, though I must admit that sometimes I would close my eyes and look inward when I felt we were threatened, in the vain hope that if there was an explosion I would save my sight.

Traffic was light so we made good time. As we approached the underpass, I noticed that the traffic had thinned out even more. Thinking back, I remember quite distinctly seeing groups of Iraqis standing in the high-walled entrances to their houses, with their metal gates partially open, just watching. When the insurgents moved openly into an area to conduct an attack, the locals would withdraw from the streets and take cover in their houses until the danger had passed. On this day, some wanted to watch the fun.

A block or two before the tunnel, where our road started to descend, a single missile flew at our convoy from a side street. The missile, probably an RPG, streaked across behind my vehicle and impacted against a fence. As I wasn't wearing a headset I couldn't hear the talk on the radio. I was in the Steel Dragons' hands. We accelerated and dipped into the underpass, speeding up the far side expecting the worst, not even having time to fire back. But nothing more happened.

Ambushes normally started with one rocket or roadside bomb. Had this first shot hit a vehicle, it probably would have killed or injured those inside. The other three vehicles would then have stopped and tried to help. This is when the main ambush would occur, with more RPGs, rifles and machine guns. But because the first RPG missed us and we sped through the killing ground, there was no further ambush.

We continued at speed, making the bridge and getting through the checkpoints back into the Green Zone.

If I were paranoid, I would have believed this was a set-up. Those at the ministry who knew I was talking to Ghadban could have informed on me. I have no proof that this occurred, and in all probability it was a random attack. When we were safely back in the Green Zone, I thanked the Steel Dragon crews and left them as they prepared to take their next customers out into the Red Zone.

The second time we were attacked was some months later, when as chief of operations I had my own four-man bodyguard, my own hard cars and two Hummers with machine-gunners standing on top. It was shortly after midday, and we were on Route Irish going to Camp Victory for a meeting: as usual, we were speeding along the highway as fast as the Hummers could go, about 90 km/h. A kilometre outside the main entrance, near what used to be the welcome sign for Saddam International Airport, a machine gun fired on us from about 150 metres away, where houses bordered a service road parallel to the highway. My vehicle's noise and armour protected me from hearing or being hurt by machine-gun fire from that range, but again, none of us knew what would happen next.

My bodyguard, all linked by radio, became even more alert and we sped up. The gunner in the vehicle in front of me was returning fire for all he was worth. Our second hard car tried to avoid the fire by driving off the highway; it hit a ditch and blew a rear tyre. In normal circumstances this was exactly what the insurgents would have wanted: one car disabled, the other cars stopping to assist. But our cars had 'run-flat' tyres, which meant that if one was shot out, you could still drive at high speed for several kilometres on the flat tyre and get out of the killing zone before the tyre tore itself to pieces. When we finally stopped at Camp Victory, the gunner in front of me opened the door to his Hummer, and out cascaded all his used shell casings. As usual, I thanked the boys, gave them a heartfelt 'Well done, fellas' and went in to my meeting, coolly pretending that everything was normal.

Who knows why this machine gun attacked our convoy. The meeting was a big one, and many convoys were on Route Irish that day. Was the gunfire meant to create turmoil on the road, which could then be exploited with a car bomb? Firing from so far away, the machine gun was obviously not the main attack. Perhaps it was meant to lure a reaction force to a better ambush position just off Route Irish.

Insurgent attacks were often very complex, and it paid to expect the worst. I always felt most tense as we entered or left the big bases, particularly the Green Zone. At each of its four major entrances, there was almost always a long line of cars waiting to be checked. Most were driven by Iraqis who lived in the Green Zone. They had to stop, show their pass, and have their car searched, both electronically and by sniffer dogs. This line, often 40 cars long, took up one of the three entry lanes. Between the lanes were concrete blast barriers, sometimes 3 metres high. Coalition military vehicles and contractor vehicles had a second, faster lane, which reduced the waiting time — and thus the risk. VIPs like me had access to a third lane, opened by radio coordination as we approached. We were waved through without any check. Very few of us could do this —

only a few generals, the ambassador and a few senior diplomats, and it was a real privilege. During my deployment, the four entrances to the Green Zone were attacked more than 12 times by car bombs.

Sometimes an attack at an entrance to the Green Zone would leave us stranded out in the Red Zone. A warning would come over the 'sheriff's net', a radio frequency that coordinated tactical actions around the Green Zone and on Route Irish. We would then choose whether to try another entrance or go back to where we had come from, both of which involved driving in very unsafe areas. Caught outside, anything was possible. We drove anywhere and did anything to get back in. But as can be imagined, the other entrances were also on high alert, and as we would get close to a gate, we had to slow down so that we weren't fired on by our own or nervous Iraqi soldiers.

A car bomb at a Green Zone entrance would normally kill 20 or 30 people at least, most of them Iraqis waiting to get in. A large car bomb let off a deep sound that rolled across the Green Zone: it was not a crack like a mortar or rocket. The closest we came to a car bomb was at the Camp Victory end of Route Irish, not far from where we were attacked by the machine gun, in the depth of winter, with rain slanting down and mud everywhere. The gunners on the Hummers were rugged up against the cold, with helmet, balaclava, jacket, body armour and gloves. We were approaching the main Victory entrance at speed and could see perhaps a kilometre in the rain. Cars were queued ahead of us, probably Iraqis trying to get into the airport. I was drifting in and out of sleep when suddenly there was an enormous explosion, followed by fire from cars burning and the start of the column of black smoke we were all so familiar with. The bomb had exploded on the left-hand side of the road among the cars waiting to get in. Though there was falling debris everywhere, including car parts and probably body parts, our third lane on the extreme right was still clear.

The bodyguard commander, summing up our options in the few seconds he had, asked no-one in particular if we should go through or stay outside. I immediately said we should charge through, which we did. We later heard that the car bomber had pulled up in the line of traffic. Two Iraqi guards had approached him, but must have become suspicious, because they were seen to turn and try to run. The bomber exploded the car, killing the guards and others in the line.

Whenever possible, I used aircraft. We flew by helicopter to Victory, particularly for night meetings, and to places that were quite close, such as Fallujah, Mussaib power station, Balad or Taji, but also to places as far as Mosul, Irbil or the Iranian border. We used C-130s for more distant trips, then local helicopters or vehicles once we'd landed.

Our party was attacked only once when travelling by helicopter: near Saddam's home town of Tikrit on our way to Mosul. We were in Blackhawks, which were, incidentally, used to ferry important civilians around with varying degrees of customer satisfaction. I would often hear the angry footsteps of a recent VIP passenger stomping down the corridor to my office to complain that they had been dumped for several days in some remote base when their helicopter was reassigned to some higher priority, leaving them stranded.

On this flight to Mosul, our two Blackhawks were engaged twice in broad daylight, probably by an anti-aircraft gun we could see mounted on a vehicle on Route Tampa, the main north–south highway. As usual, I was half asleep in the back right-hand seat of the aircraft, with my head against the window, and only became aware we were being engaged when the door gunner called to the pilot that he could see firing from the road. In helicopters, we normally travelled at an altitude of only 30 or so feet. When the pilot heard the gunner, he threw the aircraft onto its side and dropped it down to about 10 feet. I opened my eyes just in time to see the second burst of fire wink from the road. It was extraordinary that the vehicle mounting this gun appeared to be on a road that had any number of coalition convoys and checkpoints. Perhaps it was just off the road — I can't remember precisely. When we were clear, I could hear the pilots discussing going back to keep an eye on the vehicle until a reaction force arrived. As my hand moved to my microphone switch to bring some sanity to the conversation, they talked themselves out of the idea. Duelling with an anti-aircraft gun, although probably good fun in an Apache gunship, is not a smart idea in the larger, slower and less armoured Blackhawk.

My bodyguards' job was to put themselves between me and likely danger, and they did this whether they were on the road, escorting me through a group of Iraqis at a meeting, or in the midst of a rocket attack on the house. They were mature soldiers and extraordinarily skilled. They practised drills almost every day, and shot often on the local ranges, always asking me to come and shoot with them. I was only able to do this once. I always carried a rifle as well as a pistol into the Red Zone, thinking that if fate left me standing after a first attack, I wanted more than just a pistol to defend myself. My bodyguard had obviously discussed the frightening fact that the general was carrying a rifle, and the SAS commander brought the issue up with me.

'Boss,' he said, 'we don't mind you carrying a rifle, but it is our job to protect you. The first thing we will do is get you away from the bad guys. If things are going exceptionally well, then we might let you fire a shot or two.'

I guess that was only fair.

CHAPTER 7

The bright ember in the ash pit of the insurgency

Approaching the Second Battle for Fallujah, September–November 2004

Fallujah was probably the most constant focus of my year in Iraq. The first battle for Fallujah was raging as I prepared to leave Australia, and it dominated my arrival. From the strategic level, I saw Fallujah as two distinct fights, the first in April 2004 and the second in November 2004. What made the fighting different in the second battle was a period of 'shaping' in the intervening months.

'Shaping' is the term we use for actions that prepare a target, a point, a city, a country or a mind for some later activity. In the first battle of Fallujah in April, there was no time for shaping, as the political demands upon the Marines after the deaths of the Blackwater contractors came too fast. We were determined that this would not happen again.

We set about finding out as much as possible about the city, its people and the enemy located there, in case another attack was necessary. We wanted to isolate Fallujah so we could prevent the enemy's escape or reinforcement. We took every chance to attack the Jihadist leadership in the city, using precision weapons such as laser-guided or GPS bombs. We wanted to split the people of Fallujah from the Jihadists. If we could do that, the Jihadists wouldn't be able to band together with the citizens and fight us as they had in April. Also, if most of the non-combatants left the city, our soldiers had many more tactical options when and if they had to attack. Finally, we wanted to wear down our opponents so that they would be less effective in a fight.

At no stage did our shaping involve cutting off food, water, power or medical assistance in order to force the people to act in a certain way: that would have been inhumane and illegal. It did involve monitoring who was coming and going, and warning the people of upcoming operations so they could leave the city temporarily if they wished. We also staged frequent attacks, usually with bombs, on specific insurgent leadership targets within the city.

Fallujah was a bleak little city built in a 5 kilometre square on the east bank of a loop in the Euphrates River, only 20 minutes by Blackhawk helicopter from Baghdad. The Baghdad-to-Syria railway and its high embankment formed Fallujah's northern boundary. To the west was the Euphrates. A north–south highway we called 'Route Mobile' and a major traffic circle known to us as 'The Cloverleaf' contained the city to the east. To the south, there was no distinct boundary, as the city merged with the desert and farming areas in a series of increasingly dispersed houses and small businesses in a light-industrial zone.

No-one really knew how many people lived in Fallujah because, as in the rest of Iraq, no reliable census had been carried out. A figure of 300,000 came from the national food distribution program — better than nothing, but still unreliable. The city and its environs were Sunni areas, and its people had a reputation for being very independently minded. Fallujah was a hotbed of resistance to authority even in Saddam's time.

The capital of Anbar province, Ramadi, was only a few kilometres away to the west, and a number of smaller towns surrounded Fallujah. They had been home to part of Saddam's armaments and defence industry complex. None of these facilities was standing, much less operating, after the invasion and the looting.

Like many Iraqi towns and cities, Fallujah had no central business district of multi-storey buildings. The city was low: one- or two-storey buildings were the norm, with only a few five- or six-storey structures scattered through the town. The oldest, most prestigious suburbs were grouped in an area known as the Jolan district, in the town's northwest, along the Euphrates. Some of the houses were pleasant, set in parks and broader streets, but most of this area was a maze of alleyways, small shops and *souks*, or markets. Many of the alleyways were too small for armoured vehicles, and our troops soon found out that some of the older construction was quite substantial and could not be blasted apart. In the days before air conditioners, many of the walls were built 1–2 metres thick. As the oldest part of town, Jolan would have been very familiar to those whose business — legal or illegal, and over many hundreds of years — was related to moving goods between Syria and Baghdad.

The leadership of the insurgency in Fallujah initially used this older area as a headquarters. It is thought that Abu Musab al-Zarqawi beheaded the kidnapped civilian Nick Berg in a building in this area, making a film that would spread the image of Zarqawi's barbarity around the world.

To the east of the Jolan district was the new part of town: wider and straighter streets bordered by houses of a generally uniform design. The buildings were a little higher here, and the layout was more ordered, like a European or British town, with identical houses repeated monotonously. The physical differences between the closely packed Jolan and this more open area would influence our tactics in attacking the city.

Two bridges across the Euphrates linked the city to a peninsula on which the Fallujah Hospital was built. The southern bridge carried the major road (Highway 10, or 'Route Michigan') that bisected Fallujah and led to a government administrative district in the centre of town, where local councils met. This was also where the coalition had conducted its business before the April battle.

Media referred to Fallujah as 'the city of mosques', possibly to give it an image of quiet religious observance or holiness. Depending on what counts as a mosque, there were as few as 72 or as many as 166, but to me there did not seem to be more than in any Iraqi city of that size.

The only secondary industry in the city itself seemed to be dozens of very small vehicle and fabrication workshops in the alleys and small roads. Just outside the city to the northeast was a group of buildings we called the 'potato factory'. I remember wondering if it really was a potato factory — I heard it called that by my equivalent in the Marines, Colonel Mike Regner, but I never saw any reason to clarify it. The attraction of the potato factory was that it had a cool room that worked when hooked up to generators, and we soon pressed it into service as a morgue for enemy and unidentified bodies.

Fallujah was poorly drained and depended on pumps to return to the Euphrates the water that flooded parts of the city. As soon as the power went out, the pumps stopped, the water came in and the sewage pooled, making Fallujah an altogether unpleasant place to live in or fight for. Legal and illegal power lines festooned the lanes and minor roads. Someone in the Ministry of Electricity once told me that only about 20 per cent of Iraqis were connected legally to the electrical reticulation system, and even fewer were ever actually billed for the power they used.

Fallujah was once referred to by John Sattler, by now the commander of the Marines in Iraq, as 'the bright ember in the ash pit of the insurgency' — a great description. If the insurgency's base in the infamous Sunni triangle had a heart, Fallujah was it. Symbolically, by 2004 Fallujah was the centre of the insurgency. No sooner had the local people and the insurgents finished their celebrations of victory over the Marines after the April fighting than a new class of enemy began to appear. The city had always been a truckstop for foreign fighters coming from Arab and other countries through Syria, Jordan and Saudi Arabia. I remember watching for weeks the comings and goings at a restaurant in the centre of Fallujah that was used as an overnight stop for foreign fighters, and waiting for an appropriate time to hit it. After the battle in April, when the city was left without a coalition presence, foreign and some Iraqi insurgents started to stay in the city for longer periods. More flocked in as they realised that the ineffective Fallujah Brigade, not coalition troops, represented the new Iraq in the city.

The insurgency desperately needed a safe haven where they could rest, plan, tend to their wounded, bury their dead, refit their fighters, and prepare their suicide volunteers for their 'martyrdom operations'. It took Zarqawi no time at all to focus the insurgents and terrorists in Fallujah and use Fallujah as a base for operations against other areas of Iraq. He and his organisation were untroubled by local battalions or police units, whom they quickly intimidated into dispersing or cooperating.

Fallujah's location also helped the insurgency. The city was only a short car ride to Baghdad along a main highway or, if you wished to move more covertly, through dozens of back roads that curved north and south into the capital. Insurgents could get into Baghdad relatively easily from Fallujah, avoiding the checkpoints on the main roads. Fallujah also facilitated their access to Basrah and the south, and, more importantly, to Mosul in the north, along a series of infiltration routes, or 'rat lines', that ran up past the Thar Thar Lake and canal.

Fallujah was also close to many of the major electrical and oil lines that ran into Baghdad. Insurgents based there mounted attacks on infrastructure that would cut electricity and petroleum supplies to five-and-a-half million Baghdadis.

As long as Fallujah acted as a springboard for attacks against the capital and the infrastructure, it eroded the credibility of the Iraqi Interim Government and, therefore, the coming election. Fallujah was to become even more important as the election approached.

The power struggle in the city itself turned even uglier as the Fallujah Brigade and the police disintegrated. Many of the insurgents were extremists from Zarqawi's organisation or Kurds, Jordanians or Saudis from al Qaeda. Very soon, they began to impose a particularly strict form of the religious Sharia law on citizens, and to demand total allegiance. To say the least, this came as a surprise to the Sunni Fallujans. They thought they had beaten the coalition in April, yet they were now losing control of their own city to Islamic extremists.

A previous generation understood the saying, 'Vietnam is not a war, it is a country.' In the same sense, Fallujah was not a battle, it was a city. It was, and is, infrastructure, buildings, factories, houses and roads. But mainly, Fallujah was people. Fallujah's citizens suffered as badly as any others in the Iraq War but they were often regarded as less than patriots by their fellow citizens, and I was never convinced that there was real countrywide sympathy for the people of Fallujah. They were seen as perennially quarrelsome, and many Iraqis thought they brought their problems on themselves. To Arabs outside Iraq, the Fallujans were seen as Iraq's Palestinians — handy as a stick to beat the US with, but would you really put yourself in harm's way to help them? So the city of Fallujah became a symbol of resistance, and it remains a symbol today. Its people always seemed to be an afterthought. In my view, we cared more about the ordinary people of Fallujah than any other group I could identify.

There was no plan to have one fight, or two fights, in Fallujah. There was no strategy to fight in April and then November 2004. Rarely is military planning so precise. One thing happens because other things have happened; military planning must retain an infinite flexibility. I have found that the normal state of affairs in military operations, except when you are writing a version of history, is to have little ability to predict precisely what is really going to happen next. No-one wanted to attack Fallujah a second time if it could be avoided.

The pressure to do something about Fallujah started during the April fighting and intensified as the Fallujah Brigade failed to stabilise the city. In May the Iraqi Interim Government, using a number of Ba'athist generals brought back specifically for this purpose, recruited hundreds of young Iraqi males for service in this brigade. Commanders came and went and numbers fluctuated. They were equipped with vehicles, weapons, radios and uniforms that we diverted from other much more productive forces (mostly the Iraqi Police). During May, the coalition even attempted a weapons buy-back program and a series of joint traffic control points with the Fallujah Brigade. Both initiatives failed because the brigade was ineffective.

Throughout May and June, the Fallujah Brigade stumbled along but it rarely showed even marginal capability and it was demonstrably corrupt. The new Iraqi Interim Government could not continue to ignore all this, and finally it recalled the Iraqi general who commanded what was left of the brigade, a Major General Saleh. He was given a ministry job in Baghdad. Fallujah was becoming even more lawless, and in July the insurgents struck at the two Iraqi Army battalions resident in the city that were not part of the Fallujah Brigade, kidnapping and killing the two battalion commanders and an intelligence officer. Intimidation, one of any insurgency's most effective weapons, totally fragmented the two battalions. I remember two full Iraqi brigades of 4000 to 6000 troops based in Mosul being dispersed by intimidation in October and November 2004. One of them had been trained by Australian training teams.

The insurgents maintained the pressure in Fallujah in July by kidnapping the newly installed governor's two sons, forcing him to leave his job and publicly denounce the coalition to gain their release.

Only just settling in as Prime Minister, Iyad Allawi favoured continuing negotiations. He was the ultimate decision-maker now. But the insurgents in Fallujah refused to cooperate by laying down arms and joining the political process. Allawi's Interim Government, particularly its Sunni members, continually discussed the insurgent presence in the city with Fallujah's leaders, including clerics, tribal leaders and the local council. The quasi-representative National Assembly sent a delegation to Fallujah. It too was unsuccessful. No matter what was tried, the people of Fallujah were unable to remove the insurgents from their midst without external intervention.

Normally these tactical issues would have been the province of our immediate subordinate headquarters, the Corps, and we at the higher level would have concentrated on the big picture. But the particular circumstances of Fallujah made it an issue for the Force headquarters. At the request of the Iraqi Interim Government, the coalition had not conducted operations inside Fallujah since May, so that the Fallujah Brigade initiative could be given time to work. General Sanchez had designated Fallujah as a 'special zone', meaning that our forces could not enter Fallujah, and we were not permitted to fire into the city without reference to the Force (MNF-I) headquarters, except in self-defence. Even after the Fallujah Brigade collapsed, the policy of keeping away from the city was continued in order to maintain our relationship with Prime Minister Allawi. When General Casey arrived, he kept up the special zone policy.

Now that they appeared to have a base to manufacture bombs, recruit and train terrorists and suicide bombers, and to mount operations, the insurgents also dug tunnels under the city, stockpiled ammunition and fortified strong points. Fallujah became too hard a nut to crack except with a special effort, and that would require intense shaping. So from midyear until November, the Force headquarters alone ran low-level tactical operations within Fallujah. As chief of operations, the responsibility for managing such operations fell to me. And as we focused more on the 30 January election, we began to realise that there was a vital link between Fallujah and electoral success. If Fallujah were a safe haven for the terrorists and the insurgents only just outside of Baghdad, and if our enemies used the city as a base from which to control operations, to produce car bombs and roadside bombs, and from which fighters could be sent to strike at the very heart of the new Iraq, then the threat to the January 2005 election from Fallujah might be greater than the coalition could handle.

We began looking at Fallujah more analytically. Why is Fallujah important? Why do we need to get it back? If it is so important that we need to control it, is it worth attacking it? What are alternatives to attacking Fallujah? Could we not just cut it off from the rest of Iraq? Where does an attack on Fallujah sit within the overall campaign plan and the election? Could we run an election across Iraq while Fallujah remains a safe haven for terrorists to export bombs, threats, fighters, propaganda and terror across the country? What would it cost to get Fallujah back, in lives, property, goodwill and cohesion within the coalition? Would a coalition attack threaten relations between the coalition and the Iraqi Interim Government? Do we have enough troops to do everything else as well as clear Fallujah? Do we have enough Iraqi troops to put an Iraqi face on the operation? Having cleared Fallujah, would we have the Iraqi troops to then secure it? How can we look after the civilians in the city if we do need to attack? Could we split the civilian population from the terrorists? And what would we have to do to shape the city and weaken our opponents before a battle began?

This was as complex a set of decisions as could ever be imagined, and their implications were political as much as military. The politics were going to come from both Baghdad and Washington. As well, all these decisions had to be made by a command system that was fighting every day across a whole nation, reconstructing a country and an army, and also planning for the election. We could not stop the war to focus only on Fallujah.

Such a process would test the best military staffs in the world. Headquarters MNF-I, still new and ad hoc, had a long way to go before reaching such a standard. My operations division consisted mostly of intelligent and committed but inexperienced officers from several nations. In discussions with Joe Weber, I often referred to this inexperience in my attempts to increase the number of staff I had. My major support, Peter Palmer, had returned to the US for several weeks for a promotion course from colonel to brigadier-general, and then to take some leave. My few experienced individuals were in great demand almost 24 hours a day as we tried to maintain our division's output by sheer personal effort. Even basic staff functions, such as our young captains or majors translating my intentions into written orders several times a day, were often beyond us. I would pass directions by phone to some of our subordinates and then try to catch up with a written order. For the first few months of the new operations branch's existence, my aim was to actually publish a staff order before our major subordinate formation, the beautifully structured and marvellously manned Corps, had actually carried it out!

Following interminable discussion, our views on Fallujah began to crystallise. Clearly the city had the ability to disrupt the election. The months since April showed that the restoration of the rule of law in Fallujah was not going to be achieved without the coalition first establishing security. An attack was still only one of several options, but it had a complex set of preconditions that could not be taken care of at the last minute.

An attack on Fallujah would have to be synchronised with everything else going on in Iraq. When would be the best time to attack? We had plans to conduct operations against a number of cities, Samarra being the most imminent, and major operations were continual in Baghdad, Basrah and elsewhere. As well, before the election we had to achieve the logistical miracle of distributing thousands of tonnes of election materials through a hostile environment. And most importantly, we needed about six weeks before the election to conduct specific military shaping operations — this was what fighting our way to the election meant. Among other factors we had to consider was Ramadan, the Muslim fasting month, which went from mid-October to mid-November 2004, and its concluding holy days of Eid-al-Fitr (13–15 November 2004).

The Casey–Negroponte campaign plan for the period up to the January election focused on the cities and featured a 'cities strategy'. This war was about the people's will, as we and the insurgents knew. To influence the people, our military operations had to be conducted in cities — that is where the people are. We were doing this, applying the concept of the 'three-block war'.

A three-block war is an urban counterinsurgency technique: there are three components, potentially occurring simultaneously in adjoining city blocks. In one block, we might be conducting humanitarian operations, delivering medical or food aid. On the next city block, we might be keeping the peace between feuding groups, using restraint, persuasion or non-lethal weapons. On the third city block, our troops might be involved in combat operations that are as intense as in any war.

Our troops had to be able to do each of the three 'blocks': the same soldier is handing out food in the morning, keeping protesters apart at midday and fighting for his life in midafternoon. And he is required to do it yesterday, today, tomorrow and every day of his year-long tour.

Was a fight in Fallujah going to be the 'three-block' kind or something else?

Compared with the April fighting in Fallujah, we had more time to prepare, some flexibility in choosing a date, and a more demonstrable legitimacy. Under the UN Security Council Resolution 1546, the Iraqi Interim Government now ruled the country and therefore had the power to decide whether or not there would be a second battle in Fallujah. Prime Minister Allawi would also play a major part in strategic decisions. In fact, the exact timing of the November attack, when the decision was eventually made, was known only to about four persons in Iraq, and Allawi was one.

We began to realise that a battle for Fallujah would not begin as a 'three-block war', where the enemy could melt into the population. Instead it would be more like a conventional urban operation: we believed the enemy would stay and fight to protect the terrorist infrastructure they had built. We might be able to turn their strength in Fallujah — their solidification of the city into a base — into a weakness. If they stayed to defend it, the confrontation would be force on force, with small groups of soldiers fighting street to street and house to house against opposing small groups. If the attack took place, there would be savage close-quarter combat.

Much of generalship is about assembling sufficient forces in the right place at the right time. Because Fallujah looked like being more of a conventional fight than a counterinsurgency fight, we had to compare our forces with the enemy's in a more conventional manner. We estimated about 1200 to 1500 enemy in Fallujah itself, with about 1000 to 2000 in the surrounding rural areas and perhaps 400 in the surrounding towns of Karma, Saqlawiyah, Habbaniyah and Amariyah. As November approached, our intelligence estimates rose as high as 5600 insurgents in the Fallujah–Ramadi area, with 4500 in Fallujah itself. Intelligence estimates are an imprecise art form, and the only thing we would know for sure was that we killed 3000 in Fallujah itself during the battle. I remain convinced that some escaped before the assault, but I also know that others moved from outlying areas into the town as the fight approached.

Against this insurgent force armed with roadside bombs, RPGs, mortars, rockets and automatic weapons, we could assemble approximately 10,000 heavily armed Marine and army troops, and about 3000 Iraqi troops of uneven quality. We planned to establish a cordon around Fallujah and attack into the city with sufficient numbers and firepower to guarantee success, and to guarantee a brief campaign.

It was essential to make the fight as short as possible. Fewer troops might prolong the assault, which would mean more violence was required for success. The fighting was likely to be harsh, and embedded journalists and camera crews would convey it to the world in graphic detail. We didn't want to test the Allawi government's resolve to see out the fight with us. We would not fail in this endeavour. We just had to have enough troops to finish it before the political environment changed. If we got it right, there might be a week of heavy fighting and then some more time to mop up.

A severe complicating factor was that about half the US units currently in Iraq would reach the end of their 12-month tours at this critical time, in the last quarter of 2004. Tired forces would go home and fresh forces would come in — a rotation of almost 100,000 troops would occur. Logistically, the planned rotation would be a leviathan task: every major road between Baghdad and Kuwait would be jammed, and all trucks and semi-trailers in Iraq would be used to carry equipment.

The timing of the rotation came under review. Not only did we need troops for Fallujah, we also had to conduct pre-election military shaping operations, the election itself, and then manage whatever might happen after the election.

Could we bring the rotation forward? That would create many problems. If we introduced the new units before Fallujah, we would lose our experienced troops just when we needed them most. As well, such an enormous rotation didn't happen overnight. Replacement units had to prepare at home, load equipment and stores on ships, take final leave, come in by air, spend a few weeks in Kuwait doing Iraq-specific training, and then deploy into Iraq. They would then have to spend time taking over from departing units before we could declare them ready for operations. Of course, the outgoing unit would do the reverse. For the Reserve or National Guard units who would be involved at both ends, the process was even more complicated.

After long discussion and some of the best logistic staff work I am ever likely to see, Casey decided to retain the troops who had already spent a year in Iraq and were supposed to go home, and continue to bring in those who were already programmed to arrive. In addition, we asked Central Command for their reserve, a Marine Expeditionary Unit aboard ships in the Northern Arabian Gulf, and two battalions of the US's strategic reserve Ready Brigade Group: high-readiness light-infantry units. Without the political point-scoring that would surround the official 'surge' in 2007, Casey's chess game would give the US force a de facto surge or overlap of about 30,000: from about 125,000 to 155,000 by the time of the election.

The US system which mobilises the right units at the right time, trains them and transports them, is called the 'force flow' system. I took a long time to master this particular black art. For a period I lived and breathed colourful charts which illustrated the state of the move with pictures of unit badges. To any American service person these were easy to understand, but to an Australian they were initially incomprehensible. Of course, General Casey had cut his military teeth on it all.

Logistics are beautiful when they go well and ugly when they do not. There is little in between. The force flow was an interdependent logistics ballet — if you disrupted any one part of it, the chain reaction would spread throughout the US military for months or years to come. To delay one unit in Iraq would disrupt tens of other units, their training areas, equipment and staff, their ships and heavy equipment transporters. Furthermore, there were political sensitivities. It was a serious business for the staff to suggest that General Casey hold units past a previously agreed time limit. The implications for the families of these units back in America do not need spelling out. Casey had already prepared Rumsfeld and the US Army, Navy and Air Force chiefs for the possibility, and when it became necessary, he secured their agreement. Politically, it was a very tough call, but it was the right call. We would need the extra units in the months to come, whether we attacked Fallujah or not.

We still hadn't decided to attack Fallujah. If we did, our aims had to be clear. We didn't want to imitate the Russian attack on the city of Grozny in Chechnya, and obliterate it. We wanted to stop Fallujah being a safe haven for insurgents, but we needed to have a city at the end of it so that Fallujans could join with the rest of Iraq on the road to elections and a new future. As a patriotic Iraqi, Allawi didn't want Fallujah to become a wasteland, a smashed symbol of resistance with a new crop of martyrs.

Unlike our opponents, we would follow the laws of armed conflict. We aimed to clear the city of the enemy with no unnecessary casualties to the civilian population, to the enemy or to ourselves, and restore the city to a habitable state. Killing or capturing the terrorists and insurgents was critical, of course, but we had to do it in a way that ensured we'd only have to do it once. After the battle, we couldn't allow hostile groups to seep back in — this was a favourite insurgent tactic. We absolutely had to create a secure environment, repair the inevitable battle damage, restore water, power, sanitation and schools, and move the citizens back in. As General Casey said quite forcefully at one planning meeting, 'I want to see Fallujans voting in Fallujah.' Then we would follow up with a longer period of reconstruction, and restoration of democratic government and security from further intimidation for the residents of the city.

This was the overall strategy. The tactical planning was in five overlapping phases: the preparation phase we were currently in; a one-day 'enhanced shaping' phase of intelligence-led strikes on targets we wanted to hit at the last minute before the assault; then the decisive 'penetration' and 'search and attack', in which our forces would break into Fallujah and root out the enemy; then the 'humanitarian operations' where Marines would look after the physical needs of those citizens left in the city; and finally the 'transition to local control', which would go on for months after the assault.

Controversy raged around how we would regulate who went in and out of Fallujah before and during the battle. Troops, vehicles and observation posts had been in place around Fallujah since the April fighting, but they formed a less than watertight 'cordon'. Determined people will find a way through any cordon, and some adventurous or politically motivated media certainly found their way into and out of Fallujah. One of my staff identified about 50 routes joining Fallujah to the Baghdad area north of the main highway alone. There was a lot of empty space out there, and we did not have enough troops for a tight cordon.

General Casey was concerned about how tightly we would seal off Fallujah. His logic was simple and irrefutable: we did not want to allow the enemy to fight us in Fallujah and then escape only to fight us again somewhere else. The fact that our enemy seemed willing to stand and fight rather than disperse into the population was very unusual and we did not want to waste the opportunity. It would be to just about everyone's benefit if we were able to trap insurgents in the city and force them to fight to the death — or, preferably, surrender.

But we could only achieve this level of control with a static cordon, and static cordons are very dangerous for the troops manning them. The enemy can attack checkpoints one after the other by placing superior numbers at different points at different times. As a solution to this difficult problem, the Corps staff and John Sattler's Marines came up with the idea of a 'dynamic cordon': a continual series of traffic control and observation points put in place for short periods at many different points. Being fluid, they were less vulnerable. This was not the 'ring of steel' that Casey and I would have preferred, but it was a necessary — and smart — trade-off between the number of troops we had, the dangers of a static cordon, and our ability to catch the bad guys so we would not have to fight them again.

Some months earlier, I had arranged for my staff engineers to look at improving the cordon by building a bund — an earthen wall — to prevent vehicle movement except through controlled points. The original suggestion came from British sources out of their Northern Ireland experience. The Brits were reticent to suggest this themselves after the first battle of Fallujah, though, because they were perceived as having been highly critical of US tactics. So it was left to me.

My staff concluded that if we assembled all the largest bulldozers in the theatre (we had about 16 of the biggest) and worked them day and night building a 2- or 3-metre-high wall of dirt around the three sides of Fallujah that were not on the river, we could have an effective barrier up in only a few days. Casey seemed to accept this and took the details of the study on his next trip to the Marines. He returned with a negative: the Marines didn't think the effort would be worth it. Their view was that the few vehicle checkpoints would create an even greater target and result in many more Marine casualties, but my view was that it was likely to be much more effective. I was disappointed, but I could understand their logic; I was not a commander directly responsible for the lives of soldiers. I did note that in 2005, after I had left, the coalition built an earthen bund around Mosul, a city of 2.5 million people. According to the commander on the spot, it changed the nature of operations in that city by keeping good people in and bad people out.

For Fallujah, we would have to take troops from other areas in Iraq. During the assault, we would be stretched to cover our security responsibilities in Anbar province, in Baghdad and in and around Mosul. How to apportion this finite resource is the kind of judgment commanders are paid to make. What was critical was that as the battle approached and our troops were concentrated around Fallujah, the enemy did not simply step aside as we went through, move to where we were not, and attack the people in a place we had just left. This would expose the populations in those places to murderous attacks, and unhinge our own operations in Fallujah. In the worst case, after all this preparation, we may have to stop our Fallujah operations and redeploy forces to where the enemy had attacked, thus having two aborted attacks on Fallujah to our credit. This was, of course, exactly what our enemy would want.

As we developed our plans, the Iraqi Interim Government became more active. They wanted the city and its environs to not be a safe haven for foreign terrorists and insurgents, and they wanted control over the city. They could clearly see that this outcome would lower terrorist and insurgent activity elsewhere in Iraq, creating safer conditions for voter registration and a free and fair election. But they still wanted to do all this without an attack. We knew that the government would have to exhaust every peaceful option before it would authorise a military assault. And we were very comfortable with that.

But whether the coalition attacked or not, we had to start to shape the city. If we did not, and the Iraqi government suddenly authorised an attack, we would go into it underprepared and in no better position than in April. So the shaping began.

CHAPTER 8

Snowflakes come in blizzards

Shaping Fallujah, September–November 2004

As November approached, a swirl of planning built around the option of an assault on Fallujah. The entire chain of command was involved, and at each stage General Casey would see the plans and give them his imprimatur. Normally a high-level headquarters such as MNF-I would not become involved in all the detail, but as Fallujah still had 'special zone' status, the city was ultimately Casey's responsibility. Preparing possible operations there was among mine.

It has always been a most important part of generalship to know what kind of conflict you are fighting. If you think you are in a struggle for national liberation, and you choose your tactics to match those motivations and techniques, and you then find that you are in a terrorist/insurgent/criminal conflict, your erroneous tactics may have only made things worse. You may have lost before you know what you are fighting. In Iraq, the coalition's rapid and steep learning curve had blurred the traditional division of military operations between 'tactics' at the lower level, 'operations' in the middle and 'strategy' at the top. The situation was also confused by our being a coalition at war, so the 'strategic' level of war for Washington was very different from the 'strategic' level for the Iraqi Interim

Government. As chief of operations, in any one day I seemed to be working across all levels. I still had my tactical responsibilities for infrastructure security, so I still led some tactical activities and forces. But also, from my position in the highest 'strategic' headquarters in Iraq, I might be coordinating all aspects of national power one minute, and trying to hit a suspicious vehicle with a missile in the next minute.

Meanwhile, the big war continued to increase in intensity and violence. The bulk of our military forces in Iraq, both coalition forces and the emerging Iraqi Security Forces now being raised by Lieutenant General David Petraeus, were directly controlled by the Corps headquarters under Lieutenant General Tom Metz. The Corps continued to conduct what the British, from their experience in the Malayan Emergency in the 1950s and '60s, call 'framework operations'. Framework operations were our bread and butter. They were unexciting but essential activities to control the population (searches and checkpoints), and to influence the population (through 'psychological' operations such as leaflet drops or loudspeaker broadcasts). In Iraq they were supplemented by humanitarian activities such as the provision of medical supplies and food, and the overall reconstruction of an economy and national infrastructure that was in a woeful state. These operations provided the framework that supported other activities, such as our attempts to eliminate the terrorist and insurgent leadership and to protect the Iraqi population. Expressed like this it sounds straightforward and neat. Like most military operations, it was neither.

One of the most important tools in conducting any counterinsurgency is special forces units. In Iraq, Casey directly controlled most of the US Special Forces, but those assisting the Iraqi Security Forces were controlled by either Metz or Petraeus. 'Special forces' are units that have the specific training, equipment and quality of manpower that allow them to conduct sophisticated operations that are beyond most military units. Hence, 'special'. All US forces could conduct raids against our enemy, but the most difficult raids against the most important leadership targets were left to the special forces. Usually, it was special forces who conducted those raids where troops actually assaulted terrorist hideouts. At the least expected time of the day or night, they would come through doors and windows to capture or, if necessary, kill the terrorists. The head of al Qaeda in Iraq, the Jordanian Abu Musab al Zarqawi, was a particular target of special forces. If a raid was too dangerous or immediate action was needed, aircraft would strike the target with bombs. To conduct raids or guide strikes, special forces had unique intelligence capabilities to find the enemy — these enabled them not only to conduct their own operations but to contribute to just about every other military activity that was going on, especially (and here was a crucial focus for me before Fallujah) time-sensitive targeting.

Many targets in Iraq, such as members of the insurgent leadership, only became visible to us for a short time and then disappeared. Our enemy knew that we had some very capable intelligence tools, both technical and human. At one stage, having just missed Zarqawi himself, the special forces captured his driver, who spoke freely about their ways of evading our surveillance drones. The intelligence effort being put into finding a specific target hiding among the 27 million people of Iraq was enormous, but once found, the opportunity might only last for minutes — hence, in our inimitable jargon, such targets were 'time-sensitive'.

Hitting targets fast in the middle of a city requires strict rules and processes. The US rules of engagement are very specific, but they can never cover every situation. The application of these rules also needed to be supervised from the highest level down if our targeting was to comply with international law. Knowing that our conventional fighting power was unbeatable, the insurgents and terrorists fought us in other ways. They hid among the people, knowing that that would restrict our firepower. Unlike the terrorists, we cared about the lives of innocents.

The tactic of hiding among and conducting attacks from among the people is a basic element of modern 'asymmetric warfare'. In asymmetric warfare, an adversary always tries to attack your weakness, knowing it is pointless to attack your strength. But as we learnt how to fight in Iraq, the coalition was also able to play the asymmetric game, and attack the vulnerabilities of our enemy. We employed our strengths — our technology and our legitimacy — against the insurgents' weaknesses: their need to physically meet because we watched and listened to everything that went across the electronic spectrum, and the absolute immorality and illegality of almost everything they did.

If we could use these weaknesses to help us target the insurgent leadership, and then execute a precise form of attack legally, we had an effective weapon. The downside was that if we got it wrong and killed innocents, we would just make more enemies.

The ever-present question was: Is it better to attack an insurgent leader such as Zarqawi even if it involves risk to a small number of innocents, or to let Zarqawi live to kill tens of thousands of other innocent Iraqis? For me, the decision was acute and real. This was not an academic issue or a problem at some staff college, where the question is put and a clever discussion follows. Here, a decision was required instantly, and I was part of the process of making it.

New to the operations branch, my ability to conduct time-sensitive targeting was at first far from perfect. As we lost Tom Miller's and his staff's expertise, we found there was nothing specifically written down about how to carry out targeting. Most headquarters have operating procedures written down in almost nauseating detail, but we were brand new and inexperienced, our processes were far too slow, we had no yardsticks by which to judge our effectiveness, and our written records were deficient. Things were not coming together well, and Rumsfeld and Casey were noticing.

During September and October I raced to get the process back under control, redesigning it to bring it fully into line with the four major criteria of international law: proportionality, humanity, discrimination and necessity. Was the target, often an individual, positively identified? If so, how? Did the strike fulfil a military need? What weapon was going to be used and what would the collateral damage be? We needed a process to bring together the 'evidence' that supported a decision, such as current photographs or video of the target, profiles of the suspects and information on previous related incidents. As I knew I would always be doing this when I was tired, I reduced as much as I could to a checklist.

As the chief of operations, I was the arbiter of interpretations of the rules of engagement every day. Rules of engagement tell soldiers when to use force and what kind they can use. The US rules were still the same as at the time of the invasion, in March 2003, but the environment was changing so fast that the rules were being interpreted differently across the Force. There was 'constructive tension' on this matter between my staff and the well-trained US experts in the Corps targeting organisation headed by Brigadier General Dick Formica, and we needed to sort out our differences. I wanted a more uniform interpretation of certain issues, particularly around Fallujah, which would still allow us to act quickly. Among my first tasks was to codify the process, write it down and transmit it (by the ubiquitous PowerPoint) across our communications network.

Not only did I have to consider the rules of engagement applying to other coalition soldiers; I also had to think through my own role. Every soldier knew he could use deadly force to defend himself and those he was protecting whenever he felt threatened. But for me in my new job, it was more complex. In the special zone of Fallujah, all attacks (except immediate firing in self-defence) were to be authorised through my operations branch. As I was now ordering attacks, I had to consider yet again how the laws of armed conflict applied to me. Who empowered me to authorise the use of weapons such as aerial bombs and missiles? How much collateral damage was considered acceptable?

I met with my targeting chief, Colonel Brian Boyle, and our US operational lawyer, Lieutenant Colonel Al Goshie, to talk targeting in my office. I was now in the office that General Sanchez occupied months before, down the long corridor from the palace rotunda, and Steve Summersby now occupied the outer office once used by Sanchez's gatekeeper. The advantage of my office was that it was very close to my own operations centre, a very big room that we called 'Saddam's Ballroom'. My operations centre was not quite as big as the 'Battlestar Galactica' at Camp Victory but it was more than adequate, with 80 computer stations set in banks before several large screens, and it was being fitted out with more advanced screens and much more bandwidth. I moved my desk from the centre of my office up against the wall, got rid of the comfortable guest chairs, and placed the only large table we could find in the middle of the room. This allowed me to spread things out to work. The chairs were functional rather than comfortable, so no guest would ever feel tempted to overstay! The table itself was old and wobbly, and Steve was forever trying to balance it by putting paper under the legs. Across the back wall was a line of phones of various colours attached to various world nets, and I would have daily visits from the technicians who needed to fix one or another. On one wall was a loud but functioning air conditioner that, except for a few months each year, ran continually. One barred window, partially covered by sandbags, could be opened, and on spring or autumn days it was delightful to open it and to feel the breeze. The downside of opening the window was that it brought in the sound of the war from across the Tigris, or the rolling explosions of large car bombs from the entrances to the Green Zone. The only wall not covered by maps had a large video screen that Steve had managed to liberate from someone less deserving, to bring the tactical picture from the operations centre screens directly into my office.

As we sat around the wobbly table covered with rules of engagement documents and printed copies of my PowerPoint presentation, Brian and Al took a 'questioning approach'. They pointed out that certain critical questions required judgment that only I could exercise — and for which I would be accountable.

Brian said, 'Sir, you need to get up to speed on our rules of engagement before anything else. What I reckon we really need is a standard and agreed way of handling the special conditions that apply to Fallujah, and we need to pass them down to the Corps as an order.' He then asked Al to go through the questions with me, to confirm in our minds whether the current documentation that supported time-sensitive targeting reflected the way I wanted to do things.

Then it was Al's turn. When I first met him, I had found Al a little disconcerting because of his Special Forces background. We all carried pistols in the operations centre, but Al would carry a pistol plus a rifle hanging from his body armour. He gave the impression that even though he was a lawyer, he was not the kind of man you would want to meet in a dark alley. But Al was a delightful person, and so good at his job that I did not mind that he carried a personal arsenal.

He began: 'Sir, these are the questions. The first is "military necessity": Is this act that I am about to commit necessary for military reasons? The second is "humanity": Will this act cause unnecessary suffering? The third is "discrimination": Can I discriminate sufficiently between civilian and military targets? And the fourth principle is "proportionality": Am I likely to cause destruction or suffering disproportionate to the expected military gain, even against legitimate targets?'

In a past life, I had used only three principles, having rolled what Al was calling 'humanity' into the other three principles, but I liked his approach. His manner also showed that I was among a group of men who would speak their mind frankly, ethically and honestly — an essential ingredient. Too many generals are let down by yes-men beneath them.

Over the next few hours, we went into technicalities and process. There were certain types of weapons that could only be used in certain circumstances according to rules set by previous commanders. On behalf of General Casey, I needed to know every rule, then to ensure that everyone understood them. Brian raised a number of local interpretations of less-defined rules, some of which had been overtaken by events and so needed the rule to be changed to match current reality, and others that I needed to think about and take action to stop.

After this meeting, I could see the mass of work I had to do. I was very aware that it would be a gross failure if tens of analysts worked for months to find a single terrorist leader who became visible to us for half an hour somewhere in Iraq, and the part that I was to play was mismanaged and we missed him because I could not do my job.

I contemplated these sobering thoughts as I performed my other duties. I knew that my legal right to injure even our enemy was not unlimited. Unlike the insurgents and terrorists, who obeyed no rules, I could not launch attacks against the civilian population, I had to distinguish between combatants and non-combatants, and I had to spare non-combatants as much as possible. These sound logical and normal for anyone with a skerrick of humanity, but it is the grey areas that require difficult moral and legal judgments all the time. Like everything else in Iraq, little in the targeting world was ever black and white.

Also, I was an Australian officer working in a coalition with US resources and answering to a US chain of command back in Washington because it was a US process. This was an added complication. I was but a small cog in this big machine, but I had to be confident that I was operating within my Australian directive and the public statements of the Australian Defence Minister and Prime Minister. The legal minefield I operated in was similar to that of every combat soldier in Iraq, and it posed undeniable challenges.

To remind me that I was being watched from Washington, a lot of people over there took a personal interest in time-sensitive targeting. I would receive formal notes from Secretary Rumsfeld himself, written in his hand with a typed translation attached, passed on by General Casey or Joe Weber, demanding clarification on various issues. These notes were called SECDEF 'snowflakes', because they came in blizzards. I only ever saw the ones related to targeting, but they were a reminder that everything we were doing was being scrutinised. The SECDEF would ask, 'Why did we plan to hit a target at a certain time, yet not hit it until significantly later?' Often there was an easy answer: a jet was refuelling when the target appeared, or the unmanned aircraft that was sending back TV pictures had to be moved out of the way for the jet to come in, or we gave permission that the target could only be struck when conclusive evidence appeared. Even after we improved the targeting process the snowflakes did not abate, but at least we could answer the SECDEF's questions more quickly and accurately.

We could use any weapon or technique in targeting, but the two most common were raids conducted by Special Forces and very accurate bombs dropped by aircraft.

I was mostly involved with the latter. The weapon I favoured for time-sensitive targets was a relatively new type of 500-pound bomb called a JDAM — Joint Direct Attack Munition. It relied on highly accurate satellite navigation systems to hit within a few metres of the target. Laser-guided bombs were good, but sometimes they could not be used in cloudy conditions. Larger bombs might have been overkill, and smaller missiles like Hellfire or Maverick, while accurate, often lacked the necessary blast power. Aircraft could drop a JDAM through cloud, and it could 'pick up' a whole house and dump it in the street, sometimes without damaging the houses on either side, even if they had a common wall. As it best satisfied the requirements of international law, with its unsurpassed accuracy and effectiveness in cities, it became my weapon of choice.

The Special Forces task force, because of their intelligence systems, were a key part of this process. The task force regularly changed its official title, as it became too familiar to the open media, but we merely referred to them as 'the task force'. I saw the task force as a superb military creation. They had everything they needed within the one organisation, which is unusual for the military. They were very effective and, appropriately, not very visible.

One of the first tasks Casey gave me was to go to their headquarters outside Baghdad and meet the commanders. The task force had been operating in Iraq since before the 2003 invasion. Although I did not know it until later, they had been investigated for prisoner abuse, and some members had been punished. Since then, they had modified their procedures and supervision had been increased.

When they briefed me, I discovered that their main mission was to destroy the Zarqawi network throughout Iraq. They had a most sophisticated command and intelligence organisation, a detention facility, the ability to conduct day or night raids, and, through their intelligence, could offer time-sensitive targets for me to attack with bombs.

I had little to do with the Special Forces raids: my function was to know where and when they were going to occur, move other units out of their way, and report their results to General Casey.

Mine was an interesting relationship with the Special Forces, most but not all of whom were American. As I was watching Tom Miller carry out his duties, I'd wondered how we would handle time-sensitive targeting if I, a coalition officer initially without access to the top level of intelligence, ever did replace him. Tom himself came from a Special Forces background, so he was inside the tribe. General Sanchez had shut coalition officers out of highly classified matters, but Casey didn't do that with me. I had been sent to Iraq with a written directive to be the chief of operations, requiring me to obey legal orders given by my coalition boss. Targeting was central to my role, and for targeting with Special Forces, I would need access to that higher level of intelligence. If I was somewhat surprised that Casey gave his Australian chief of operations responsibility for time-sensitive targeting using mainly US Special Forces, bombs and missiles, the task force leaders themselves were absolutely astounded!

The command elements I dealt with were all Americans. I was not a commander in any sense, but in some capacities I spoke and acted on behalf of the highest commander in Iraq, so even though I was not a US officer, Special Forces had to deal with me. Initially this was difficult for them. Being a culturally secretive organisation, they could not comprehend having to work through a non-US officer. Working through any staff officer is hard enough for Special Forces. Like all really good soldiers, their supreme confidence sometimes betrays a touch of arrogance. But working through a coalition officer just did not compute. Establishing trust even with Australian Special Forces is hard enough if you are not one of them. To do this as a coalition officer with someone else's Special Forces was going to be very difficult indeed. And, of course, the Special Forces commander could still, rightfully, bypass me and go straight to Casey.

So my big problem with the task force was credibility: as a non-US officer, and as the leader of a new and inexperienced operations branch. I was trying to establish credibility without my most experienced US adviser, Pete Palmer, who was still on leave. At one frustrating stage, when I was trying to improve my branch's functioning and meeting considerable push-back from the task force, I suggested to General Casey that he pass the task force from us down to the Corps, who were better organised and staffed. Casey was emphatic that this would not happen. My suggestion was naive: Casey controlled the task force exclusively because their results against the enemy leadership were strategically important, and I had to improve my staff's ability to manage them on his behalf. I couldn't delegate this one.

But I was steadily getting into the swing of heading the operations centre. I dominated the centre with my voice and my presence as I trained new operators. Staff experience was knee-deep in shallow water and the war was not waiting for us to get ready. This was on-the-job training in the extreme. I would perch on the front desk with my back to the three screens and, as information came into the operations desk, I would call for silence and 'conduct' the process. I would ask the recipient to tell us all the information: a contact with the enemy here, a convoy that needed assistance there, a threat warning that applied to a group or an area, a TV news item branding us all as war criminals, an attack on an oil pipe or electricity line. I would then say, in a very loud voice, 'What are you going to do with it? Who wants that info?' And I would run the basic staff functions like a tutorial. 'Talk to such and such, get a joint view of the information. Who else needs to know just in case? Make sure that you call our day chief of ops, check the info with the unit, get a press release moving, call me and tell me, get a crisis action team up and get me a plan.'

As time went on I needed to train fewer people, or I had more experienced people posted in. Then a posting cycle would occur and again I would face an enthusiastic but inexperienced group of young men and women. The induction process would begin again.

The operations centre was all about detail. If I told someone to do something, it could not be left at that. There was always a cascading need for subsequent actions. If I assumed that what I said had been done, and directed subsequent actions only to find out the first action had not occurred, the result could be, and sometimes was, the death of our soldiers in the field. This was a deadly serious business, and mistakes would always occur, but my job was to minimise them.

Slowly but surely the reservists in the room learnt their jobs and became confident in what they were doing, relying less on the few regular soldiers. The three enormous screens on the front wall of this once-grand ballroom in Saddam's Palace controlled our lives. They brought in General Casey's face, like some bizarre Big Brother, several times a day. Miraculous electronics brought the Predators' view of the latest battle, day or night, and the graphics from the Blue Force Tracker. One of the big screens was usually divided into nine civilian TV channels broadcasting perceptions, fantasy and lies from the outside world. The three one-star officers, the 23 colonels and the 250 majors and their subordinates in operations branch had lives that revolved around this room. Behind them were our offices managing the flow of forces throughout Iraq and the dozen other sub-functions that made the big machine grind along.

Minute by minute, information on targets came in to the intelligence system. I would receive several briefings on how targets were developing throughout the day — mid-morning, mid-afternoon and finally about 10pm or 11pm. In the first brief we might look at five targets, which would narrow down to two or three by the second brief and then one or two by late at night. If a target came together, it would come together quickly and briefly, so the talking had to be done beforehand. These targets had to be hit quickly, accurately and, above all, legally. And they had to be fitted in with all the other responsibilities I had, and all the other calls on my time.

As I've already noted, the coalition's technical intelligence ability in Iraq left the insurgents and foreign terrorists no choice but to meet in person. This was a vulnerability we aimed to exploit, but it was not easy. We might assume a particular cell had to meet at certain intervals and in a certain area. The problem was to discriminate between the meeting of a terrorist cell and the meeting of any social group. This was particularly hard in Fallujah because we couldn't enter the city to conduct raids or observe. In Fallujah, we had to 'stare' at areas around the clock, mostly through an unmanned Predator, looking for signs of meetings.

Terrorist leaders knew we were watching and listening. They used deception to trick our intelligence, and sensibly limited the duration of their meetings. They conducted many activities, especially meetings, under cover of darkness, so time-sensitive targeting was done mostly at night. Because of this, the task force worked on what they called a 'reverse battle rhythm'. Their intelligence people worked during the day, finding and preparing targets, and their assault troops slept during the day and conducted their raids at night, which was the opposite to a traditional military unit. I often joked with my staff that it was okay for the Special Forces to work a reverse battle rhythm — it just meant that I worked on a 24-hour battle rhythm.

The tempo that had tired me out in April as I followed Tom Miller around had not slackened off now that I was doing the job. I would start work at four or five in the morning and go through until at least midnight. And every day, of the four or five hours I set aside to sleep, I would lose at least one for time-sensitive targeting. Every now and then, about once every two weeks in the middle of an intense targeting activity or a fight, I would miss a whole night's sleep. This was my routine for most of my year in Iraq. My fatigue was so relentless that I desperately needed my system of checklists.

To keep my focus, I had to draw on all my experience. Many years before this, when I was an instructor at the Infantry Centre, I kept my flying skills current by flying a rescue helicopter based in the city of Newcastle. One weekend a month I would sleep at the helicopter base and be on 24-hour call for emergencies. From a deep sleep, within minutes I had to be in the air and flying with the crew on board. The transition from deep sleep, through receiving information on the nature of the emergency, flight planning, and then a lot of low-level night flying in an aircraft with only one pilot in the era before night vision goggles, gave me experience in managing such situations. I had refined my concentration techniques in various military situations since; it was not rocket science, but it did require a degree of self-discipline and judgment. I kept using those mind-numbingly simple lists to organise myself.

When a time-sensitive target was found, the US colonel who headed my night shift in the operations centre would call my XO, Steve Summersby, in our little house by the pond. Steve would emerge from under the stairs to wake my bodyguard, who were sleeping in bunks in the living room, then come into my bedroom to wake me. My clothing, body armour and weapons were laid out before I went to sleep, so that we could be instantly on the road. Five to eight minutes later we were in the headquarters. Brian Boyle, as head of targeting, would normally stay up after midnight, watching the targets develop and looking after my interests, then sleep a little longer in the morning. Al Goshie, our operational lawyer, would join me when I arrived in the operations room.

The three of us would form the targeting team. As I dumped my helmet, weapon and armour into the hands of my bodyguard, I would be handed a proforma of what we had to do and factors we had to consider. The special forces liaison officer, using the task force's intelligence, would then present the case to strike. Steve would produce a cup of tea for me, for which I was forever grateful. I preferred tea; coffee was too much of a stimulant. If I did get back to bed, I didn't want to spend the rest of the night staring at the ceiling.

By now the operations staff would have passed the target to the air operations centre in Qatar, which transmitted it to a pilot over Fallujah. My targeting section and my air section were linked to Qatar through the military equivalent of an internet chat room. My staff in Baghdad and the air staff in Qatar, as well as pilots in the air, could watch all the steps in the process, ask questions, seek clarification and keep themselves in the picture. I often thought of those pilots, sitting in the dark of their cockpits listening to the chat and to the sound of their own breathing in their oxygen masks, high above Iraq with a variety of bombs on their wings. Often their sorties would be six hours long, punctuated by trips to an airborne refuelling tanker, then a return to base with their bombs still on board if they were not given a target. I always felt that my years in Army Aviation — that supposedly bad career move — gave me an extra sliver of appreciation for what those pilots were doing.

Once we knew more about the target, the commander who 'owned the ground' was then asked to give 'ground clearance', a formal acknowledgment that he did not have troops who might be endangered by a strike. For Fallujah, this was John Sattler, the commander of the Marines in Anbar province. I often spoke to John on targeting issues in the wee hours of the morning. As aircraft alert and ground clearance were occurring, I talked some more to the Special Forces staff about the background to the target and why it should be hit. This took a few minutes, but quite often I needed to clarify an issue if I was not convinced that the target was clearcut enough to me or if I wanted to go at it in a different way.

Meanwhile I could look at the TV-like pictures that were coming down from the unmanned drone. Normally these were on one of the three big screens at the front of the operations centre for all to see, but as soon as we began a targeting process we brought the picture down to my desktop computer in the second row of the tiered seating. There were still many staff who were not cleared to such high levels of security. As the target developed, I was often given very sensitive intelligence that allowed me to make a strike decision with far greater certainty. All the while, the targeting staff monitored the chat room and called out to us as the various working parts moved into alignment.

A critical part of the targeting process was the collateral damage estimate, or CDE. It brought up the fundamental legal and moral considerations of proportionality, humanity, discrimination and necessity. The CDE told us the number of people likely to be killed in the strike. Specialists in Qatar and Florida produced a CDE for every target, based on many different factors. The production of the CDE had been a problem for us initially because it came too slowly. Once we put more specialists onto it, its efficiency improved.

I was familiar with discussions in the media about 'collateral damage' and knew that our processes were questioned and sometimes ridiculed. I had watched Australia conduct its targeting using our jets during the 2003 invasion, and had read General Tommy Frank's book, in which he describes how he did his targeting, his attitude to collateral damage, and the intelligence that found and tested the targets during his 'conventional' type of warfare. In counterinsurgency, the term 'collateral damage' can prompt cynicism from the uninformed, who see it as military techno-speak sanitising the impact of war on ordinary people. Nothing could be further from the truth. For those who do not have the luxury of criticising without offering an alternative, the term 'collateral damage' is practical and well understood. The process saves thousands of innocent lives: if the CDE was too high, we had the option of not striking the target.

We did not employ the term to dehumanise what we were doing. In Iraq we were reminded of the consequences of our actions immediately: as we watched bombs hit, the screen would flare silently and the wind would slowly blow away dust clouds to reveal the wreckage. Within an hour of the strike, some Arab network would broadcast pictures of the scene and assessments by so-called spokesmen in the local hospital, listing the number of women and children who had been 'slaughtered' by the 'crusaders'. Of course the network commentary and the 'doctors' did not criticise the terrorists or insurgents for holding their meetings in the midst of their own families or neighbours.

We did everything we could to avoid killing innocents. The coalition did not fight just for the sake of fighting. General Casey and his field commanders did not want to aggravate an already difficult situation, and their first guiding principle was often expressed as the old medical dictum: 'First, do no harm.' There was a continual search for any approach that did not involve bombs and bullets. A bullet achieves its effect by transferring kinetic energy to a human body, something that does not go far in winning the heart or the mind. In Iraq we searched for the 'non-kinetic' approach, the approach that used anything rather than force, but it was not always possible. Examples of the non-kinetic were: buy weapons back from the population rather than conducting searches in homes that disrupt daily life and risk civilian casualties; rather than kill bomb emplacers, create employment to counter the insurgents who offer money to the unemployed to plant roadside bombs; use police rather than heavily armed soldiers to enforce the law; provide essential services to the people so that they see some benefit from our occupation. Other agencies conducted a range of humanitarian operations that we supported when the threat was low.

Nevertheless, when it comes to significant levels of combat, international law accepts that some innocents might be killed. As long as we apply considerations of proportionality, humanity, discrimination and necessity both legally and morally, the fault for the death of innocents lies with those who chose to wage war from the bosoms of their families. Even if I had a positive identification of a terrorist leader, I still did not have the right to just bomb him. I still had to consider proportionality, humanity, discrimination and necessity. If our own morality, and our own law, are not enough to guide us, there is also self-interest. Every time we kill an innocent, we make more enemies for ourselves. Ironically, in the short term, this logic did not necessarily work against the insurgents, but in the longer term, their illegality and brutality has started to earn them their share of enemies among the people of Iraq. The slaughter of innocents in the tens or hundreds of thousands is, to them, a tactic. They solve any resentment that may arise from their actions with even more violence — they simply kill anyone who objects.

I do not accept that there is any moral equivalence between what I did and what our enemies did. I was acutely aware of the consequences of our actions. It is not necessarily the process that makes time-sensitive targeting difficult, although that is difficult enough. It is being able to make decisions when you know what their consequences are.

Once I'd received the CDE, the military necessity of striking the target had to be weighed against the number of innocent people who might die. I used a standard set of criteria to assist me. One was the knowledge that a terrorist car bomb may kill dozens or hundreds of innocents, and one terrorist technician is capable of producing any number of these bombs. Each enemy cell could attack the Iraqi population once or twice a week. A member of the leadership is capable of instigating even greater carnage by coordinating subordinates who can then kill and maim.

The decision to strike was never taken lightly, but it had to be taken quickly. If a terrorist meeting looked as though it was about to break up before the official CDE was ready, I had to estimate a CDE and recommend a strike (or not). I was accountable for that judgment. In fact, the targeting team would be negligent if we missed an important target by taking the safe route and waiting for the formal process every time. This decision about collateral damage is no different in law from the decision made by a lieutenant platoon commander crouched down on the side of a road calling for an air strike on a position from which the enemy are firing at him and his troops. I just did it in a much more comfortable place while drinking Steve's tea.

Once we'd ironed out the early problems, the CDE would usually arrive promptly, comparing the impacts of 500-pound and 1000-pound bombs with other weapons for the target in question. Sometimes the facts did not line up nicely. Intelligence may not have been convincing, or the CDE was uncomfortably high at the time the attack was proposed. For example, if a target was in a residential area then the CDE would be high at night. If possible, it would be best to wait until daytime to strike it. But of course for certain types of transient targets, such as leadership meetings, delay might mean losing the targets for days, weeks, even months.

The best thing the insurgents could do for us, and for the innocents, was to gather in the open away from buildings and other people. In these cases, the CDE was low or zero and the decision was very simple. The only time I was involved in such a straightforwad action was when a large group of insurgents gathered in farmland to the south of Abu Ghraib in the middle of the night, having arrived in buses to recover a large cache of weapons. This occurred only a day after intelligence reported the likelihood of a significant attack on the prison. Our action went for several hours and used most weapons we had, as well as the Special Forces in their 'Little Bird' helicopters; it resulted in the death of 60 to 100 insurgents

Sometimes I'd have to make the decision within 20 minutes of waking up. If we knew the target to be enemy, the decision was not so much 'if' as 'how' and 'when'. If there was no technical intelligence to confirm that the target was a specific enemy, but there were other more general indications, then there was more complex judgment involved. Did the pattern of activity indicate that a particular meeting was military in nature? Could it be a Fallujah book club or a sporting committee meeting on the roof of a known enemy house at 3am with bodyguards outside and sentries posted at the end of the street? Did the associations they made during the day as we 'stared', following them around, indicate that they were enemy? Did they visit houses in which we knew hostages had been held?

The responsibility for making these judgments was extremely taxing on me. Once, as we drove into the operations centre, I remember thinking, without any sense of irony, 'God, let there be special intelligence so that the decision will be straightforward.' What we called 'special intelligence' gave me a higher degree of certainty. But usually, I had to rely on patterns and an accumulation of evidence. If there was a 'reasonable' probability, in the legal sense, that the target was enemy, and if the CDE was acceptable, I would recommend the strike.

As a staff officer, my decision was not technically a decision, but a recommendation to my boss, General Casey. Executive authority remained with commanders. So I would make my recommendation, then ring Casey and put the case to him as I saw it, normally without the detail. He then made his decision, either approving the strike or directing his own course of action. If necessary, he went up his chain of command. Rarely did Casey reject my recommendation, but it did happen. And on occasions I differed with the task force commander about whether to strike or not. On these occasions there was 'robust discussion', to say the least. There were also threats of bypassing me and going directly to Casey. Once or twice that did happen.

When I first started hitting targets, after seeing the impact and the immediate post-bomb period, I had to approve the media release that accompanied the strike. The torturous process of making the strike decision, then observing the sudden, noiseless flaring of the target as the bomb hit, and seeing the damage and who came to the rescue and where they went, was all-important. I could then report to Casey on the effect of each strike in a highly classified briefing the next day.

The terrorists and insurgents might have subscribed to the old saying that 'there are no rules in a knife fight'. But there are rules; they just did not obey them. In fact they institutionalised the transgression of international law. My feeling was that the media did not scrutinise our adversaries' actions as carefully as the coalition's. For any faults we may have had, the coalition represented the rule of law. It was right that we were held accountable. But so should the other side. My quarrel with the media was that, on certain occasions, the insurgents seemed to have been given licence to fight the way they did because they were fighting the US and the coalition, or resisting an occupation. But barbarity is barbarity, no matter who perpetrates it.

As October wore on, our intelligence could see that the terrorists were going to stay to defend their base in Fallujah. Because of this, it became increasingly important to shape Fallujah by separating the residents from the enemy.

From October onwards, we dropped more pointed leaflets, we made broadcasts from aircraft and we filled the media with warnings. We staged nightly attacks against the leadership within Fallujah, which encouraged some residents to leave. Our greatest allies in this endeavour were, much to our surprise, the insurgents themselves. They went to Fallujah to hide among the people, but committed mindless acts of violence against them. They set up local religious courts and Fallujans were tried and punished, even tortured and executed, if they did not commit to extreme fundamentalist Islamic ideology and Sharia law. The Sunnis of Fallujah had no desire for any of this, and their exodus gathered pace.

As we noticed what was occurring, we tried to hasten their departure. We increased our leaflet drops and broadcasts, and often told the enemy who we had killed. We either stated or strongly implied that the killing was the result of betrayal, and indeed it often was. Betrayal was a constant and, I was assured, successful theme. There must have been some level of paranoia in the minds of enemy leaders, because they moved three times a day, escaping death by seconds and watching others die around them. We played on this fear.

We continually told the people of Fallujah and other cities of the evil of those in their midst, particularly the foreign fighters. Like most people, Iraqis are very parochial. They suspect foreigners and admire strength and success. As we achieved victories and put the pressure on Zarqawi, we broadcast on local Fallujan radio or dropped leaflets saying: 'Foreign terrorists will stay until Iraq has burnt to the ground — Do not let these criminals destroy your future.' At that time, Zarqawi's network was only getting into its stride, but had publicly claimed responsibility for 62 attacks that had killed 26 coalition soldiers and 478 Iraqi security force members, and probably a far greater number of Iraqi civilians. One effective presentation was our message: set against a picture of dead terrorists who could still be recognised. 'Someone has been betrayed. Who will be next?' Or we would say, even before we attacked Fallujah, 'Be warned — Do not share Fallujah's fate', and set the warning against a picture of

Zarqawi. Another effective presentation was a leaflet showing pictures of insurgent leaders with the message, 'These criminals are wanted by Iraqi authorities', and, on the back, a safe pass for those who would give information. Though the success of this campaign was difficult to measure, it seemed to be sowing the seeds of doubt within insurgent and terrorist groups.

We also held out carrots, publicising the fact that Fallujah was missing out on millions of dollars of development funds — they would only appear once the terrorists were gone.

As the end of October approached, leaflet drops and broadcasts advised Fallujans to leave for their own safety because the Interim Iraqi Government intended to conduct 'direct military action' to rid the city of terrorists. Secretary of Defense Rumsfeld made public statements of resolve, saying that the situation in Fallujah would not conclude with a ceasefire. The world press assisted by going into a paroxysm of uninformed speculation about what the attack would look like and when it would occur. We also made sure Fallujans heard our media releases, put out normally within an hour of a strike occurring. Here is a typical one:

MNF-I STRIKE KILLS ZARQAWI ASSOCIATE

FALLUJAH, Iraq — A precision strike in northwest Fallujah, conducted at 3 a.m. October 26 by Multi-National Force-Iraq, has taken another toll on the Zarqawi network. This strike on a Zarqawi safe house further erodes the organization's capability to conduct attacks on the citizens of Fallujah and Iraq.

Multiple sources reported that a known associate of the Zarqawi network was present at the time of the strike.

Zarqawi terrorists continue to endanger the lives of the people of Iraq, by conducting operations in residential areas and exposing the civilian populace to harm.

Recent strikes and raids targeting the Abu Musab al Zarqawi network have severely degraded its ability to conduct attacks and have effectively reduced the influence of its terrorist leader as made evident by the recent merger of the Zarqawi network with al Qaeda.

The United States has offered a $25 million reward for the capture or death of Zarqawi in continued demonstration of its commitment to rid Iraq of terror.

Part of the shaping for Fallujah was trying to kill or capture Zarqawi's lieutenants. They all had specific target codenames, which I grew to know as we watched them. The permanent leader of the Zarqawi network in Fallujah was Umar Hadid, known as the Emir (leader) of Fallujah. As one of the three most prominent terrorist leaders in Fallujah (Sheik Abdullah Janabi and Zarqawi were the others), Hadid had about 1800 fighters of his own.

Unable to capture him because of the prohibition on entering Fallujah, I made a sustained effort to kill him and launched several strikes as the task force delivered the intelligence. One I remember distinctly was on a house belonging to Hadid's brother Abu Walid, himself a propagandist for the terrorists. Hadid was visiting, and when all the information lined up, I hit the house with a JDAM. The house exploded around him, and his brother was killed, but Umar Hadid walked out of the rubble.

The next time we found him, he was in one of the many houses he personally owned in Fallujah. I hit the building with another single bomb and again he escaped, but we were fairly certain we'd wounded him. Later we had intelligence that he was in another house, and I again authorised a strike. As the bomb was in the air I received confirming intelligence that he was at the site. The house exploded around him again, and again he walked out. As we reviewed images of the strike, we could see a figure, probably Hadid, emerge from the rubble and cross to the far side of the road, where he stood among the neighbours who had come to dig him out.

Finally, he went to a house where I could use several JDAMs at once. We got a good clean hit and could see no survivors. We were confident that we had killed him.

Almost immediately, we heard chat on the phones saying, 'Abu Umar has become a martyr.' But then, within a few hours, we overheard other chat saying he had only been wounded and was going to Jordan for medical treatment. Which was the truth, which the attempt at deception?

During the actual fighting in Fallujah some weeks later, the enemy propaganda machine announced that Hadid had been killed heroically leading his men against US soldiers. This was not our belief based on our special knowledge, but some months later a new insurgent brigade was formed south of Baghdad, and it was named 'Shaykh Umar al-Hadid'. New brigades tended to memorialise the dead, so we remained convinced that we had killed him in the house. This new brigade claimed responsibility for a particularly murderous action on the Suwayrah Highway near Salman Pak, so his tradition lived on, even if he did not.

Fallujah was just one of many operations we were running over this period. My daily battle rhythm as chief of operations finished each night with a meeting of my own staff from about 8.30pm to 9.30pm. This was also shift change time in the operations centre, so both shifts were present. I could give direction on what we were going to do in the next 24 hours based on what we had done in the last 24. I could also pass on to my staff what General Casey had said at our earlier evening meeting. After tidying up any other loose ends, from about 10.30pm onwards, I reviewed all the orders that were going to be issued that night, which would take me at least an hour. I then looked for ways to escape to bed.

I was feeling the pace by now, and tried to find ways to maximise my sleep time. As our competence in targeting improved, I would give the approval to strike a target, and then, in the few minutes before the bomb hit, I'd hand over to Brian Boyle. The rule was that if all went well, I was to be briefed as soon as I arrived back in the headquarters, at four or five o'clock in the morning, but if something went wrong, I was to be called back immediately. Only once did we have a bomb go astray: for mechanical reasons, this bomb did not guide itself after release from the aircraft. Fortunately it hit open space and caused no casualties. On another occasion, I had directed the strike aircraft to use a 500-pound bomb, having used the 500-pound bomb CDE figure to make my decision. The post-strike report stated that a 1000-pound bomb had been used, which of course may have hurt more innocents. Thankfully it made very little difference, because we were hitting a target in the sparsely populated south of Fallujah. All the same, I directed an investigation into how it had occurred.

So we tightened the screws on Fallujah. Time-sensitive targeting and special forces raids depleted the enemy leadership in Fallujah and Zarqawi's network in Mosul and in Baghdad. Sometimes we hit two time-sensitive targets per night and conducted a number of raids in both Mosul and Baghdad. On many occasions, having gone through the targeting process, we ended up not striking at all. Once or twice we hit three targets in a single night, which consumed all my meagre sleep time.

When this happened, it multiplied the effect of my tiredness. Unlike a military exercise in Australia, this war did not go on for a polite two or three weeks and then return to peacetime routine. For me it went for a full year, and for many of my US fellow generals, it went longer. The consequences of what I was doing were enormous and the need to be accurate in what I did was paramount, but throughout it all, I thought of four hours as a very solid night's sleep.

For one period of a few weeks, I would try to get a nap in the office sometime mid-afternoon when my energy levels were at their lowest, by telling Steve Gliddon to keep everyone out. I might fit in about a 20-minute nap — not much, but better than nothing.

In retrospect, I seem to have managed the fatigue surprisingly well. I used to find it most demanding late at night, after our last meeting, when a line would form beside my station in the operations centre to show me complex orders that had to be released that night. I was the only person in the headquarters, apart from General Casey, who could actually release a formal order that made people and units do things. Every order that went out was published under my name. In the early stages, before we started to achieve some level of competence, particularly before Peter Palmer came back to Iraq as a newly promoted Brigadier General and became my right-hand man, I was not able to delegate this task very easily. With some officers I could trust the order to be right, but with others it required detailed reading, for which I had little patience at 11pm.

Despite being tired, I cannot remember ever losing my temper, which for many people is the real indicator of exhaustion. I was quietly angry often enough, but it would have been fatal to lose control. I was tough with people when necessary, and I removed several from their positions because they were not up to it. My tiredness and the importance of the issues also meant that I had little time to stroke people's egos — but it was still very important to do it. Often I had to revert to tough love, and my verbal counselling, often conducted from the front of the operations centre in the presence of all staff, was direct, to the point, but never personal or nasty. My voice might have boomed, but it was never 'raised'. I led by commitment to our cause, I tried very hard to talk to the action officers directly and not through their bosses, which gave the junior officers great satisfaction and released their bosses for important work, and I made a point of praising good work as publicly as I criticised work that was not up to scratch.

I had told Anne about the intensity of what I was doing when I was home on leave. After I returned to Iraq, she was concerned and rang my brother Maurice, a doctor, to ask him how long a person of my age could work at that intensity with such pressure on less than four hours' sleep. Anne reported to me in one of her daily emails, with some delight, that Maurice assured her that I would probably survive the year!

When we did get things right, it was very satisfying. We believed we wiped out the enemy leadership in Mosul twice and about one and half times in Baghdad. We hampered the technicians who built car bombs and planned insurgent raids. We killed or captured those we called 'facilitators' or fix-it men, as well as those who controlled the money, disseminated the propaganda or ran the recruiting. We did not defeat the insurgency, but we started to see signs that we were making it less effective: car bombs were blowing up prematurely or not blowing up at all as the experience levels of technicians dropped; young and inexperienced insurgents were being put into leadership positions; foreigners who had come to Iraq to die in martyrdom operations were being given other roles, for which they were less suited. Counterinsurgency is all about attrition over the long term, so every little bit would contribute to the whole.

The insurgents in Fallujah had always assumed we would attack, and as noted earlier, to our surprise, they stayed in Fallujah and prepared to meet us. We had expected that as we built up the pressure on the city, our enemy would melt back into bigger cities like Baghdad and avoid a fight. But instead they fortified the city with barriers and roadside bombs. They dug fighting positions, built trenches and reinforced buildings. They adapted the tactics we had seen in Chechnya to the local environment. They used defence in depth, consisting of rings of fortifications, so we'd have to break through more than one line. They coordinated the fields of fire of various weapons to interlock in the places they predicted we would be. They built alternative positions so we would have trouble knowing where they were. They trained and rehearsed battle drills. They had radios down to even the smallest group — unusual for such an enemy. They called in mortars using mobile phones. They located their medical facilities close to the frontline — this is a very important morale issue with any fighting force, even one that relies heavily on suicide as a tactic.

They practised their battle drills mainly at night. One night a group of insurgents moved into an open area in the southeast of the city to conduct live mortar training. We watched the first few rounds go up, then focused on the instructional class. We very quickly attacked them out of the dark using an armed Hercules gunship (an AC-130) with the callsign 'Spectre'. No graduates from that class would confront us in the assault.

One night, the Corps decided to move a large number of armoured vehicles from south of Fallujah along the road that formed the city's eastern boundary. A group of armoured vehicles moving at night can be a terrifying sound, even if they are on your side. You struggle to tell how far away they are, how many there are, or what direction they're moving in. The sound comes in waves. Even several kilometres away, it chills the blood — especially if you think they are coming for you.

Though we should have had our finger on the pulse, my staff and I were not fully aware of this activity. Nor did anyone really appreciate its consequences. It was late September when this happened, and we had not yet decided on an assault on Fallujah, but the insurgents thought their time had come. They activated their radio and mobile phone network throughout the city: this was the backbone of their command-and-control system. We watched them deploy. One large group, up to 100 men, moved to a bund in the open southeastern sector, probably thinking that the night cloaked their activity. We had an AC-130 airborne for another mission over Fallujah at exactly that time and, with no danger of any civilian casualties, it attacked this group, wreaking havoc. Later that night, we watched them bury the dead in long trenches in Fallujah's Cemetery of the Martyrs. We did not strike at the funeral, but we could have, quite legally. We explained that decision by saying that if we watched, we could learn more about who moved where, who was linked to whom, and where they went. And indeed, we did gain important information about an insurgent leader by tracking his vehicle as it carried him to a hospital to visit the injured.

Although it hadn't been planned this way, the move of the armoured column had let us both cause casualties and study the insurgents' plan for the defence of Fallujah. On the rather flimsy assumption that anything that works once will work again, we decided to conduct another 'feint', this time deliberate. In military terminology, a 'feint' is an attack that is not pressed home and should not result in casualties to our side. Its aim is to create an impression of real peril in the enemy's mind. A well-executed feint will entice the enemy to deploy into battle positions and communicate, and we see it all. If luck is with us, they may even offer us targets.

To work, the feint has to be convincing — often you have to partially join battle. The effect on your own troops is delicate. Commanders and soldiers have to understand that this is a feint, and they are not to engage in close combat and risk their lives. Many feints in the history of war have gone wrong because combat has been joined and the feinting force, normally a small force, is repulsed, with casualties. This does not inspire confidence in the leadership!

A feint could have a secondary purpose: it could be used to mislead our enemy about our ultimate plan of attack. On its own, this would justify the effort. And third, it could be a full rehearsal. Many of our soldiers had not conducted such a big and complex activity since they had been in Iraq, so we also saw this feint as a live-fire training exercise.

As we enthusiastically began planning the feint, it began to concern me that we still didn't have a final plan for our real assault. What if we conducted the feint from the direction that we later decided would be the real one? The enemy was not stupid, and would watch and adapt.

I accompanied General Casey to the first briefing of the feint plan from the Corps planners. In essence, the feint would resemble the attack on Fallujah the previous April, so it would suggest to the enemy that we would repeat those tactics. The feint was going to be at night, following leaflet drops and artillery and mortar fire on selected targets, with much noise and movement on the north, east and south, yet trying to focus the attention of the enemy on the southeast of the city. Tanks would be deployed on the north — the tanks are normally where the main thrust of an attack is. All intelligence tools were ready to acquire information, and aircraft would fly over Fallujah to take advantage of any targets.

As General Casey heard the detail of the planned feint, he began to show a little unease. He discussed approaching from the north in some detail, perhaps betraying a predisposition to use this approach for the actual attack. He asked how many tanks were going to be used to create the deception, how close they were going to come to the northern edge of the town, and how the railway and its high embankment would affect the tanks' movement and noise. The number of tanks was small, from memory, only eight or so. The effect of the railway and the embankment had not been taken into account fully and Casey asked the right questions — this was a strategic commander going right down to the tactical detail. The plan did not specify how close coalition troops would come to the edge of the town during the feint. Having discussed these issues and resolved them, Casey approved the plan.

The feint, called Operation Phantom Eclipse, took place on 14 October. It went off like clockwork. Leaflets were dropped, the artillery was fired and the armoured vehicles were manoeuvred. But within Fallujah, there was almost no reaction. The enemy command and control stayed quiet; there were no significant deployments. We suspected that the rail embankment to the north had masked the sound of the tanks. One or two local enemy commanders made calls asking what was going on, but that was all. They certainly knew we were out and about, but they had learnt from the previous accidental feint, and showed considerable discipline.

That night, we learnt a great deal — though perhaps more about ourselves than about the enemy. We continued to study the enemy dispositions throughout Fallujah, and we compared them with Chechnya and with the battle of Hue in Vietnam — which was the last significant urban assault conducted by the Marines.

The insurgents were not defending on the edge of the city, where their forces could be destroyed by our superior fire over open ground. They had some light forces on the edge, but their first line of defence was a block or two into the city, among the houses, where the long range of our weapons was of little use. By drawing us in close, they could fight us house to house. But because they didn't know what direction we would come from, they had to cover all approaches to the centre of the town. Whether they could hear our tanks in the north during the feint or not, they had obviously been influenced by how we had operated in April, and had now set themselves up appropriately.

Deception, as I had been reminded on the oil pipes, is probably the hardest type of military operation to get right. At a late stage in the planning for the feint, it occurred to me that even if we conducted a near-perfect feint and withdrew without becoming engaged, the enemy might tell the world we had attacked Fallujah and failed again. The courageous defenders of Fallujah, along with its loyal and brave citizens, would have thrown the crusaders back from the ramparts of the city for a second time. There was nothing we could do about this possibility, given that the planning for the feint was well advanced, and I am ashamed to say that I approached it in the best of military traditions: I hoped it would not happen.

The other possible 'own goal' in the information war was if the embedded media revealed the attack as a feint. Or, if we didn't tell them it was a feint, when we withdrew after a partial assault they too might assume the coalition had failed in Fallujah again. So we did tell our embedded media teams the intimate details of the feint, but not until the very last moment, so there wouldn't be a leak. There were rarely media leaks on operational matters, advertent or otherwise, but I do remember one or two journalists being 'unembedded' because they were not careful enough.

Before the feint, a Marine platoon commander briefed his troops with his embedded journalist present. He told them when they would cross what he called the 'start line' for a feint attack — it is normal to use the term 'start line' for a feint as well as for a real attack. When the attack was not pushed home and it became obvious that it was a feint, one journalist made a formal complaint that he had been lied to and used for propaganda purposes. He said he had been led to believe it was a real attack because of the use of the term 'start line'. Perhaps the platoon commander had been less than clear in his briefings. He may have assumed the journalist would have understood him. But we had a rule never to lie to the media or use them as a tool, and the rule had been followed.

When we finally decided to attack and analysed the options, we decided, ironically, that the best direction to attack from was the north, where we had put the tanks during the feint.

As chief of operations, I had to run a 'rock drill', so called because in less sophisticated days rocks were used to represent units that were moved around on a dirt map to show what everyone was doing. Our type of 'rock drill', held in a big room with all the players present to ensure overall coordination, looked at how we at the strategic level should prepare and synchronise events to help the soldiers doing the fighting. As I grew more experienced in this job, I began to build up a list of what we needed, and by the time we started to look seriously at Fallujah I had a standard set of 42 preconditions.

I'd learnt a lot from my infrastructure security days. As I had the best overview of anyone in headquarters, I thought I could simply make everyone aware of these 42 preconditions, and force, encourage or cajole them into taking responsibility for the ones that related to them. Thus we'd get a well-synchronised operation. To the surprise of none of my staff, when I tried to do this I was studiously ignored.

For a time, this produced some tension we could all have done without. One example was my ongoing attempts to get a supportive fatwa, or religious ruling — against the insurgents — from somewhere in the Islamic world. We needed to counter the anti-coalition fatwas that were being issued with great regularity by unknown and possibly bogus clerics. I could see no reason why we should just sit back and take these blatant propaganda hits. The initial suggestion of getting a fatwa came from the US Embassy, and everyone acknowledged that it was a great idea but difficult to achieve. I thought we should at least try.

When I put this idea repeatedly to the general concerned, he treated the suggestion initially with ridicule, then with disdain, and finally with outright hostility. He voiced his objections to me in a very ugly incident as we left that morning's post-BUA meeting, to the amusement of all my colonels, who were waiting for me in an adjacent conference room. The confrontation occurred at the same time as I was trying to encourage everyone to tone down their bad language. I entered the conference room and began the meeting by pompously announcing: 'Well, as you have heard, I have had a prick of a morning. I promised myself that I wouldn't say "Fuck" till at least 1100 today ... and it's only 0945.'

By not throwing ourselves into obtaining a fatwa, we missed using it before the battle in Samarra, in October, and missed again for Fallujah. By the time the election came, we managed to get an authoritative fatwa from Egypt against those who were trying to defeat democracy. Of course the fatwa did not bring the enemy to their knees, but it did enable us to publicly counter Zarqawi's claims that democracy was anti-Islamic.

In October in the lead-up to Fallujah, my 42 preconditions process was not even partially accepted. But each day in the generals' meeting after the morning BUA, I would stubbornly go through progress on each of the preconditions. Again, this did not endear me to some of my comrades. I joked that I feared the wrath of my fellow generals more than I feared car bombs in the Red Zone. My bodyguard joined in the joke and suggested that perhaps they should face inwards as I moved around the palace to protect me from my colleagues. Regardless of how sophisticated and technologically advanced this war sounds, military commanders and their staff are human, with foibles and faults. Sometimes it was better to maintain working relations than it was to be right. Drawing that line was very difficult, particularly in a coalition. But it was a tough headquarters and the issues were big. We were all very tired and my fellow generals could never be described as shrinking violets.

I no longer have the full list of the 42 preconditions: it resides, rightly, in the US classified computing system. But the 42 preconditions were the basis of the rock drill that I conducted before major operations, so we would know what we had to do before crossing the start line. Some of the headings were 'Political Support', 'Reconstruction Funds', 'Population Controls', and 'Iraqi Army Units'. With every one, I asked the question: 'Have we met this precondition?' The answer could be 'yes', 'no', or 'not applicable'. If the answer was no, which it often was, we had to explore the consequences. It was a hyper-rational way of doing things, but it was aimed at understanding and minimising risk for the soldiers on the ground. It had several great benefits — everyone knew the plan, everyone knew their role in the plan, everyone knew everyone else's role in the plan, and everyone knew the risks. Its main shortcoming was that, while we staff had been immersed in its complexities for weeks, others who were coming into it fresh, distracted by day-to-day fighting and other demands, had to quickly adjust their focus to take it all in.

The preparation for the attack on Fallujah involved a huge rock drill, second only to the one conducted for the election, and included Iraqi government and military representatives. The difficulty of running a rock drill in one language is high; running it in two, stopping for translation and side conversations as one Iraqi explained the process to another, was very challenging. To add another complication, we needed to withhold some very sensitive detail from our Iraqi friends, such as the date and concept of the attack.

Humanitarian assistance was one of our 42 preconditions. Morally, it was a particularly important issue for Fallujah. We cared a great deal for the people of Fallujah, as victims of the jihadists who occupied their city. Legally, we were required to provide for those affected by the assault. The coalition had enormous resources that we could put into humanitarian assistance, and the Allawi government, from their then meagre budget, provided US$2 million specifically for humanitarian aid. I remember thinking that this was a very small amount for the Iraqi Government to be putting in, but I quickly moved onto problems that were more immediately my responsibility.

The humanitarian supplies we prepared for Fallujah included immediate food for 10,000 people, which would have to suffice until we could assess the real needs in the city. Although we suspected that most Fallujans had left, we could not work on that basis. In Kuwait we had another 220,000 meals ready. We had 15 days' supply of bottled water on hand and we assembled medical kits to support 20,000 people for 90 days. More kits were en route from Denmark. We had 1600 blankets on hand and 12,600 'livelihood packages' (toilet paper, non-prescription medicines, soap, tea, sugar, chocolate), and 15 tonnes of medical equipment ready to be delivered to the Fallujah hospital. To meet our obligations to Fallujah under international law, we put together a civilian medical evacuation system, totally separate from our military system, to take wounded or sick civilians to a Jordan-sponsored hospital between Fallujah and Baghdad until the civilian facilities were re-established.

After our experience of fighting in other cities, especially Najaf and Sadr City in August, the use of the mighty dollar as a weapon against the insurgency was well advanced. We had more than US$100 million in reconstruction aid ready to be spent on Fallujah. It was to be dispensed by the Iraqi Government, and was to provide electricity, water, sewerage and schools; we hoped it would be seen by the people as coming from their government. The residents who had left would not return until their children could go to school, so we earmarked US$6.5 million to get schools ready. We had reconstruction teams ready to manage the reconstruction and so create thousands of jobs for Fallujans. We expected that Fallujans' quality of life would improve dramatically within six months of the battle.

Iraqi Security Force soldiers in one of the first unarmoured vehicles delivered to them in 2003: an early name for the Iraqi Army (Iraqi National Guard, or ING) is still painted on the side. Vehicles like these offered no protection against insurgent assaults.

'We might let you fire a shot or two...' At a range firing a Polish-produced AK–47, the main weapon used by the Iraqis and their enemies. The excellent oil and electricity protection force training camp at Taji, where this photo was taken, was closed down, showing our lack of vision in providing essential services to the Iraqi people.

Mussaib power station, old and Russian-built, was the main electricity supply for Baghdad. The staff worked wonders in getting it to function at all.

Helped by an interpreter, I talk to some trainee oil guards. I assume that the orange dummy bomb in the foreground is for teaching them how to defuse explosives, not make them.

General George W. Casey Jr, Commanding General of MNF-I from July 2004 until early 2007. Good commanders are intuitive, and Casey usually took the right option, using his own gut feeling. When this war is concluded, I hope George Casey will continue to be recognised as the great general that he is.

Front   **IZ D7644**

Someone has been Betrayed!

Zarqawi

IZ D7644

Back

Abu Al-Shami   Umar Baziyani   Muhamed Lubnani

We were betrayed by Zarqawi!
WILL YOU BE NEXT?

IZ D7644

An example of a psyops pamphlet. Whenever insurgents betrayed each other we publicised it.

Meeting with Shayk Khalid, the chief imam of Fallujah, after the November battle. He hated the US occupiers with a vengeance, but softened after a few months of occupation by Zarqawi's extremists.

Visiting the Korean soldiers in the Kurd lands near Irbil. The Koreans would encourage Iraqis by saying, 'We were in a worse state than you in the '50s, but now we are a rich, prosperous, powerful democracy.' The indomitable Colonel Chun is on the extreme right wearing glasses.

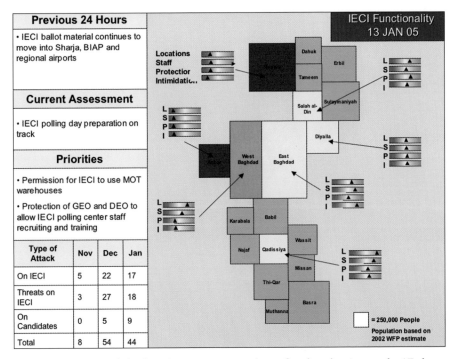

Our PowerPoint slide showing our preparedness for the election, only 17 days out. In the colour scales, red is bad and green is good. In the final week before the election, there would be 800 attacks, with 260 on election day itself.

A billboard in Baghdad encouraging people to get out and vote. By the third election in 2005, 12 million of 14 million eligible Iraqis voted.

LEFT: Eight million brave Iraqis came out to vote on 30 January 2005, protected by wire lines such as these. The Iraqi Army and Police performed brilliantly.

BELOW: The 'money shot' from the elections. Voters weren't allowed to take babies into the polling booths, so a woman has given her child to an Iraqi soldier. Possibly staged, but not necessarily.

The first eight ballot papers from the January 2005 election were presented to the eight Commissioners of the Independent Electoral Commission of Iraq. The IECI's Chief Electoral Officer, Dr Adil, made a gift to me of Ballot Paper number nine — a great honour.

My farewell from the operations centre, April 2005. Peter Palmer, my deputy, is on my left. Steve Hashem, on my right, looks serious but had just conducted a very funny farewell 'roast'.

The day after I returned from Germany in August 2005, Air Chief Marshall Angus Houston, on behalf of the US Secretary of Defense, presented me with the official medal for the US Legion of Merit. Anne was invited to the function. She has been with me forever in a way that I never deserved and I have often rewarded her with absence and worry.

Major General A.J. Molan AO DSC, for 'command and leadership in action' awarded the Distinguished Service Cross by Australia and the Legion of Merit by the United States of America.

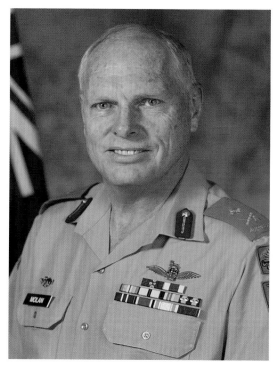

*

By late October we got confirmation of how many Fallujans had left the city. Initially, when a target was hit, hundreds would gather to help dig out the survivors. As time went on, the post-strike crowds had grown smaller, until eventually no-one was appearing. We hoped this was because the insurgents and terrorists had worn out their welcome. We started to look at marketplaces, water and medical distribution areas, mosques on Fridays, movement through checkpoints, and even who was hanging out washing to dry. There seemed to have been a self-initiated evacuation, exactly what we wanted.

General Casey still had to decide the timing of any assault. On 30 January 2005, the day mandated by the UN for the first free election in Iraq, the people of Fallujah should be able to vote in Fallujah. Working backwards from then, we would have to provide security for the elections, manage the election logistics, register voters, assemble staff to man the election, help return Fallujans to their city after the attack, rebuild the city, secure the city after the attack, and, of course, conduct the attack itself. It was dizzyingly complicated. We assumed a great deal, and applied equal measures of judgment and hope. At the rock drill, I remember expressing little confidence in our ability to do it and offering 'work-arounds', or alternative plans, for those parts that were likely to fail. There is an old military saying: hope should never be the basis of planning. But in the absence of anything else, informed hope can be another word for judgment. War is risky.

General Casey set the date for the attack at the end of the first week of November 2004.

CHAPTER 9

Slow is smooth,
smooth is fast

The attack on Fallujah, November 2004

This attack would not be a three-block war. It would be a hybrid: a set-piece conventional assault in the middle of a counterinsurgency war. This was the kind of assault veterans of World War II and Vietnam would have recognised: a division-level assault of 13,000 US and Iraqi soldiers, supported by tanks, artillery and aircraft, backed up by humanitarian assistance and the rule of law. It would be conducted against a well-armed, entrenched and fortified enemy in a city where there could be any number of civilians. So while this was part of a counterinsurgency, it was not quite the Malayan Emergency or Northern Ireland.

In our planning we studied the fighting in Hue during the Vietnam War and applied the lessons learnt there. Middle-aged veterans of Hue were brought to Iraq and spoke to the assault troops and the planners. As it turned out, the lessons that came out of Hue were exactly the same lessons that came out of the November Fallujah fighting.

I was constantly amazed at how the US soldiers and

commanders were able to manage the complexity of what we were doing. I'd seen how difficult three-block war could be for the generals, but it is much harder for the soldiers who fight it. Now, soldiers who had constantly switched roles from peacekeeper to aid provider to suddenly being in the middle of a firefight were preparing to go into Fallujah as assault troops. In no time at all (one US Army armoured brigade only arrived from Baghdad a day or so before the assault), they had to understand a plan which was going to test their flexibility of mind, attitude and discipline to the extreme.

I will tell the story of Fallujah as I perceived it from Baghdad, but no account can be complete if it sidesteps the viciousness of any serious urban combat. Urban fighting is ugly, violent in the extreme, and often tragic. I will try to do it justice, to honour the troops who fought so well.

Three US soldiers died from non-battle injuries the night before the attack, when a bulldozer preparing a road for the advance of armoured forces rolled over into the Euphrates and its two-man crew was drowned. One soldier who tried to rescue them also died. I thought at the time that this was just another tragedy that would be overtaken by the momentous events of the next few days. May none of those soldiers ever be forgotten.

For three months I had 'owned' the Fallujah battlespace, but as soon as I handed over formal responsibility, first to the US Special Forces for their one-day 'enhanced shaping' phase and then to the Corps for the assault, I was for the most part an observer. My only duties were to watch and anticipate events, report to General Casey and the Allawi government about what was going on, and keep an eye on the rest of Iraq. And then, when Mosul exploded in our face soon after the Fallujah battle began (more on that later), most of my attention went to finding Iraqi battalions I could move to Mosul, along with some US troops, to recover that northern city without limiting what we were doing in Fallujah.

General Casey launched the Fallujah assault on 7 November 2004. It was officially called Operation al Fajr, an Arabic word meaning 'dawn', selected on the advice of Prime Minister Allawi, I imagine to indicate the start of something new. The name we had been using during the planning phase was Operation Phantom Fury, and many who fought in it still know it as that.

We had assembled a formidable combination of air and ground forces to trap, then kill or capture the insurgents and terrorists in Fallujah. The trap was formed with a thickened 'dynamic cordon' around the city — not watertight, but effective enough. The Marines, by nature a light force designed to operate from the sea, were reinforced by army units with heavier vehicles and artillery. Marine and US Army battalions who had been involved in the August fighting in Najaf would break into the city and fight from house to house, helped by the army's Abrams tanks and Bradley fighting vehicles. The US Army operated about 450 M1 Abrams tanks in Iraq at any one time. I was most familiar with one parked under its own shadecloth near an entrance to the Green Zone. That 70-tonne tank sitting in the heat, with its 120mm gun — a single black hole in the front of the turret — was always a welcome sight. Its commander would sit in his hatch in the tank turret, fully kitted for combat in the 30°C heat, with an incongruous dirty yellow Esky to cool his drinks. The smaller M2 Bradley fighting vehicle, of which there were about 600 in Iraq at any one time, carried infantrymen who could dismount to fight on foot when required. It was the most capable vehicle of its kind in the world, with superb sights, allowing crew members to see over long distances day or night. Infantry of any kind were always delighted when Abrams tanks and Bradleys rolled up to support them.

Meanwhile, the army brigade from Baghdad, the 2nd Brigade — known universally as the 'Blackjack Brigade' — would command the cordon with some of its own troops and an agile Marine light-armoured reconnaissance battalion.

This was truly a mixed force. Marines were commanding army, and army was commanding Marines. In the planning phase, we had been wondering how the army and the Marines, with different weapons and vastly different cultures, would coalesce in Fallujah. The idea was that the army, designed to fight 'heavy', and the Marines, designed to fight 'light', would complement each other. Marines were equipped to dismount and fight on foot and counter close-in attacks, while the army had heavy armoured vehicles, firepower, and much more night-fighting equipment. They would both be supported by artillery and aircraft.

The tactical plan was for simultaneous assaults across the entire northern city boundary, beginning from behind the railway and its embankment. In the newer, more open parts of Fallujah to the east, the assault forces would spear through very quickly on several axes, bypassing strongpoints so as to disrupt the insurgents' command and control network and stop them concentrating. In the older parts of the city to the west, the troops would fight house to house, clearing everything they found and bypassing little. We planned to draw as many hostile groups as possible into combat, and to engage one particular leadership group who were thought to be in the older sector.

This was what we called a 'divisional-level' battle, based around the US Marines 1st Division, which wore the stars of the Southern Cross on its shoulder patch, alluding to its World War II history in Australia and the Solomon Islands — they were a long way from Guadalcanal now. The aim was to tie up the enemy on a broad front, so they could not redeploy to fight us in stength. This would essentially be a fight run by junior leaders and small teams combining infantry and tanks. Our assaulting forces would use firepower precisely and judiciously, but more freely now that most of the population had gone.

We did our best to make this operation different from the April one. The April battle was joined bit by bit, and without the benefit of long and careful planning and shaping, or clear political guidance and support. In April, the coalition only employed four battalions, and then attacked from four directions at once. Most of the male population of Fallujah fought against the Marines in April, and those who did not fight made the battlefield very complicated just by being there.

This time, the majority of Fallujans had left. While this made it easier for us in one way, it also meant coalition forces would be up against many more hardcore insurgents and foreign fighters, who were occupying fortified positions and had well-rehearsed battle plans.

To prepare for propaganda attacks from a hostile media, General Casey gave me one very important task. He directed me in no uncertain terms to ensure that there was no more than a one-hour turnaround between an allegation appearing in the media and our response being fired back. An example might have been a headline saying, 'Coalition fires on mosque in Fallujah'. Within an hour, we would have to find out where the mosque was, when the event happened, if the firing actually occurred and, if it did happen, why. We were not to deny anything immediately, nor investigate everything in such detail that we could only reply five days later, far too late for the media cycle.

I was aware that the Western media would scrutinise and broadcast the November battle live to millions in the US and around the world. Experts would second-guess and closely examine everything we did. My memory tells me there were about 60 media outlets represented in the assault force by about 90 reporters and cameramen. We had given no direction on this, and the size of the media contingent surprised us when the Marines told us what they had organised. It certainly surprised General Casey that the Marines, under their own steam, had embedded a media crew into just about every assault company. Our surprise was not about having something to hide. Our concern was just that at some stage the media would get something wrong, not necessarily through malevolence but through honest error, as they had about the 'start line' incident during the feint in September. More media could mean more unhelpful errors. But the US Marine Corps looks after its image carefully, and its embedded reporters were normally better than the blow-ins who turned up just before major battles or events — they had a greater chance of understanding what the soldiers were trying to do if they were living with them and sharing the dangers.

I had been steadily growing more involved in the information war, and Casey's one-hour turnaround of facts was a manifestation of this. But it was not all about the facts; sometimes it was also about the hardware. A few days before the assault, we saw what appeared to be an outside broadcast van, complete with satellite dish on its roof, hidden behind a house in Fallujah. I kept an eye on it from high above as we conducted our shaping operations. It moved infrequently, and we assumed it was being concealed until the attack and would be used then. At roughly the same time, we were approached by the Middle East news network al Jazeera, who told us through Central Command in Qatar that they had journalists with the insurgent forces in Fallujah and asked us to respect them. Of course, we said, we would respect them as non-combatants, but if their journalists were moving with the enemy we could not guarantee their safety, just as we couldn't guarantee the safety of Western media embedded with coalition units. Rather optimistically, we suggested that it would help us to respect them if al Jazeera could just tell us where in Fallujah they were! It was a long shot and probably worth a go, but al Jazeera are obviously not stupid and we heard no more about it.

We decided that the outside broadcast truck, if that was what it was, was not part of any known media organisation, so we waited until it was unoccupied, then destroyed it with a missile.

For many months now I had seen daily examples of the information war running in a parallel reality to the actual war. The information fight required less physical courage and sacrifice, but was just as important as the combat on the ground. Brigadier General Erv Lessel, who headed the strategic communications section in my operations branch, often reminded us of the dictum that 'public information turns tactical success into strategic victory'. I liked to look at it from the reverse: there is little point in winning the fight if no-one knows, cares or believes what you say.

We were confident about winning the physical fight. The only question was at what cost. On the other hand, I was not so confident about winning the information war. We knew that the inevitable battle damage to the city, along with civilian casualties, would be the focal point of both Western and Arab media. So when we responded to a specific accusation, we would have to get it right. Otherwise the next news grab would be that we were lying and covering up. We would be pilloried when we were not right, but more so if, after investigating an allegation against us, we still got it wrong. No-one would ever believe that we had just made a mistake.

It was my responsibility, then, to find the truth and find it quickly. This sounds straightforward enough until you remember that those who had the answers to our questions were in Fallujah fighting for their lives. In the military, we try to do everything through the chain of command. That is, we do not go directly to anyone's subordinates; we go through their boss unless there is a very good reason. This was one of the few times when I felt justified in ignoring the chain of command and reaching well down into the ranks. I would find it very difficult to convince those at the sharp end that a story in the media was as important as the physical fight they were in, but I had a one-hour deadline and that deadline was an order from the CG.

Another significant glitch in disseminating information was related to the video footage produced by our unmanned Predator aircraft. Predator footage was often decisive in disproving allegations made against us. But it includes data on heights, speeds and angles, from which the enemy could gain information on the performance of the sensors. So that data needed to be stripped off the video before it could be publicly aired. We needed to do this quickly, but sometimes it took days to send it back to the US and then have it returned — by that time we had been tried, convicted and hanged by the media. To my knowledge, we did not speed up this process until after I left Iraq.

Meanwhile, General Casey directed the Corps commander, Tom Metz, to form a large team of information specialists to follow the assault troops into the city and immediately document what the insurgents and terrorists had been doing in Fallujah. With documents, still pictures and video, we would record every transgression of international law. Dick Formica, the head of targeting in the Corps Headquarters and a most effective officer, headed this team very well and produced excellent evidence that we duly disseminated to the world. But from my perspective at the coalface, it seemed that most of the European networks, and the BBC and the US cable networks, were unreceptive to the evidence we found of torture, murder and intimidation by our adversary on a vast scale in Fallujah. And of course, the Arab networks had absolutely no interest in what we were saying. But still we had to produce the information, if only for the record.

The assault on Fallujah began with the best Iraqi battalion, the 36th Commando Battalion, securing the Fallujah hospital on the evening of

7 November, supported by a Marine light armoured reconnaissance battalion. My staff and I watched every step, as it was beamed live by video from our Predator drone, and backed up by the Blue Force Tracker, showing the position of all friendly forces. I had taken a step back from my physical and mental involvement with Fallujah, and was surprisingly dispassionate as we watched the Corps run the tactical battle; there was little I could do now. My natural paranoia cautioned me against focusing too closely on Fallujah, in case we were caught out badly somewhere else. An uprising across the rest of Iraq such as we had experienced in August would have tested us. This had been an issue at the rock drill. If I had been the enemy, it is exactly what I would have done.

We watched the assault go in. In taking the hospital first, we removed one of the greatest sources of enemy propaganda. This was the hospital from which so-called doctors had contested my version of the strikes we had made in Fallujah over the previous months. Often within an hour of a strike, a white-coated 'doctor', unknown to any Iraqi medical authority in Baghdad, appeared live on Arab TV speaking from the hospital in a very sophisticated broadcast. It was good to remove that source of enemy propaganda, but more importantly, we needed the hospital to consolidate medical support in our hands for any remaining citizens of Fallujah.

The main assault occurred the next evening. In order to establish ourselves in the city, we had planned that the first 12 hours of this battle would be in the dark — this would allow us to take advantage of our superiority in night-fighting equipment. The enemy had only a few night vision devices, mainly Russian equipment, captured US equipment or commercial equipment purchased in Europe.

The day we entered the city, 8 November, was referred to as 'A-Day', or Assault Day. Four Marine and two army battalions, backed up by several Iraqi battalions, moved into the city from the north, passing through the steep rail embankment in gaps blown by large aerial bombs. Night always poses its own challenges, particularly if you are trying to move large numbers of armoured vehicles in an orderly manner. I have participated in numerous night exercises, and despite the proliferation of night vision devices and even GPS navigation there are always traffic jams, especially if an enemy can use mortars or rockets against choke points. I watched the bottleneck from my electronic perch as hundreds of armoured vehicles tried to get through a few gaps in the embankment. In many cases, the infantry dismounted and kept the assault going on foot — their heavy tanks and trucks caught up with them some hours later.

After the troops moved into the edge of the city, fighting began across the entire northern boundary. Initially, the troops moved fast. The original plan was to reach the centre of the city in 72 to 96 hours. Then the western three battalions would hold, while the eastern three battalions crossed the main highway and swung west, pinning the insurgents against the Euphrates.

From my operations centre in Baghdad, the attack looked neat and tidy once the traffic jams were sorted out. I could see that progress was slow and deliberate in some parts, but consistent with the plan. In other parts of the city, progress was very fast indeed.

In the critical Jolan area on the northwest corner, the old area of Fallujah, the 1400-man Marine battalion 3/5 under Lieutenant Colonel Pat Malay cleared every house, one by one. The battalion commander elected to use all three of his companies as he squeezed the enemy out in front of him. He destroyed many enemy fighters directly, and used indirect fire and close air support selectively to avoid casualties among his own troops. In the newer areas to the east, which had wider and straighter roads, battalions pushed on as fast as they could. Their objective was to dislocate hostile groups and separate them from each other, disrupt enemy command and control, and prevent enemy groups from concentrating in larger numbers or redeploying. This also worked well.

That's how it looked on Blue Force Tracker. To the soldiers and Marines in the city, there was nothing neat and tidy about this fight. This was not like the cut and thrust of the 2003 advance on Baghdad. This fighting would start in a street or a house, then go up the street as houses were secured by brute force or were sometimes bypassed to keep the speed of the advance going. The fight would then move in a different direction. When pushed, the enemy would hold firm or push back, and the fighting would spread in that particular area in any direction and with little apparent logic. It was all down to the individuals on the ground.

Because friendly fire is not at all friendly, every single soldier had to be aware of what was commonly called the 'geometry of fire'. We had emphasised this in our preparation. In the chaos of this attack, the danger zones of weapons were stressed and stressed again. There were some incidents of US forces firing on their comrades, but a great many fewer than I had expected. At least one was from a 500-pound bomb that landed too close, causing casualties but no deaths. These troops were experienced. Most had fought in urban environments, albeit less intense than Fallujah. Their commanders had a healthy paranoia about hitting their own troops, and they led well.

As we had predicted, the infantry and the tanks were a battle-winning combination. The saying is 'same axis, same speed', meaning that ideally, tanks and infantry would move towards the enemy from the same direction at roughly the same speed, as the roads allowed. Sometimes a tank would be a little ahead or the infantry a little ahead, but normally they would be as tight as possible, protecting each other. Tanks would lead assaults down a street, with the Bradleys or the Marine APCs and armoured Hummers close behind, often accompanied by the ubiquitous 7-tonne trucks loaded with ammunition. The ammunition usage rates were as high as we expected.

If the tanks were a little in front, insurgents would either wait and go for the vulnerable rear of the tank or only attack when the infantry followed. On our side, the soldiers would try not to be sucked into a close fight, but often they were fighting at close quarters before they realised it. The tanks would be called up to use their heavy guns if those on foot could disengage and move back to a safe position. But often the infantry could not disengage, and the tanks fired in very close proximity to the dismounted troops. Those close to the firing tanks were deafened, often for days.

We expected the enemy to mix their weapon types the way they usually did. They would initiate contact with a US squad, using rifle fire and the odd bomb detonation, which might create initial casualties and cause our troops to deploy. As our troops took cover and returned fire, enemy marksmen armed with Dragunov sniper rifles would target our commanders and radio operators. To break this impasse, we might move armoured vehicles into the middle of the fight. The insurgents would then attack them with barrages of RPGs.

With our tactics successfully preventing them from concentrating in numbers, the insurgents dispersed into small groups and fought to the death from fortified houses, mosques and hospitals. Or they would sally out and flow around the Marines until they hit a hard position and could go no further. Often insurgents would lie in ambush, letting the Marines enter houses and then engaging them inside. No artillery, tanks or bombs could intervene in this type of contest. The Marines had to fight from room to dimly lit room to clear a building, often hampered by the casualties they took in the initial burst of fire. Sometimes, as we had seen in Baghdad and Mosul, insurgents would lure our troops into a house and then blow the whole thing up.

This was an old-fashioned, close-quarters fight — pistols, grenades and anything else that was to hand. There were even accounts of knives and bayonets being used. Where possible, armoured vehicles saved coalition lives by blowing holes in the sides of houses or pushing over walls to allow the assault troops access from an unexpected direction. Small-unit tactics and junior commanders were applying the key ingredient of such fighting: tactical patience. Never rush things. Manoeuvre to get into the best tactical position. 'Slow is smooth, smooth is fast' — if you rush things, you wll ultimately pay — was a Marine saying burnt into the junior commanders' minds.

The insurgents often sacrificed their younger, less-skilled fighters first, holding back the seasoned professionals until they knew more about our intentions. They used imaginative and clever IED ambushes, and even used live bait, such as a group of insurgents in full view, to lure our troops into a killing ground laced with explosives. Their core fighters were very good, and were prepared to fight to the death. I remember intelligence briefs that described the most fanatical fighters as 'Islamo fascists', a delightfully confusing term. There was a widespread belief among coalition troops that the most fanatical of the enemy used mind-altering drugs. Perhaps this was true. It is more certain that those who had decided to fight to the death had taken large amounts of painkillers to anaesthetise themselves and keep on fighting while wounded. Before the battle was even joined, they attached tourniquets to their arms and legs loosely so that if they were injured they could immediately pull them tight and keep fighting. Many individuals required more than what might be considered the normal number of shots to stop them, giving credence to the long-held view that the 5.56mm bullet from the standard US M-16/M4 rifle did not have the stopping power that such close combat required. I remember one instance, not in Fallujah but in Mosul, where an insurgent was shot four times — once in the testicles — by 5.56mm bullets and still had enough strength to fight hand-to-hand with a US soldier. He did not give up until his face was smashed into the concrete floor and he lost consciousness.

Another key to success in this kind of fighting was never to make an uncovered move. Every activity, from moving up a street, to assaulting a house, to recovering a casualty, had to be conducted by one group while another covered them. An assault on just one house might require a squad of about ten soldiers to assault the house, a squad to cover them, a squad ready to follow them in, and two other squads to surround the house and prevent escape or reinforcement. Often, a fight would start with the enemy inflicting an initial casualty on our troops. Our response was to recover the casualty, which might take some time, and then destroy the enemy. One of the most common uses of the squad automatic weapon, a light machine gun carried by each fire team, was to provide the cover fire while the others were picking up a casualty from a room or a hallway. A full magazine of 100 rounds might be fired in one long burst into a room, which was sure to burn out a new barrel, but we had lots of new barrels, and that kind of storm of fire would allow a casualty to be recovered.

Another saying, used to make the complex as simple as possible to exhausted and frightened men, was 'Assault, Security, Support'. Once an assault went in, its flanks had to be secured, and then it could be supported. Behind the immediate fight, reinforcements waited on foot or in armoured vehicles to support their mates or move in a new direction as the scrum developed. The Marines' ammunition-loaded 7-tonners were ready to move forwards to the assault troops or evacuate the wounded to triage and medical stabilisation points just to the rear. The Marines had what they called 'Shock Trauma' platoons, and often casualties were in the ST platoon within minutes of being hit. That was the support. But other brave troops, caught in the initial burst of fire in a dark room, bled to death before their mates could get them.

Except for the first night's advance on the Fallujah hospital, Iraqi troops were held in reserve for specific tasks. One of those tasks was clearing mosques — that was work for Muslim Iraqis, not infidels. Insurgents had fortified, stored weapons and supplies in, or fought from 66 of the 166 or so mosques in the city, so the Iraqi battalions were soon busy. Under the laws of armed conflict, once insurgents opened fire at our troops from a mosque, the mosque lost its protected status. If we had to attack a mosque, US combat cameramen filmed such incidents so that we had evidence to counter the inevitable propaganda that accused 'crusaders' of defiling a religious place.

I remember seeing a TV broadcast where media embedded in one of our units videoed artillery shells bursting in the air between the minarets of a mosque. This did not look like a proportional response. The Arab networks took the video and attached the kind of commentary we expected, claiming indiscriminate firing on places of worship in contravention of international law. I worked the phones. The truth was that the artillery was firing on targets close to the mosque but behind it. It was the camera angle that gave the impression that they were firing on the mosque. And the reason air-bursting shells were being used was that they caused less damage than shells that buried themselves in buildings before exploding. To their credit, most of the embedded Western media understood this perfectly and reported it accurately.

In the attack's initial stages, the enemy used mortars against us some 60 times. The Marines detected each one, using radar that picked up the mortar round's high trajectory. On the first day, many of these were very effective. We could only return fire at the mortars 47 times, because we were following rules of engagement that directed us to protect any population that might still be in the city. As the assault progressed, however, we confirmed that there were very few locals in Fallujah, so we could respond more vigorously.

Psychological operations (or 'Psyops') were active at the lowest tactical level. As one Marine commander told me, 'We used the Psyops loudspeaker systems to wake them up in the morning by telling them that we were coming to get them, and we put them to sleep at night calling out names of mujahideen that we had killed from captured lists taken off bodies.'

Air power and air surveillance were critical. Coalition aircraft were stacked up over Fallujah or on call day and night. This included the AC-130 we had used so successfully in the shaping phase. Armed with accurate, direct-firing 105mm guns and smaller quick-firing 40mm grenade launchers, they were devastatingly effective, and were my weapon of choice whenever a bomb was inappropriate. Sitting high up in the Iraqi sky were all sorts of jets (F-16s, F-15Es, F/A-18s, F-14s, and even, I am told, some British GR-7s), their wings laden with bombs waiting for a target. Close air support was often very close — in technical terms, 'danger close'.

Around and under the 'fast movers' were the slower, unmanned surveillance drones such as the Dragonflys, Pioneers and Predators, sending a stream of pictures back to all levels of command. Sometimes as many as eight drones were looking at a single fight. There was also a way of relaying the images seen by the pilots to the fire controllers on the ground to confirm the target. Air-attack controllers with the ground commanders could then confirm that what the aircrew were looking at was what the ground controller wanted hit. Typical targets were described as 'snipers in a minaret', 'insurgents firing from buildings and courtyards', 'insurgents in blocking positions', or 'insurgent machine gun positions'. The sharing of images was an innovation; in the past a controller on the ground would only be able to describe a target verbally, and any misunderstanding between him and the pilot could kill our own troops, or civilians, or waste a bomb.

In the first week of the attack, the air element conducted 622 missions, a quarter involving precision bombing close to our troops.

Only seven of those missions were pre-planned at the very start of the assault. The rest were organised in quick time on fleeting targets, showing the real flexibility of the US Air Force.

Aerial bombs have a decisive impact. If you hit the right place with an aerial bomb in a ground fight, that part of the fight is normally over. The danger, of course, is that it is easy to hit your own troops.

In peacetime exercises, we would never drop a 500-pound bomb closer than a few kilometres from our own troops. At that distance, the concussion from the bomb could still knock you back if you were in the open, but the shrapnel was unlikely to hit you. Even if the bomb was dropped long or short, the chance of friendly casualties was less if you were a few kilometres away. In Fallujah, using the super-accurate GBU-38 JDAM, some bombs were dropped at less than 100 metres from our troops. Some of the blast was absorbed by the buildings, and the shrapnel was contained somewhat by the walls. So if you were trying to hit an enemy position that was only 100 metres from your own troops, and the data passed to the aircraft was even slightly wrong or the bomb malfunctioned, the risk was enormous. But on some occasions, the effect of such a bomb on the enemy would be considered so decisive that the risk was accepted.

After the first few days, I was dividing my time between the operation in Fallujah, our attempts to get troops to Mosul, catching up on routine issues that had been on hold during the planning and targeting frenzy of the last three months, and planning for the election that was now only two months away. Once I was drawn back to the Fallujah fight by media accusations that our fire caused minor damage to three health clinics. After much thrashing around for reliable information, I was able to determine that in two cases, the insurgents had used the buildings for offensive firing positions, so we fired on them. In the third case, the clinic was in a much larger building which we had bombed after insurgents had fired from it. This so-called clinic had not been used as such for many years and was not on the list of protected medical facilities the Interim Iraqi Government had given us before the assault. At least we had the facts, even if no-one was interested.

Insurgents had placed bombs throughout the city, waiting for our troops. Many of the berms and barriers that had been built to try to channel our forces into killing grounds had explosives buried inside them. In the middle of one night during the early shaping phase, I had recommended to General Casey that we attack some berms using an AC-130 to detonate bombs that might be inside. Casey had rejected my suggestion, and I concluded that suggesting anything new at 3am was never a good idea — but we did start targeting these obstacles after I raised it with him at a more civilised time.

Once we started to do this, I watched an attack on a suspected roadside bomb position by an AC-130. We'd expected the secondary explosion that indicated that the shell from the AC-130 had hit a hidden bomb, but what we saw was truly terrifying. The AC-130 round fired into the berm caused a series of explosions which ran along each side of the road for about two city blocks and then rippled out to about a block on either side, then back up in the opposite direction. The enemy had prepared a superb ambush of buried artillery shells and joined them together like a daisy chain waiting for our troops to move into their midst. Somewhere in the area would have been a suicidal trigger man waiting to make his final contribution to jihad.

Much to our surprise, the Interim Iraqi Government declared the city secure on 13 November, after less than a week of fighting. The assault phase of the operation was planned from 7–11 November, but the fight would continue in a very serious way for six more weeks.

Given the speed of the initial assault, we decided not to swing the eastern battalions around and push the enemy up against the Euphrates, but kept all battalions clearing straight through to the southern edge of Fallujah. Then we needed to back-clear the entire city. Although this was a surprise to no-one, it was particularly hard on the troops. A city can never be cleared in one pass, and already insurgent groups were re-emerging. The Iraqi troops were very active in countering this.

Fallujah would take a similar time to clear as had Hue in 1968, four to six weeks. The conditions for the soldiers were appalling. Apart from the danger of combat at close quarters, the soldiers could not be pulled out for a meal, a rest or a wash. Most combat soldiers conducting such operations were exhausted by stress and physical exertion, had loose bowels because of the unsanitary conditions — dogs and rats ate bodies in streets awash with sewage — and their own clothes were filthy with dirt and blood, so every cut and scratch quickly became infected.

Statistics for two separate days, 23 November and 10 December, reveal the prolonged ferocity of this long fight and its effect on the soldiers. On 23 November, two weeks into the fighting, my notes remind me that we killed 95 enemy. We had no coalition members killed and only one wounded. It was a tough day for the Iraqi units, though: they had seven soldiers killed and 42 wounded. In these first two weeks we had suffered a total of 61 soldiers killed and 552 wounded.

On 23 November we bombed nine targets, six of which were insurgent-occupied buildings. A prowling AC-130 responded twice to insurgent attacks and fired twice, my notes recording that it used 18 105mm artillery rounds and 57 40mm rounds. We estimated that on 23 November there were fewer than 200 insurgents in the city. We had killed 2175 and wounded an unknown number. The total number we killed would rise past 3000 (that was the number of bodies recovered). In these first two weeks of fighting, we had detained 1801 suspected insurgents, so not every member of our opposition was a martyr. Of those we had detained, about half were released for various reasons; we had 974 on hand by 23 November.

On 10 December, five weeks after Assault Day, the fight was still going strong and it was the same soldiers who were fighting it. I recorded that we hit two targets from the air with four 500-pound bombs: they were buildings occupied by insurgents. The price we had paid in lives so far was now 72 dead and 648 wounded, of whom 293 were lightly wounded and would return to duty. I noted that we found the body of one person identified as a 'civilian', and 66 'civilians' who had been wounded. The exact status of these civilians was always difficult to determine. If they were not armed, they were considered 'civilians'. Wounded or displaced civilians were detained for some time and questioned, and if no case could be made against them they were released.

By 10 December, the troops had fought through the city twice, and were clearing specific trouble spots a third time. Every single building in Fallujah had been entered and every room had been inspected. The stress on the troops of this house-to-house searching and fighting for six weeks was extreme. For the brand-new Iraqi troops, it was an introduction to the nastiest type of fighting that can be imagined.

The question should always be asked: Was this a fair price to pay for the removal of a safe haven for insurgents and foreign terrorists, and for the first vote in Iraq?

Compare it with Hue, where the Marines fought for a month, losing 580 killed and almost 1000 wounded. In military terms, we described Fallujah as a strategically defensive fight that used offensive tactics. We were attacking Fallujah to restore a status quo that would allow us to conduct an election. The attack was conducted with the authority of the legitimate Iraqi government. Lazy members of the media, looking for an easy line to offer their editors, trotted out the old headline that we destroyed Fallujah in order to save it.

One Marine battalion commander told me of a reporter who came to Fallujah some time after combat operations had quietened down, and only wanted to see a destroyed city. The commander personally escorted the reporter to a row of shops that were pretty well intact. The Marines had actually taken casualties preserving the shops, which they did because the people would need them. This reporter, however, was only interested in six to eight destroyed houses nearby, and that was the only story that went out, even though the commander explained that the destroyed houses had been used by the insurgents for ammunition storage and had been booby-trapped. The commander said he had only found about 1000 civilians in his sector: about 350 in an apartment block complex and others in smaller groups. He was proud to say that his troops were not responsible for the death of one civilian.

But the headlines screamed that Fallujah had been destroyed. Repeated often enough, that became an accepted fact: the city had been wantonly destroyed by US troops, and the bodies of women and children lay thick among the ruins. I admit that the damage was visually spectacular — I could see this in hours of staring down from my Predator drone viewpoint. I remember quite clearly the first time General Casey visited after the heavy initial fighting finished. He came back and briefed us that evening, which was very important for the generals in the Green Zone, who could not look down on the fight, as I could, from a Predator. In this meeting there was no levity.

'I have to say that I have never seen anything like this,' he said quietly. I had been offering my daily technical count of the number of buildings I could see destroyed, and had even suggested that we go public with it to counter criticism. My count of buildings destroyed was roughly correct but I had separated the facts from the emotion, and Casey said rightly that we would not use the count at this stage. 'Keep counting and perhaps we will use it later,' he told me.

What he had seen on the ground was the result of a 21st-century military fighting through a relatively modern city. Although he had not visited every part of Fallujah, because the fight was still going on, it was visually overwhelming. 'I understand the figures,' he said, 'but what you see as you drive around there is the greatest tribute to our soldiers and Marines that I could ever imagine, because this has been a tough fight. And I can imagine the effect it is going to have on the media.'

He was right, of course. The impression of destruction would be even more marked on reporters who were looking for damage, wanting it to be there. We had prepared ourselves as much as possible for the accusation that we had destroyed the city, but facts and emotion are two different things, and Casey brought this home to us. It now became even more important to find some way to get this into perspective.

Some months earlier, I'd had my Australian intelligence officer in the operations centre get the imagery analysts to count the number of structures in Fallujah, so that we at least had a starting point. The analysts came up with a total of 17,432 structures before the assault, a figure I accepted but could not personally verify. Comparing imagery over time, we were able to count the structures destroyed or severely damaged by direct strikes in April and the lead-up to November. To these were added the structures that were destroyed during the November fighting. They came to fewer than 10 per cent of the 17,432. In my view, it was less than honest to say that we 'destroyed the city', but perceptions are everything.

Our decision to attack Fallujah had been justifiable on political grounds, and what we found in the city after the attack confirmed our decision. The information that Dick Formica's team found and offered to the world illustrated the importance of the city to the insurgents and the terrorists, whether the world was listening or not. We counted 653 IEDs found or detonated in Fallujah during the fight. This was a very high number in a very small area. We found 19 'factories' producing roadside bombs and car bombs. This production capability was far more than required for use in Fallujah; the surplus was obviously going to the rest of the country. Had we not removed this safe haven, Fallujah-manufactured car bombs may have torn the guts out of the Iraqi election day.

In one factory we found 'chemical cookbooks' — instruction manuals for the production of chemical devices. This facility also had a quantity of chemicals known as 'blood agents'. The discovery had nothing to do with weapons of mass destruction: the scale was too small and the types of agents were different. But the find showed that the terrorists were experimenting with chemical weapons to be used against the coalition or the Iraqi people.

I had become used to the extraordinary number of weapons washing around Iraq. I'd been astounded at the tonnes of weapons that we had taken away from the Imam Ali shrine and nearby houses after the Najaf fighting in August. But Fallujah was an arsenal of significant size, even by Iraqi standards. We documented 229 weapons and ammunition caches. One out of every five city blocks had one, and these were big caches. Again, this was far in excess of local insurgent requirements.

Some of our most spectacular finds were the eight hostage houses or torture chambers, popularly referred to as 'slaughter houses'. They were recognisable from the execution videos that had been made in them, the blood spatters and bloody handmarks on the walls, and the sand that had been used to soak up the blood. We uncovered the National Islamic Resistance Operations Centre, the insurgent equivalent of my operations centre in the Green Zone. In several of these facilities, we found laptops with evidence of executions on them.

In another part of the city there was a well-equipped insurgent TV station, in which were made execution and recruitment CDs for distribution well beyond Fallujah. By 13 November we had found one live hostage — shackled and starving, but still alive — and five dead hostages in Fallujah or its surrounds. Three of the dead were contractors working for the big US logistics company KBR.

We also found three safe houses for the entry of foreign fighters into Iraq. This confirmed our view that foreign fighters, such as Zarqawi, played a key role, through locally formed religious councils, in the imposition of more extreme forms of Sharia law.

We had 16 foreign fighters in detention: six Egyptians, four Syrians, two Saudi Arabians, and one each from Jordan, Libya, Yugoslavia and Britain, plus any number of passports referring to other individuals. It was impossible to say how many of the 3000 who were killed were foreign fighters.

By any measure, the loss of Fallujah was a severe setback for the insurgency. But despite our cordon, many of the leaders left the city before the final assault and, from outside the city, exhorted their foot soldiers to continue the struggle. Zarqawi even criticised those leaders who remained in the city, including the religious leaders, for not fighting enough. This was something we tried to capitalise on, making sure that every defender of Fallujah knew exactly where their brave leaders were, and what they were saying about the defenders' efforts.

But to concentrate only on the violence of Fallujah, as most people did, is to seriously miss the point. The fight in Fallujah was inseparable from the January 2005 election. We never saw it as a climactic battle. By the time it started at the tactical level, I was engaged in the next two to three fights. 'Fight your way to the election,' Casey had said. Had we not removed Fallujah as a terrorist safe haven, staging the January 2005 election — not just in Fallujah but right across Iraq — would have been unacceptably risky.

No Fallujans will ever thank us for fighting through their city, but the battle brought some benefits to the new Iraq. Foreign fighters were either captured or killed, and their flow into Iraq was disrupted, at least for some time. The Iraqi Security Forces played a real role in the recapture of the city and served courageously and proudly. The chances that upper Euphrates areas such as Haditha and Qaim could achieve some economic progress were increased because they now had access to Baghdad. The rule of law was re-established under legitimate civilian authority in Fallujah itself. The attack was a public display of determination by the Interim Iraqi Government and the coalition, and enhanced the Iraqi government's credibility. It was a message to every Iraqi that it was time to commit to one side or the other. Very soon after the battle, we saw its effect in Ramadi, where the people attacked the insurgents. The mayor, fearing the imposition of Sharia law and fearing the impact of military operations on his town, said to us, 'We do not want what happened to Fallujah to happen to Ramadi.'

I did not have the luxury of quiet contemplation of events before, during or after the battle of Fallujah. I had no trouble, however, recognising how central to our enemies' philosophy was the pure expression of hatred.

Killing innocents in large numbers to play on the humane instincts of Western audiences was their central tactic. In Iraq, the one group Zarqawi hated more than the Americans was the Shi'ites, because he believed Shi'ites were apostates, rejecting the true stream of Islam. He attacked them mercilessly. Zarqawi and his ilk offered the Iraqi people nothing but a return to the 12th century. To see the total absence of modern thought behind this insurgency, you only needed to look at the Zarqawi treatise on the evils of democracy issued the week before the 30 January election. Since I had arrived in Iraq I had been looking for one single impressive idea behind our enemies that was not blind hate within a distorted Islam, so I took some time to read this treatise. Even allowing for the hurried translation, this was not even undergraduate stuff. It was puerile and was rejected by the vast majority of the Iraqi people. What Zarqawi said was that democracy was evil because it gave power to the people while, under the Koran, only Allah can have such power. I read this and recalled witnessing the largest Muslim nation in the world, Indonesia, with 240 million citizens, embracing democracy with vigour.

Obviously not prepared to rely on the substance of his arguments, in the same breath as Zarqawi issued his treatise, he also issued a warning: 'Vote and you will die.' Again, I could find very little scrutiny of this preposterous position in the world media.

When the fighting was finished and the reconstruction began, a large number of personnel from various superior headquarters wanted to visit Fallujah. Their reasons were normally quite legitimate. General Casey had gone down early in the second week of fighting to convey his appreciation to the soldiers and report back to Washington with the authority of an eyewitness. Prime Minister Allawi visited on at least one occasion that I remember. Casey's deputy, the British Lieutenant General John Kisely, managed the reconstruction and visited often, making things happen by pure force of personality. Brigadier General Steve Hashem, the officer in charge of civil military operations within my operations branch, frequently travelled to Fallujah to direct, cajole and encourage. United Nations staff wanted to go but could not get permission from New York. Much to their frustration, they had to settle for a briefing from me in the Green Zone. I hadn't visited Fallujah since the fighting. My mind had moved on to two issues — Mosul and the election preparations — and I had no intention of going to Fallujah unnecessarily and being labelled a military tourist. Three months later, in March, only weeks before I left Iraq, and when the situation had settled down, I did indulge myself and visit.

The Interim Iraqi Government, at John Kisely's request and urging, sent teams of engineers to Fallujah once things were secure. They assessed the total damage at US$493 million and, as a result, offered the people of Fallujah US$110 million in compensation to rebuild their houses. The government claimed it had no more to give. I was disturbed by this, and would like to think it had more to do with incompetence than with a malicious attitude towards the Sunnis — the government was Shi'ite dominated. I was close to the coalition officers who were involved in negotiations with the government. They were deeply frustrated with Iraqi officials and politicians. To be charitable, I would say that their immaturity in government meant that they were only able to focus on one issue at a time, and the issue of the moment was now the election.

Our involvement in Fallujah left us vulnerable in many other places, a risk we had anticipated but had no easy answer for. My attention was diverted from Fallujah at about the two-week mark in November, as the enemy struck in Mosul. We suspected that those who escaped from Fallujah during the shaping phase, including Zarqawi, had headed north to divert us. The initial slaughter of the people of Mosul by the terrorists was horrific, but — and this is one of the more subtle human costs of being in a war — I found that I was more than used to this by now. I remember one night when the terrorists attacked and captured about 26 of the 34 police stations in this city of two-and-a-half million, killed the police who resisted (most, sensibly, ran away), and looted each station of its weapons. They followed up with retribution killing on a terrible scale. As each day dawned, we found lines of bound and executed bodies.

We had left two Iraqi brigades, each of about 3000 personnel, in Mosul during the Fallujah fighting in the hope of guaranteeing security alongside the police. These two brigades had been targeted by a long intimidation campaign, and we found out too late that they were ineffective. Our only answer was to move other Iraqi troops up to Mosul, and several police commando battalions under Iraqi command. Each night we flew Iraqi troops by CH-47 helicopters from Baghdad up to Mosul. Many of the commandos did not want to go, and, once there, did not want to stay.

Fortunately, I had on my liaison staff a very capable Arabic-speaking American, Colonel Bob Newman. I also had a Marine liaison officer, Colonel Tom Duhs, in the Ministry of the Interior, looking after the police, and Colonel Jim Hamkins, who was my liaison officer with the Ministry of Defence. These three facilitated the reinforcement of Mosul. As I tried to get battalions ready to go north, I could get no effective assistance from the Iraqi leadership, but I had to do something. It was easy to identify the units needed, but very hard to get them to move. I would get every promise from every Iraqi officer, and then nothing would happen. We finally forced one battalion to go by forcing the commanding officer to bring his soldiers to the Green Zone and dispatching them at night by helicopter. The first commanding officer accepted the inevitable as we shipped his troops out by air, but then unwisely sent about 70 unarmoured vehicles up to Mosul by road. These vehicles were badly ambushed before they had gone 50 kilometres, probably betrayed by someone on the Iraqi staff. I admit that sometimes I felt real despair.

The Iraqi attitude was a continual puzzle for me. We were keen to hand over control of as much as we could, but they seemed reluctant to take responsibility. I could more easily understand their hesitancy to fight than I could their reluctance to give money to Fallujah. In Saddam's army, the leaders had been historically unwilling to get into a fight. When things became tough, the Sunni leadership abandoned the Shia soldiers. We tried to bring new Iraqi battalions into the April fighting in Fallujah much too soon, and they refused. We did it differently in Samarra and in Fallujah in November, and it was somewhat more successful, but far from perfect. The Iraqi Army battalions in November were better equipped and better trained, and they had US advisers who were willing to enter combat with them. But our police commando battalions, who did not have permanent advisers who shared the risk, did not trust us — it was obvious. Because they had no US cadre within the battalions, we had no way of showing our commitment to support them. In their view, we were sending them to a strange part of this big country to fight a better equipped enemy.

The lack of support coming from the Iraqi military leadership can also be explained. Signs of initiative in Saddam's Iraq were never rewarded. In fact, anyone who showed initiative or a willingness to take on responsibility was viewed with deep suspicion, and was often caused to disappear. The way you survive under a dictator is to stay unnoticed — I had seen similar things under Suharto. This attitude had been prevalent in Iraq since at least 1968, probably longer, and had impacted on the spirit of a generation. We were not going to change this in a year or two.

After more failures than I like to recall, my three colonels solved the problem for me. They would stick with each battalion's commanding officer to prevent any second thoughts, until the troops were in the right place at the right time. After a few very tense incidents, we worked out a system that made the Iraqi higher command responsible for their own troops. The deployment of Iraqi battalions worked out better, as the Iraqis could see we were not going to dump them into a situation they could not handle, and the level of trust increased. But they always had the capacity to surprise us.

No two fights are the same, and it takes time to adjust any force to a specific fight. The US military that had been built up with the prospect of defeating the Russians on the north German plains, and had brilliantly defeated Saddam's army in 2003, was in 2004 being widely criticised by armchair strategists (some in uniform in Iraq) for not having adjusted fast enough to the counterinsurgency fight. I almost scream in frustration when I think of the discussions I have endured over the years in the Australian military about whether we should have a heavy or a light force. The experience of Fallujah taught me that whatever the force is, it must be able to fight in a modern conflict with what it has and it must be able to adapt faster than its opponent. In Iraq, in the second year of the war, the US military was adapting from being the best conventional force in the history of warfare into a counterinsurgency force. But then, in Fallujah in November 2004, they were required to adapt back again and conduct a traditional conventional assault on a city for a counterinsurgency objective.

They did so wonderfully. There were exceptions, of course. Some individuals could not adjust from the three-block war mentality and used too much or too little firepower, but my observation was that the dovetailing of the army's 'heavy' forces with the Marines' 'light' forces worked superbly in Fallujah, as it had in Najaf a few months before. Yet for the millions in the world who gained their knowledge of the war from the media, the courageous and moral actions of thousands of these troops were overlooked. A video of one US Marine shooting a wounded enemy gave this battle its enduring image. But it was ever thus.

Just before I left Iraq, in March 2005, I accompanied my civil affairs staff on one of their regular Monday visits to the Reconstruction Council meeting in Fallujah. We flew down to Camp Fallujah without incident, escorted by two Cobra gunships. Our convoy, a few Hummers and some trucks with the Marine protection element, prepared for the short trip from the camp to the town.

In the balmy spring sun, I leant on the side of the armoured Hummer, enjoying the warmth with my helmet off, only the weight of my body armour and my pistol and ammunition reminding me that I was in a war zone. After months of operations-room gloom, I felt I had emerged from the dark.

My musing was disturbed by the commander of the Marine security detachment, a lieutenant, who apologised that the convoy would be delayed because two of the vehicles had flat tyres. I had already seen the crews unload the vehicles and begin working on the offending wheels. I was in no hurry.

The lieutenant really just wanted to talk, and I was happy to listen. He'd heard Australians were in his convoy and was keen to get to know us. This was the start of his third tour in Iraq, including the invasion. Each tour was about six or seven months long. On leave before returning to Iraq this time, he and a friend from Okinawa had arranged to fly to Australia for a holiday, travelling on one of the US military aircraft that regularly cross the Pacific to the Australian Air Force base at Richmond, just west of Sydney. His mate had to pull out of the trip at the last minute, but the lieutenant decided to go by himself.

He had arrived in the middle of the night at Richmond, about 40 kilometres from the Harbour Bridge and the Opera House. In the dark, he walked the few kilometres from the airbase to the local suburban railway station and waited for the new day's first train to Sydney. On the train he met an Australian couple who put him in touch with another couple living in a Sydney beachside suburb. He stayed with them for a few days. He then met an Australian girl who had her own flat at another Sydney beachside suburb, and spent the remainder of his leave with her. As he chatted for a few minutes with me, or moved up and down the convoy encouraging the soldiers in their work or ensuring security was tight, like hundreds of thousands of other young men in Iraq, foreigners or Iraqis, his mind was on the job, his body was with his men, but sometimes his heart was a long way away.

My mind should have been more on the job too, because having spoken to this young Marine, I got back into the Hummer and managed to inflict a wound on myself — on my body, but much more on my pride. I always checked that the combat lock on the Hummer door stayed unlocked, because a very common cause of premature death was being trapped inside a vehicle on fire or in water. In checking the lock as I got into the vehicle, I managed to jam my thumb. On the scale of injuries in Iraq it was non-existent, but it hurt like crazy. I offered a quiet obscenity and sat in the back seat with my precious blood pouring from my thumb. Then, to preserve the relative cleanliness of my body armour, I did what was natural — I put my thumb into my mouth to stop the blood going everywhere. As I did this, the US driver, the vehicle commander and the machine gunner, who had not seen the sacrifice I had just made for the Iraqi people, all turned around to welcome me into their vehicle.

What they saw was a foreign two-star general sitting in their vehicle with a pissed-off look, sucking his thumb. Much to the mirth of my bodyguard, this was passed around the convoy radio network at the speed of light.

We arrived at the meeting hall in the old government centre, near what was called the 'Pizza Slice', a wedge-shaped city block. Here there had once been a restaurant I'd suspected of being a foreign fighter staging post. We had watched this restaurant for weeks before hitting it one night after all the staff had gone home and it was likely that there were only foreign fighters present, sleeping the night. The hit did not set off any secondary explosions that might have indicated that it was being used to store munitions, but it burnt fiercely. I would have liked to go and see the ruins in person, but that would have risked not only my life, but the lives of my bodyguard, and really exposed me as a tourist. I would spend a year in Iraq in this bizarre form of modern war, without ever seeing the results of my actions with my own eyes.

The weekly Fallujah Reconstruction Committee consisted of about 20 eminent Fallujans around a central table with others sitting along one side of the room, and a few of us coalition types watching from our side. The meeting was entirely run by the Iraqis and was translated for us by several shifts of coalition translators, dressed in US Army camouflage clothing. I still missed the great advantage of being able to speak the local language, as I had in Indonesia.

The meeting was delightfully mundane, parish-pump politics continually interrupted by the interpreters, who insisted on translating every single use of the common phrase 'In the name of God the most gracious, the most merciful', which peppers any Arabic conversation. As a result, the meeting crawled. At one stage the head of Iraqi Police, a major general, was giving his summary of the security situation in the preceding week. Again it was routine, but one incident had occurred: a bus on the outskirts of Fallujah was boarded by an armed insurgent group who checked papers and then got off. I noted that the police chief said that 'security in the city is 100 per cent', which may have been accurate but seemed to be tempting God, the most gracious, the most merciful.

However, I left that meeting with more positive than negative feelings about Fallujah. The people were returning and were looking to the future.

Prime Minister Allawi's successor, Ibrahim Jafari, often used the old saying, 'The tree of democracy is watered by blood', and Fallujans have made an abundant contribution to the watering of the tree. Between December 2004 and March 2005, 90,000 Fallujans voted with their feet and moved back into the city. In August 2005, the city had 180,000 citizens. Fallujah was, at that time, as secure a town as you could find in Iraq, and was self-governing.

After several weeks, Mosul also settled down and we were into the shaping operations and logistics of the election. The election had never left my consciousness during the frantic months since

September. Doing one hundred things at once, we had kept preparations for the election steaming along. Now we would launch into a series of military operations to lay the ground for the elections and build on our success in Fallujah. Without successful elections, the sacrifice of tens of thousands in places like Fallujah would be for nothing.

CHAPTER 10

'You vote and you die'

Iraq's first free election, January 2005

I had been responsible for planning our support for the election since May 2004 — by default. When my infrastructure security job had put me into daily contact with the civil affairs soldiers, they had brought to my attention how little planning was being done for security for the election. There were some great ideas around, but no real planning. So I'd put together a small planning team, of five US civil affairs majors and one or two Australians.

We were not the only people who had fallen behind. Just as with infrastructure security, the military at the lower levels were saying, 'We don't do elections.' They saw it as a civilian responsibility.

Yet wasn't the election our reason for being in Iraq? Everyone knew that to fight for the sake of fighting was pointless. Of course we would win every military fight. But if we were only in Iraq to kill terrorists, we would never win, because there would always be new terrorists. If we were going to win the war, we must turn insurgents into citizens with a stake in their own country. Politics was the way to do this, because politics is the main peaceful means of dealing with differences in any society. The role of the military in modern counterinsurgency is to protect the people and the political and economic processes, and that was why we were fighting in Iraq. We had lost about 900 US soldiers and many ordinary citizens since I had been in Iraq, and to then have a failed election because of a lack of organisation would have been unforgivable. This was recognised in our campaign plan, but had no real purchase yet at lower levels.

Successful elections were not only important to justify our sacrifice. If we had failed to reach this first of many political milestones, who knows if we could have held the coalition together throughout 2005; Iraq needed to conduct three elections to satisfy UN requirements, and delaying the first of them may have lost us at least a year in progress towards the other two. Our very legitimacy in Iraq was tied to the conduct of elections on an agreed timetable. If we had failed through sheer incompetence, our opponents would have claimed it as their victory.

The UN had given us the timetable. During the occupation from April 2003 to June 2004, the Iraqi people had been represented to the occupying powers by a Consultative Council appointed by the CPA. This was followed by the non-elected Iraqi Interim Government from July 2004 onwards, under Prime Minister Iyad Allawi. In the circumstances, and with hindsight, this was a remarkably successful government. The election that my majors and I were now considering was the first step in a delicate electoral ballet that had to be conducted in the midst of the equivalent of a bloody riot. A successful 30 January 2005 election would replace the appointed Iraqi Interim Government with a 275-member Iraqi Transitional Government. This government would then draft a constitution by mid-August 2005, and this would be put to the people by mid-October 2005 in a nationwide referendum, the equivalent of the second national vote. Having established their constitution, the transitional government would then run, by the last day of December 2005, a third national vote in eleven months. This election would produce Iraq's first 'normal' government, elected under its own approved constitution for a 'normal' period of time.

So the January election was the first step in defining the political life of the new Iraq. Some claimed it would also define the future of the Middle East and the world. Perhaps they will be proven correct over time, though certainly there seems to be no risk of democracy catching on in the Middle East in the short term. The significance of this election in Iraq was reflected in the pressure I was feeling from Washington through the US Embassy.

Since Iraq had emerged as a nation out of the carve-up of the Ottoman Empire after World War I, the pendulum of democracy had swung back and forth, until finally Saddam had taken over, running a state based on oppression and intimidation. In Saddam's Iraq, elections usually delivered a 99 per cent vote for him — so clearly elections do not equal democracy. I remembered a tongue-in-cheek comment made by an Indonesian military friend during Suharto's time when we were talking about computers, most of which at the time were under military control. Because of this, election results always went through the military. My friend joked that the Indonesian armed forces were so efficient in their use of computers that they knew the results of Indonesia's elections even before they had been held. Saddam was at least as efficient!

As we prepared, I continually stressed that Iraq was not going to become a democracy on 30 January; it was going to hold an election. This first step was going to be hard enough. We could hope that Iraq would become a democracy, but that would take time, and only the Iraqis could decide that.

History tells us that it takes decades, if not centuries, for people to acquire the habits of democracy. Iraq did not have centuries or decades, only half a year to organise an election. As good men and women tried to find a path to democracy, fixed firmly to their throats were insurgents and terrorists. We all knew it would not be force of arms, but the people of Iraq, plus the concept of democracy and time that would defeat the insurgency. Yet in the immediate future, our opponents were determined to throttle the democratic life out of Iraq by violent means. We were certainly going to have to fight our way to the election.

Back in May, between fights on the infrastructure, my team began educating me about the election. They sat me in front of charts and diagrams of extraordinary complexity and explained that the election would be conducted under a proportional representation system in which 7000 Iraqi candidates would run for office on more than a hundred 'slates', or party-like organisations. It was estimated that 14 million citizens were eligible to vote (Iraq's population was 27 million). They would need at least 5400 voting centres and the entire process would have to be staffed by 180,000 electoral workers. This monumental task was to be run by the Independent Electoral Commission of Iraq, the IECI. When my majors and I started planning, the IECI had nominated its eight commissioners and was training them overseas, but as an organisation it did not yet exist.

We were to plan how to provide the military security for an election. It is true that armies normally do not 'do' elections, but we could offer the IECI what no-one else could: the ability to plan and to make things happen, not just security. It was the Iraqis' election, but we could establish security around the vote itself, and around the recruiting and training of the 180,000 staff and the massive logistics. This was going to be a big task indeed.

Opinion polls had shown that a large majority of Iraqis wanted to vote. Consistently, 80 per cent in non-Sunni areas indicated their intention to vote (access to Sunni areas to conduct such polls was more difficult). But just because people had said they wanted to vote did not mean they would or indeed would be able to, and at this early stage I did not have an IECI organisation on the ground to reassure me. As a general, I am paid to worry constructively. The more I knew about the state of the planning, the more concerned I became. I was going to rely heavily on my small group of majors.

Australia is one of the few countries where attending a poll is compulsory and those who do not are fined. We consistently have 90 per cent-plus participation. Most countries have voluntary voting; their participation rate varies, but 60 per cent is not an uncommon turnout. In these countries, there must be some incentive to come out and vote: a sense of civic duty, a commitment to a party, a high dissatisfaction with the current government. In Iraq, voting was not compulsory. And because of the high level of violence in many parts of the country, the decision to leave your house could at any time be a life-and-death one. How, then, could candidates campaign? How could the people know what the parties were offering? How could you assemble an official list of voters, which is essential for any credible election?

We soon realised that the election was going to consume us for months, even if we only did the security. First, a voter list or electoral roll was needed. Then individual voters on that list needed to be registered, and then the list had to be put up to challenge. Somewhere there also needed to be a period of campaigning, a period of recruiting and training election workers, a period of logistic activity as ballot papers were distributed and booths set up, and then perhaps, an election day. And every step needed security.

General Casey asked me to give a presentation to the other generals, a 'show and tell' on the election. I wanted to bring the essential questions to the front of their minds. If it was at all feasible to conduct an election in the midst of violence, was there a level of violence beyond which an election would not be feasible? Would we have to smash the insurgency down to some acceptable level by January 2005 to allow Iraqis to vote on election day? If so, what was that level?

Other questions flowed from this. If there was only a very small turnout on the day, say 15 per cent of the 14 million Iraqis who were eligible to vote, could we say that the election had met an acceptable standard? Probably not. Would 50 or 60 per cent be acceptable? Probably yes. What if 50 or 60 per cent of the 14 million voted, but no Sunnis voted? Would that be an acceptable election? And what election-related activity could the coalition soldiers take part in without being accused of compromising the entire process — this was to be an Iraqi election run by Iraqis.

These were the big questions I considered for months in my spare time between fights in various cities and on the infrastructure, and there were no neat answers. Often, we thought we had answers, but as the election came closer, the answers changed. What I came to realise was that success would depend a lot on how many people voted and who they were.

Everyone assumed that most of the Shi'ite men and many of the Shi'ite women would vote, because the Shi'ites had been oppressed for years — they had the most to gain. Likewise, we all assumed that every eligible Kurd, man and woman, would vote, and probably in larger number than the Shi'ites because as a society they were smaller and very well organised.

Then there were the Sunnis. Their leadership, unlike the Shia leadership under the widely respected Grand Ayotollah Ali al-Sistani, was not centralised, so it was very difficult to talk to them as a group. What passed for their formal leadership, particularly at places such as the 'Mother of all Battles' Mosque in Baghdad, was essentially the local chapter of the insurgency. Although we knew that these clerics were part of the insurgent leadership, we could not touch them because the Allawi government, probably sensibly, was unwilling to risk alienating more moderate Sunnis. There had been strong indications that the Sunni rank and file were prepared to vote, but on the day, they were likely to do what their clergy told them to do.

Elements of the Sunni leadership had been saying that the non-participation of the Sunnis would invalidate the whole democratic process. 'Compromise with the Sunnis or risk the credibility of the election' was their line, direct or implied. The other 80 per cent of Iraqis wouldn't accept this menacing ultimatum. Ambassador Negroponte took a hard and courageous stand against this, stating publicly and frequently that 20 per cent of the population voluntarily removing themselves from the democratic process for their own reasons did not invalidate the votes of the other 80 per cent.

Our strategy was to work around this hurdle, and not to rush the Sunnis. January was the first of three elections for the year; Sunnis could ease into participation at some later time as long as the first step was successful. As individuals, Sunnis could run on non-Sunni slates. Sunnis could also be among the group that wrote the constitution even if not one Sunni voted. Whatever their participation rate in the first election (it turned out to be only 4 per cent), our hope was that it would increase in the second and third — and it did. We hoped that as they saw the benefits, and their clerics realised it was better to be part of a process that was working — and that was inevitable — their participation would increase. Our aim was not to confront them now, but to show them that democracy was the way of the future.

One of my greatest challenges, which I recognised from well before the 'show and tell', would be to keep the division commanders in step with election preparations while they were in continual combat. The election, of course, was not their immediate concern. My job was to ensure that, when they finally did focus on the election, everything would be ready. The division commanders, being busy men, did have an unfortunate habit of not reading what was prepared for them about the election. Then, feeling that they were unaware of preparations, they would complain to Casey that we were not producing anything for them. Casey would then come back to me and ask why we were not doing anything for the division commanders. I responded by simplifying my election updates into a regular bulletin, and making sure these got to the complaining generals. The commanders then complained that I was treating them like idiots and giving them too much information! Adopting my best submissive attitude, I just kept on doing what I could, confident that at some stage these busy guys would realise that the election was serious. Such is the life of a humble staff officer. I wonder if I was such a prig as a division commander. My ex-chief of staff at the 1st Division assures me that I was!

The election machinery started to grow around us. The IECI commissioners came back from their overseas training. The UN advisers turned up. The non-Iraqi staff were hired — there were some Australians among them in key positions. The Iraqi staff appeared, organised offices and began compiling lists of voters.

Suddenly a monster of an organisation was mushrooming around us, and we had to link into it at every level. Many in the IECI were inherently hostile to the military. Our principal link to the IECI was Squadron Leader Jim Xinos, an Australian Air Force officer embedded in the US Civil Affairs unit and working as a liaison officer with the IECI. Jim spent all of his six-month tour ensuring that what we were doing and what the IECI were doing were aligned, and he was able to win the trust of the IECI and positively influence their (and our) actions.

I had to assess how much security the elections needed. How many troops would we need on the streets, and how many would we be able to get? If there were not enough, what was our Plan B? We realised from the start that the close-in protection of the polling stations had to be done by Iraqi troops. Otherwise it would be said that the foreign coalition had rigged the elections. But when I first started planning, nothing like sufficient numbers of Iraqis had even been recruited, much less trained.

Even at best, we anticipated having only about ten Iraqi troops or police at each of the 5400 polling stations. This was the age-old counterinsurgency conundrum: we had to create security everywhere, but the insurgents only needed to pick a handful of places to concentrate their forces and create mayhem. We could not fortify each polling station with sandbags, razor wire and obstacles — no-one was going to come out with their family to vote in a bunker. Were we going to have to defend the area around each polling station from mortars, which might fly a few thousand metres, or from rockets, which might go many kilometres? Were all areas of Iraq likely to have the same level of threat and need the same level of security?

So, although it was no-one's preferred option, we had no choice but to use coalition troops. The question was, how close to the polling stations could we put them so that they could be available but not compromise the integrity of this Iraqi-run election? What were the other tools, such as population-control laws, that we might be able to use to help our soldiers on the ground? What was the worst thing the enemy could do to us on election day and how could we counter it? Most of this we did not know, and there were some things we could not know until the event itself.

Given that we couldn't literally 'defend' every polling station against every threat, we had to create a security environment where a small number of soldiers and police could handle an immediate problem. So our security strategy for the election was simple: beat the enemy down before the election, have a small number of Iraqi troops at the polling stations with more capable coalition troops in close proximity, and exercise population-control measures.

Four to six weeks before 30 January, after Fallujah, the Corps began to focus specifically on the election. Nothing in Iraq ever stopped so that we could plan at leisure, and nothing was sequential. I used to say, as things spiralled around me, that if you cannot keep 100 balls in the air you are in the wrong game. We rolled out of the August combat against Shia militias in Najaf, into combat in Tal Afar and Samarra, then into Fallujah, and at the same time into operations in Mosul. We then launched into what we called the Ramadan offensive in November and December. Compared with this tempo, election day might have seemed to most coalition soldiers like a day off.

I would eventually have to hand over election security and logistics to the Corps, which had the troops and logistic units and controlled most of the Iraqi units. As the election approached, the question of when planning would cease and doing would begin became an issue. I was reluctant to hand over responsibility, because I felt the Corps were still absorbed by combat operations across Iraq. Perhaps I was more tired than I thought, but I made a wrong call. General Casey indicated, in less and less subtle ways, that he wanted the execution to start, and I disagreed. We faced off on this for a few days, but I have always been very good at accepting the inevitable and finally got the boss's message. When the chop in responsibility was made, the Corps was well into it and did not let anyone down.

We had already seen that we would be doing much more than election-day security. When I heard the size of the logistic effort that was going to be required, I was astounded. It was enormous. Among our reservists in civil affairs we were lucky to have a specialist in world air freight, who told us how many tonnes of election material were required. All of it was being manufactured and printed outside the country, all had to be flown into the country by cargo aircraft and disseminated by smaller aircraft, helicopters or trucks in the face of hostile action. The tonnage was translated into cargo jet loads, and again I was staggered. The insurgents didn't need to bomb polling stations; they could wreck the elections by going after truckloads of ballot papers. Once again we went into a planning huddle. The IECI were not on top of it, but we felt sure they would call on us eventually, and when they did, we had to be ready.

I assessed that the worst threats to election day itself were car bombs, mortars and rockets, in that order. To stop the car bombs, we increased our focus on searching for manufacturing sites and restricted the enemy's ability to move the car bombs to their targets by increasing the numbers of roadblocks and patrols. We gave the highest priority for our night-time strike activities to car bomb makers, and had some success. To combat mortars and rockets, we saturated likely launch areas, or 'boxes', with ground troops and helicopters. Controlling the threat early was the key. If there was carnage early on election day, even at a small number of polling stations, a willing media would carry it into people's homes and no Iraqi in their right mind would come out to vote for the rest of the day.

The division commanders, for all their complaining, picked up the ball at the right time and focused on making it all work on the day. As commanders they were brilliant, and it inspired me to see what they achieved. They were assisted in no small part by Australian Major Matt Jones in the Corps headquarters. Matt had achieved, and deserved, such a level of trust at the Corps that he was responsible for all their election preparations.

At one stage, about six weeks from election day, when I was thinking about little else, I received a call from a colonel at the office of the Secretary of Defense in Washington.

'I have been asked to give you a call,' he said, 'to find out what you guys are doing in relation to assisting the Iraqis to run this election.'

By this stage, of course, we had helped the IECI plan the elections, we had provided security to the process of compiling the voter rolls, we had fought in Fallujah to ensure the election could be held, we were running the logistics, we had just started operations in the Upper Euphrates to halt the flow of arms and foreign fighters into Baghdad, and we were about to run the first of the rock drills that would complete the coordination. I was amused that someone in the SECDEF's office was just now focusing on the election. I knew that Rumsfeld himself was up on everything that was going on, as I had heard Casey brief him, so this query must have been coming from his junior staff.

Deciding to have a bit of fun, I replied, 'What election?'

I strung this poor colonel along for several minutes, saying I'd have to find someone who knew who was responsible for the election in our headquarters.

'Now when is it again?' I asked innocently. I could feel the colonel's tension increase as he imagined that he or his military superior would have to tell the SECDEF that no-one in MNF-I had done anything about the election.

'I tell you what, I'll find a name you can speak to, and get him to send you an email,' I said.

Beneath my mad mischief, I was a little incensed. However, in the first line of the email, I apologised to the colonel, admitting that I was responsible, then listed what we had already achieved. I subsequently heard from an Australian in the SECDEF's office that I'd sent ripples up and down the Pentagon corridors, something I had not expected to achieve in my time in Iraq.

At the start of December, I was very worried. For some reason, the election preparations were just not working at the Iraqi end. Something was seriously wrong in Baghdad.

The dysfunction of the Iraqi Interim Government was readily apparent. Coordinating the diverse ministries was a nightmare. The Ministry of Food held the only reliable population list, on which the electoral rolls were based. They also owned the food warehouses from which we wanted to disseminate the tonnes of voting equipment. The Ministry of Education owned the schools that we wanted to use as polling centres. The Ministry of the Interior owned the police. The Ministry of Defence nominally owned the army troops, although most had been passed to the Corps, so we felt assured that they would be in place. Of course Defence had to be in the process, because they were Defence and this was Iraq. The US and the UK embassies were vitally interested because they had invested lives and money in this country. There were also many intelligence bodies, some Iraqi, some US and some UK. The only thing we did not have in this mix of 'stakeholders' was journalists, and we might have had a few of them for all I knew. And from my experience of working with the oil and electricity ministries, we would definitely have insurgent spies inside any group we put together.

Major General Ayden Khaled Qadir, a policeman in the emerging Iraqi force, had been nominated to run the election security. Ayden was my counterpart in Iraq, and despite not sharing a common language, we had become friends. He had been attacked several times while going about his duties, once when I had insisted that he come into the Green Zone for a meeting. I'd felt very guilty ever since. I had helped him get accommodation for his family, and he now lived in a humble house in the Green Zone. I had sponsored him to get a pass that meant he could come through one of the faster entry lanes, so that he did not get ambushed waiting in line. He was one of the few Iraqis I met who had never served in Saddam's army.

But as 2004 drew to a close we had a problem. Ayden had ceased to communicate with the other parties who were going to make the election occur. It was becoming apparent that he and his officers lacked the confidence, and some of the skills, to perform their task. They were not protecting the election mechanisms being established around the country by the IECI: the testing of the electoral rolls; the recruiting and training of electoral workers; and the start of the election logistics. Iraqis had been killed and election facilities bombed. The police were either not doing their job, or doing it for a day or so and then disappearing, leaving the facilities and people vulnerable. The enmity between the police and the IECI was now palpable, and it threatened the whole election.

Whatever was going on, I had to get everyone talking again. We had already made a significant contribution. Over the last few months, we had planned in excruciating detail, offered those plans to the IECI, and adjusted the plans under their direction. The IECI were polite enough to be grateful, and recently we sensed a mellowing of the anti-military bias among some of the IECI staff, assisted by Jim Xinos working in their midst. They were now prepared to take up any offer of assistance, realising they were not able to do it themselves in the time available. And then, in accordance with the principle that this was an Iraqi election, we had stepped back to see what the Iraqis and the IECI would do.

But now, in the crucial last weeks, I saw that nothing much was happening. We did not have time to be gentle. At this stage in December, the Iraqi agencies were not speaking to each other, let alone working together. I discussed this with General Casey earlier, and he had spoken to the government, but that seemed to have been ineffective. We had decided not to act at that stage, but now January was approaching and there was still no progress, and time was running out. At General Casey's direction, I set up a coordinating body that we called the Iraqi Election Execution Committee.

Committees are not the most exciting of God's creations, but they can serve a purpose. This committee had a simple brief: make the election work, and do it quickly. Everyone was represented, from the various government ministries to the intelligence agencies, the coalition military, the embassies and the IECI. I directed that it meet twice a week. Steve Hashem, who ran the civil affairs unit, had been allocated a South Korean colonel, and tasked him to head up his election section. The colonel's name was In-Bum Chun, and his appointment was to prove one of Steve's best moves. It was very difficult to seize or be given authority in this cross-cultural environment, and even harder to project your personality through an interpreter. Colonel Chun was able to do this better than most; all he needed was some cover from above.

Amid the logjam, I visited one of the committee's routine meetings in a small and noisy conference room at the Ministry of the Interior building, just on the edge of the Green Zone. My bodyguard and Steve Gliddon, my new executive officer (he had replaced Steve Summersby), got me there with their normal efficiency, and I went in.

It was absolutely packed with participants and spectators. It was normal that the staff who had worked on an issue would sit around the walls, back from the main meeting table where the principals sat, so they would not have to be re-briefed later. The result was that many meetings became very crowded. In a headquarters atmosphere, where meetings are everything, those who worked on issues for long hours wanted to see the results of their work. Some meetings could be great sport. It could be more fun to watch your boss grapple intellectually with your issue than it was to be working in some hot rat-hole in the bowels of an ungrateful headquarters.

At this committee meeting, though, the crowds were there but the principals were not. It was a circus. The room was stinking hot, the noise from inside and outside was a babble, and the antagonism was boiling over. Colonel Chun, chairing the meeting, was doing his best, but things had seriously stalled. No decisions were being made, not even simple bureaucratic ones.

I am not very good at committees at the best of times. I was continually tired in Iraq, and therefore even less disposed to waste my time and everyone else's on pointless meetings. But this was the only group of stakeholders we had and, because this was an Iraqi election run by Iraqis, I did not have the option of dismissing the committee and taking over. So after observing most of the meeting, I took Colonel Chun aside for a quiet word.

We came back in, and I made an announcement. With Colonel Chun's agreement, I would now chair the committee. I said that the next meeting would be tomorrow and I had something very important to announce, so the principals had to be there. As I spoke, Ali, an Iraqi who had been my interpreter for most of the time I had been in Iraq, took over from a UK Embassy interpreter who had been struggling to do the entire meeting. Ali was a fine young man and all of us in the Australian group loved him greatly, but his English was not good and his ability as an interpreter was not even as good as his limited English. He was a dentist who had been trained in Jordan. As an interpreter, he was probably a very good dentist. But we would not have exchanged him for anyone even if we had a choice — which we did not, because even barely competent interpreters were scarce.

So there was absolutely no guarantee that anyone at the meeting understood a word I said. But they would have picked up my attitude. Having made the announcement, I left to try to figure out how we could make this all work.

Virtually on election eve, we faced two enormous problems: first, no-one trusted anyone else; and second, no-one in the room believed elections were actually doable. As a result, no-one was prepared to take any risks, even moderate risks, or make any commitments. There was no sense of pride in how far we had come, and no sense of purpose about what lay ahead for the Iraqis if we could just get through this gate.

The IECI staff were as bad as anyone. As they were the key players, this was serious. Dr Adil Al-Lami, the Chief Electoral Officer, was being advised by some young non-Iraqi advisers who distrusted everything we or the Iraqi military and police did. Ultimately I think they grew to trust us, and Dr Adil proved over time to be a true man of independent mind, but at this stage he did not know how much faith he could have in us. The police, from

Major General Ayden down, were terrified that we would force them onto the streets to be slaughtered. The army always believed they should be running the election, and were not going to be told what to do by the police, whom they despised. Mind you, the police were too scared to ever tell the army what to do. The Ministry of Food was not going to put its warehouses at risk just for some concept of democracy that it neither believed in nor understood. And the Ministry of Education was extremely reluctant to risk the lives of its teachers and the existence of its schools for what it worried might be a passing fad of 'freedom'. The Iraqi intelligence agencies implied that they knew something about everyone, so no-one was willing to say much when they were around. And the UK and US embassy reps sat against the wall and simply watched, accompanied by a raft of spectators who loved a bit of public drama. The spirit of the Iraqi people had been beaten down by Saddam's heavy hand, and this was the result.

Over the next 24 hours I pulled myself away from whatever else was concerning me, sat down with my staff and talked with whoever I could. Colonel Chun assembled a list and timetable of urgent actions. I contacted all the principals and told them they must be at the meeting or I would complain directly to Prime Minister Allawi or to my newfound ally in a dozen things, the overwhelmingly effective Deputy Prime Minister Barhem Saleh.

At the appointed time the next day, I arrived at the meeting. Word had got around to all the staffs that there was likely to be even more sport today than normal. So the small room was packed, not just with the principals, all of whom were there, but also with every staff officer around the headquarters who had a passing contact with election preparation. The room was already stinking hot and the noise was substantial.

I looked at this for a moment, then walked around the room asking each person who they were and why they were here. Ninety per cent I threw out. Some argued. Most went quietly. Slowly but surely I got the room under control and we were down to the principals around the table and about five observers: one each from the US and UK embassies, the head of the election section in the Corps, and one or two others. I then left Steve Gliddon outside with my bodyguard to keep the noise down.

The room could now see that I meant business and had some authority. I told everyone I would chair every meeting from now on. I asked Colonel Chun to go through the agenda. We had everything written in Arabic and in English, and we passed out both copies. We had diagrams, timetables and a list of actions in both languages. On the agenda was every issue we needed to cover to get the show back on the road.

I got everyone to reintroduce him or herself (the UK Embassy representative was a civilian woman), then I made a speech. I remember thinking that I needed to say something inspiring now, and I had a go at it, but Ali was still interpreting, so much of the effect was probably lost. But what I did get across was that the night before, in a car bomb attack in Anbar province, we had lost a substantial number of soldiers. I played on this, the sacrifice, feeling overly dramatic but keeping the sentences very short for Ali's sake. I reminded these Iraqis how much they had suffered, feeling it was pretentious, at the very least, to be telling any Iraqi about suffering.

'We have invested the lives of our children in this country,' I said quietly, with Ali probably mangling the translation behind me. 'The biggest weapon that we have against the terrorists is this election. The election must work. No-one will stop it working. We will not fail through not trusting each other.' I then spent some time talking about how we would make it work, hoping to create confidence in its achievability and value. This election was worth dying for, and people had already died for it. It sounded a bit corny, but I was getting the nods around the table that I wanted. Ali was keeping up, and every now and again others would assist him by adding a word or two in Arabic.

I asked Dr Adil to speak. He deferred to his English-speaking adviser, who laid down the problem as they saw it. Mainly, they were worried that there was not enough security provided for the election infrastructure they were building up around the country, and for the newly recruited staff in the regions. The adviser described in some detail and with great passion one regional electoral office that had police protection, but then the police left, and gunmen arrived and killed some of the volunteers.

This was emotional stuff. Dr Adil jumped in and accused Ayden's police of not doing their job. I cut this off quickly and got Ayden to answer specific criticisms. He finally accepted responsibility for election security but pointed out that he had the responsibility but no authority, and was going to be blamed when security failed — not to mention his larger worry, that he and many of his policemen might be killed. Once we deployed his police, he said, 'Who will feed them and pay them? If they are not fed and paid, we might be able to deploy them initially, but they will go home after two or three days because they have no food or money to buy food.'

I got Ayden to agree to get a plan up within a few days. We already had it written and I knew he would accept it. But would the IECI accept the plan? 'Yes,' they said, 'that was all we were asking for.'

'We will do it,' I said. 'Let's move on to the next issue.'

Over the next three hot and tiring hours we went through every issue. Most were between the police and everyone else. My staff took notes and made up a 'to do' list that I could later work my way through with all concerned. I kept each conversation quick. No enmity was allowed, no raised voices. By the end of the meeting, everyone could at least see that things might happen, that someone was in charge and that I was committed to making the election work. There was still no trust, little commitment and very little belief, but we had made a fresh start.

After two or three meetings, we began to achieve results. Ayden's boss, Interior Minister Falah Hasan al-Naqib, was willing to do anything except provide actual assistance. He confirmed Ayden's authority but was reluctant to pay a stipend to the police so that they could buy themselves meals. I also proposed to Naqib that we pay each deployed policeman a 'democracy bonus' as an incentive to keep them on the streets at the critical time. But he procrastinated until it was too late. After the election, when things had gone well, he decided to pay them a very small amount, which I regarded as an insult. There was not much enthusiasm for this election from some elements at the political level, as well as at the working level.

To raise confidence, Ayden and I put together a complete plan for election security which he presented to the committee. When the committee members saw the plan, they started to shift from mild interest to vague commitment. They began to think the election might just be achievable. I tried the same thing with the education ministry to get them to join the fight, but failed. So I went directly to Deputy Prime Minister Saleh, who achieved exactly what I wanted by sheer force of personality. We invited the IECI's logistics contractor onto the committee as the election date approached, and started to hear the full range of his problems as well.

Once we began to achieve some goals, the attitude of the key people, quite predictably, changed. The IECI grew to trust us, particularly when I passed along to the commissioners some intelligence we'd received that an attempt was to be made on their lives. We changed their routine, increased the number of weapons their bodyguards carried, and provided money to hire more bodyguards. The commissioners were given an adviser to organise their personal security, through whom we passed intelligence. Their bodyguards, normally members of their family, cousins and uncles, were given some training. The insurgents' plot had been to ambush them at the entrance to the Green Zone, so we quickly got them entry passes and started surveillance measures against suspect individuals. The trust built.

A year later, I introduced myself to a diplomat at a Canberra social function. On hearing my name, the diplomat said: 'I know you. You ran the election committee in Iraq and threw everyone out and then made it all work. I read it all through our diplomatic cables coming back in from our embassy in Baghdad.' I felt pleased, but a little bit cautious. It is like checking who is at the far end of a video conference before you get too outspoken. You cannot be too careful!

Rescuing the election process required more than just the constant massaging of everyone's ego and the constant reinforcing of success. Every now and again, it required a short, sharp word to quieten those who just wanted to hear the sound of their own voice, or who did not want to work with the others. It also required a significant dedication to the task, at least during daylight hours. This still left the rest of my 20-hour day to run the war.

At this time, Lieutenant General Abdul Kadr, an Iraqi tank officer, was the leader of the new Iraqi Army and was determined that his troops would vote. He alerted us to a problem that we were all too busy to notice. Given how busy his troops would be on election day, how would they be able to vote?

I took his query to our committee. Many in the IECI hadn't overcome their deep suspicion of any military, particularly the Iraqi military. When I raised the issue, they were unwilling to allow Iraqi soldiers to vote on 29 January, the day before the election. They decreed that soldiers were like anyone else and had to vote on election day. This effectively disenfranchised large parts of the army, because the soldiers were invariably protecting polling stations where they were not registered as voters. I failed to change the IECI's mind.

When I told Abdul Kadr, he asked if he could come to our committee to try personally to change the decision. Abdul Kadr was a tall man, and on his new Iraqi Army uniform he proudly wore the old Saddam-era badge of the armoured corps. I had first met him in the office of another senior Iraqi officer only eight months before when he was a brigadier general, and he occupied nothing more than a desk behind the door. His superior introduced us and told me what a fine officer Abdul Kadr was and how, as a tank commander, he had survived the destruction of many tanks in combat.

Since then Abdul Kadr had overtaken his former superior, and was now highly valued. He had spent some time as the military commander in Fallujah but was now back in Baghdad as the army commander.

In an impassioned plea, Abdul Kadr said he was 60 years old, the commander of the new Iraqi Army and a lieutenant general in a country about to embrace democracy, yet he had never voted in his entire life. He argued that if you wanted true democracy in Iraq, and if you wanted your soldiers to see themselves as citizens before they saw themselves as soldiers, you had to let the soldiers vote. Abdul Kadr reminded the committee that even civilian remand prisoners would be able to vote.

'Do not deny my soldiers the right to vote and have them end up like me, 60 years old and having never voted,' Abdul Kadr pleaded.

The IECI rejected his plea, but — such was the way of things in Iraq — apologised to him with great regret.

This episode made me stop and think. I had been moving at one thousand miles an hour now for the better part of a year, and had not realised just how far Iraq had come in a very short time. The invasion had ended in April 2003. Looting had occurred for a few months. Then the insurgency had to be faced. The occupation had ended in June 2004 and the UN, Iraq and the coalition had agreed on this pathway to a democratic future. The election we now faced was the culmination of it all. And here was a practical, albeit bizarre, example of progress. Perhaps for the first time in Iraq, a general, the head of the Iraqi Army, had pleaded with a civilian committee for something, and then had accepted its decision, even though that decision went against him.

Our police security plan won the Iraqi cabinet's approval. In the committee, we were seeing results. Once the plan was approved, I wrote and had translated an order for Ayden to send out to all police and military units across Iraq. I offered it to Ayden. But by this time, his confidence was growing and he had the taste of both responsibility and authority — he had already written his own order, and it was more culturally appropriate than mine. It was published across the nation.

As the election got closer, we were meeting daily, and were solving significant problems each time. Members got into the rhythm of making decisions without referring back to anyone and without minutes or records. I missed only a few meetings and most of the principals were attending most of them. Every now and again there would even be a bit of humour in the meeting, but overall it was serious business. We received regular reports about election workers and police being killed, buildings blown up, and employees kidnapped. I had been in Iraq for almost a year now, and was surprised by nothing. If there was any humour in the meetings, it was often focused on Ali. Someone who knew the words would cut in on his interpreting, or one of the intelligence people who spoke good English would take over for a time. Once someone got up on Ali stumbled along, made him sit down in a chair and treated him like a child, much to his embarrassment.

But we got things done and Colonel Chun ruled the agenda like a warlord, crushing anyone who drifted off focus, and always producing an action sheet at meeting's end. If someone had not finished what they said they would do, or what we had asked them to do, there was a good-natured ribbing or a stern word of disapproval. Colonel Chun would report to me late each night with the results and the proposals for the next day. Slowly, others in the committee took responsibility and the momentum started to build, and ultimately it became an Iraqi committee truly run by Iraqis for the future of Iraq. In weeks, the Iraqi spirit had re-emerged. It was a great feeling to undo a little piece of Saddam's evil.

In the last weeks, things came together. We had established a voter list with 14 million names on it. We had tested it and offered it up for public challenge. We had printed and constructed tonnes of ballot material overseas and assembled it in distribution points in neighbouring countries, then flown it in and distributed it by road across the country. We protected the IECI, using Iraqi troops and police, as they employed and trained 180,000 election workers. We were far from perfect in everything we did, but our failure rate was acceptable. We had helped the Iraqis put their face on the election and complied with the IECI's delicate unwritten rules. With only a few days to go, we deployed the Iraqi Police and soldiers to their locations. Some had gone home after a day or so, but they were now back and looked like staying in place. We were helping to feed and support them, and our troops were backing them up with quick reaction forces and anti-rocket and mortar patrols, giving them confidence to stand up to the insurgents. We had done our best to keep car bombers off the streets. We had driven down the insurgency to a point where, we hoped, the Iraqi forces could handle it on election day. We had removed the insurgent safe haven of Fallujah, among other operations across the length and breadth of the country. It appeared that we had fought our way to the election.

All we needed now were voters.

*

I was still determined to get one deception operation to work. In doing so, General Casey let me put together a small planning group, but insisted on retaining ultimate control.

Our idea was about eradicating car bombs, or at least convincing the insurgency that they had to use them before election day or miss their chance. We had limited their manufacture by securing Fallujah, among other operations, but we knew there were more out there, being stored in sheds or garages or workshops, waiting to be used against the voting stations.

Casey and I went to see Interior Minister Naqib to put to him certain aspects of our plan. We were subjected to one of Naqib's infamous meetings. Every issue but the one that needed discussion was raised, visitors unknown to us entered and left the office and were introduced and kissed on both cheeks, and a ten-minute meeting became a culturally sensitive three hours. When the crowd was reduced to a workable number, we moved from the outer office to the inner office and spoke to the minister about the way we might lessen the use of car bombs on election day.

This would require, I explained, a total ban on all but military and police vehicles across Iraq for election day and a few days before. This was a drastic measure for a nation of 27 million, but Naqib took the proposal to the cabinet, which agreed. Ostensibly, the aim was to prevent the use of car bombs on election day, but our real aim was to force our enemies into setting them off earlier. They would have to move the cars into place before the ban, so giving us a greater chance of intercepting them. Extending the total vehicle ban over several days also fed into a general view that the election might be called early. It all meant that attack squads would have to move near voting stations days before the poll, thus increasing their vulnerability.

The plan was complicated and its success would be difficult to assess, but we were able to detect the early movement of insurgents into the cities from surrounding towns a full week before the election, and we stopped some of them. They did detonate an abnormal number of car bombs a few days before the election, causing carnage in certain areas, but I cannot remember one car bomb going off on election day itself.

The night before the election, I was asked to brief Ambassador Negroponte. Both he and Casey had moved from the palace rotunda, which was assessed as vulnerable, to a more protected part of the palace, but they still occupied offices opposite each other. They were further away from the operations centre now so it took me longer to get there. It was the first time I had visited this new centre of power. Jim Jeffrey was there, as was the embassy staff member who was responsible for monitoring election preparations. I assumed I was being asked to brief because later that evening Negroponte would be speaking to President Bush.

After exchanging pleasantries, we got down to business. The Ambassador was up to speed, having been well briefed by his own staff, who had attended every meeting of the Election Execution Committee. He then surprised me by asking if I was confident.

I hadn't thought about it. Confidence was not an issue; we had no choice — we were into this and it was going to occur. I replied that despite what we had achieved, there was no way anyone could know whether the election would work. We could not predict if the enemy would smash enough polling stations early enough to deter people from voting. I said that the last thing we wanted was images of mortar and rocket fire carried by the world media, or the smell of burning rubber, benzene and flesh from car bombs. But my biggest uncertainty was over the Iraqi Army and Police: would they stay on the streets? I repeated my view that if our enemies had not made a significant impact by about mid-morning, it may be too late for them to deter voters.

I didn't speak like this to shock Negroponte; it was merely how things happened in Iraq. This was a man who knew the ways of the world, so he was not fazed. The four of us spoke of a few other things, the visit ended and Steve led me on the long journey back to my office.

Privately, that night, I was feeling deeply anxious: about what specifically, I did not know. It was my normal feeling just before big activities. I tried to console myself that there was nothing else I could do. It was around this time that the two large rockets I referred to previously came through the roof of our building and hit a room only a few metres from the operations centre. It was an ominous start to election day, and it reinforced the humming undertone of paranoia I lived with for the whole year in Iraq.

Having got this far, I now had to run election day itself. I had long been dissatisfied with our slow information movement in an age when the media worked directly via satellite. Since Fallujah, we had been regularly turning information around within Casey's one-hour deadline. But on election day, if we took some heavy hits in the morning, the quick spread of bad or inaccurate news could keep Iraqis at home and ruin the entire project.

I decided to try a system of positive reporting. All levels would send situation reports on the hour, every hour, to the strategic level. They were to be 'sound bite' reports mentioning positive and negative issues; if we wanted more, we would come back and ask.

When I proposed this, you would have thought I was asking the Corps to sell their children. The controversy went up and down the chain of command for some days — not from the commanders, but from their staffs. I had directed a rehearsal of the reporting system several days out; predictably, it failed. I raised this to commander level, starting with Casey and then contacting each of the key commanders across the country, impressing on each the importance

of the reporting in 'converting tactical success to strategic victory' —
Erv Lessel would have been proud of me. We tried it again and the
response was better; then we did a third rehearsal and it worked well.
Their initial reluctance reflected the fact that the closer soldiers are
to the fighting, the less interested they are in the information war.
But information flow, on this day, was no afterthought. It stood right
in the centre of our strategy.

January 30, election day, was cold but clear. We had worried about
snowfalls in the mountainous Kurd lands, because they might stop
people leaving their homes in this predominantly secure and safe
area. Luckily, the snow held off.

The clouds also held off across the rest of Iraq, so our drones
would be fully effective. The first report we got in the operations
centre was drone video of long lines forming all over the country,
beginning in some areas up to an hour before the polling stations
opened (they opened at 0730). The next report was of mortars being
fired near a booth in Baghdad, but casualties were low and a quick
reaction force moved against the enemy. At 0630 I received the first
of my hourly reports, which was comfortingly boring, and by 0730
things were still looking good. By 0830, a number of incidents had
occurred but nothing disastrous, and I began to feel that we might
have a victory here. By 0930 there were more incidents. One of our
snipers had killed some insurgents who set up mortars in front of his
hiding place. He shot them dead before they could fire.

For some reason — and this astounds me to this day — I had not
considered the threat from vest suicide bombers: individuals who
hide explosives in a vest under their clothes and enter a polling
centre. The first vest suicide bomber report came in about 1030, or
perhaps 1130, and despite my surprise, my first thought was: 'Too
late, you've missed your chance.' If they had really wanted to make an
impact, the enemy should have used the suicide bomber at 0730.

Throughout the early afternoon, the vest bomber reports came in thick and fast, but they were not stopping the voting. I saw on our media screen a shot of family groups walking to vote in Baghdad — fathers, mothers and children — as though it was anything but the most dangerous city in the world.

Once again the majority of the violence was limited to the central four provinces of the Sunni triangle. The other 14 provinces, mainly Kurdish or Shi'ite, were quiet enough. We had a running count of the incidents, and while the count was high, the voters were not deterred. But in Iraq it was what you did not see and know that got you, so I was still worried. There were no cars around because we had banned them, so the roads were being used as playgrounds; soccer was the most popular game. We spied on these games through our drones or heard about them through the breathless media reports. Anbar province was ominously empty of voters. The Sunni clerics had prevailed, and the Marines' excellent and innovative work to get election workers in and allow people to vote was being rewarded with minimal participation.

By mid-afternoon I was cautiously optimistic. The operations room was crowded as people came and went. We started to discuss whether we would get an acceptable participation rate, but there was no way we could make any estimate yet. The Sunnis had stayed away in droves but the Kurds had voted to a man and woman. The Shi'ites seemed to have reacted to a fatwa that al-Sistani had put out saying that it was the religious duty of every Shi'ite man and woman to vote, but it was still hard to get an overall feel. The polls closed at 1730 but some had such large numbers still demanding to vote that they stayed open. Our hourly reports told us about the closing of the polling stations, the securing of the ballots and the start of the first count. Most media reports were comforting, but they knew less than we did. I was amazed to hear that even the BBC had said something positive about the war. Once again I was feeling good — which put me on edge.

It was at this stage that I received our first report that something had happened to an aircraft north of Baghdad. I decided not to phone the boss until I'd heard some more. The next report said two Hercules transports were missing. Air traffic control was saying it had them on radar but lost them soon after they took off heading for Balad, a short distance north of Baghdad. Then we heard that the two aircraft were British C-130s. I rang General Casey and passed the information to CENTCOM and the Joint Staff in Washington, emphasising that the reports were still unconfirmed. We set all the normal systems up and found that it was faster to get a heliborne quick reaction force from the Marines in Anbar than from Baghdad, so the Corps activated that even though we did not yet have a location.

Two aircraft, the reports said, and big ones. Someone must know more. I moved drones from looking at the election to searching for the crash site, and soon we found the wreckage of one aircraft. What about the second? For more than an hour now the reports had consistently said two aircraft. A transiting helicopter reported smoke in an area that was different from the confirmed crash site and could feasibly have been the second. I moved another Predator to try to find the smoke. More details came through. Every now and again I got the election cell to give me a quick update; things were still going okay.

Finally, our control tower confirmed that only one C-130 had departed at the time in question, but we continued to get disturbing reports from multiple sources that there had been two aircraft and that the second crash site had been seen, or heard, or even found. There was only one aircraft we could find out anything about, but strangely enough, when I left the operations centre just before midnight, about six hours after the crash, we had just received another report about the mysterious second C-130.

The first aircraft was, tragically, very real. I saw the Predator video showing us the wreckage and watched on the Blue Force Tracker as the quick reaction force built up around the crash site. The British C-130 had taken off from Baghdad for Balad with its crew and, I think, one passenger in an aircraft that could carry 60. Because Balad is so close to Baghdad, it had not climbed to height, instead flying very low and very fast. By sheer bad luck, it passed over an enemy group who had RPGs; they fired one and apparently hit the C-130 in the wing root. The wing was ripped off and the aircraft hit the ground. All were killed. The insurgents were probably as surprised as we were.

I noticed that we'd had a report from an Apache helicopter pilot who traded fire with an enemy group in roughly that location early in the afternoon. I hoped for all our sakes that the information had been passed on to the C-130, but I doubted it. Securing the crash site took us the rest of the night and all the next day, and the investigation soon began. When I left Iraq two months later I had still not seen the formal results.

But overall it was a great day for Iraq, and generally this was recognised across the world. I could not believe the transformation of the Iraqi Army and Police. On this day, they had fought for their new country. In front of their own citizens and the critical gaze of the world, assisted by four to six weeks of direct coalition shaping operations, the Iraqi Security Forces defended election day against 260 attacks, a daily attack figure not exceeded until late in 2006. Although there was bloodshed at some polling stations, not one of the 5200 stations was penetrated by the insurgents. Forty-two of the attacks were vest suicide bombers, but all were stopped before they got into the booths. A few polling stations were closed for a short time, but no polling station was disabled by the bombers.

We heard extraordinary stories about the 'martyrdom' of Iraqi soldiers and police. It was strange to hear 'our' Iraqis talking about 'martyrdom', because until then it was a term I had only ever heard from the insurgents and terrorists.

As I read stories of extreme heroism, I thought that if these were Australian soldiers they would be nominated for the highest gallantry awards. In two of the stories that I particularly recall, soldiers or police were providing security at a polling station for a long line of Iraqis queuing up to vote. Those who had voted proudly displayed their purple fingers — this was done to prevent multiple voting. On each occasion, the soldiers or police spotted someone who showed signs of being a vest suicide bomber approaching the line, and charged the individual, running through the line of voters and wrestling the bomber to the ground. On both occasions the bomb detonated, killing the bombers and those apprehending them, but without great harm to those queuing to vote.

An Iraqi battalion commander was walking through city streets with his small bodyguard, moving from one polling station to the next to visit his men, who were dispersed in small groups. He saw more than ten armed insurgents running along a parallel street, evidently to attack a polling station. With no other options and no quick reaction force available, he and his bodyguard attacked the insurgents, killed many, disrupted their attack, and gained time for a coalition reaction force to get to the scene. He lost his life doing so.

A journalist reported a vest bomber's attack that had killed and injured Iraqis waiting in line to vote. The casualties were taken to hospital or the morgue. But the remains of the vest bomber's body were left where they fell. The voting line re-formed and, as they moved past the bloody spot, the voters spat on the remains.

I read these stories in my little office at the back of the operations centre in the days following the election. In my role, victories were mainly measured in bureaucratic terms. As I read, I felt a genuine envy for these real soldiers who were fighting for their people and their country.

★

The election was also a dramatic strategic victory for the Iraqis and their allies. We had conducted a complex organisational, logistical and social activity in the face of months of violent opposition and 260 attacks on election day alone, yet Iraqis still voted. The participation rate was soon determined: 58 per cent of eligible voters! In any country where voting was voluntary, this was an acceptable figure. The Sunnis did not vote, but we were ready for that and we had some perspective on it. They would vote in greater numbers in the second election, and in the third. I did not see anyone of any substance try to make an argument that Sunni non-participation invalidated the January election.

When we woke up the day after the election, the Iraq people had taken a giant step towards a democratic country through an election that was relatively free and relatively fair. Suddenly, people wanted to talk politics and Iraqi soldiers and police were heroes. They had defended their country — they had finally had a public victory. They realised that there were no appropriate medals in the new Iraq to give those who had displayed uncommon valour, so they set to work coining them. The day after the election, 2000 people appeared spontaneously at the gates of the Al-Numaniya Military Training Base and volunteered to join the Iraqi Army. The Iraqi generals were ecstatic and the police walked tall. Even Zarqawi was quiet for a few days.

We had the messages ready for the media. If we'd prepared messages for a disastrous failure to vote, I did not see them. But soldiers like me are professional worriers; although a frightening number of people spoke about 'democratic transformation in the heart of the Middle East', those in the coalition who used these kinds of words spoke quietly, and in private.

It was obvious that the insurgents did not win the election, but as General Casey said to us, they didn't lose either, and we had no way of telling how badly they had been hurt. Only their reaction over time would give us the answer to that.

★

My year in Iraq peaked, in my mind, on election day. But I still had
to get through February and March before I could switch off to go
home in April. In the months leading up to the election, I had been
driven by the need to bring the diplomatic, political, military,
information and economic strands of this war together on that one
day. Fight your way to the election, Casey had said to us, and fight
our way to the election we did.

I had intended to get everyone in the team together on the night
of the election and say something stirring, but the war did not allow
that: we were busy searching for a crashed C-130.

The day after the election, reports were still coming in and there
was a lot of tidying up to do. There was still a buzz in the air. That
night, at the evening shift change conference in the operations centre,
I said what I could to mark the occasion. I thanked everyone as much
as I could. I meant it from the bottom of my heart, but felt that my
words were inadequate. I mentioned a bunch of people personally,
mostly US civil affairs soldiers or coalition soldiers attached to the
civil affairs unit. I was still far too close to it all to understand the
magnitude of what we had done. There is never a time to pat yourself
on the back in Iraq. Every time you feel good, it is really
complacency. Feeling good just proves that you do not know what is
going on. As soon as you think that you have achieved something in
Iraq, the enemy will come from nowhere and blow your arse off.

I had tried to think ahead in each operation, and had cultivated
the keenest sense of what I called 'constructive paranoia'. I was
anticipating, and had planned for, retribution against those who had
voted and still had the purple ink on their fingers. The shooting
down of the C-130 reinforced my fear that there was something out
there that neither I nor anyone else had thought about. So I was still
coiled.

Luckily, this feared retribution against voters did not occur. When we got the final results in, we realised that we had done something special. At the CENTCOM vidcon on the day after the election, I gave my immediate post-election report. When I finished, General Abizaid was overly generous in his praise of the coalition. He said, 'I have seen many operations in the last few years including the invasion of Iraq and the Afghanistan battle and now these elections, and I believe that this [the election] was as complex an operation as any of them.' At the BUA, Casey and Ambassador Negroponte were present at the palace end of the vidcon. Casey personally and publicly congratulated me, as did the ambassador and others.

We knew that democracy was not just about a vote. Democracy is about institution-building and winning the trust of minorities so that they believe that even if their candidates lose, their rights will be respected. If this election proved one thing beyond a shadow of a doubt, it was that Iraqis were not rejecting democracy.

Many had been killed on election day, but fewer than we expected. More had been killed on the long journey up to that day. But we had got through the first gate of the campaign plan, and with a bit of style. Things are tough enough in Iraq in 2008 as I write this, but if we had fallen at the first election, who knows where Iraq and the coalition might be today? Could we have held the coalition together if we had failed at the first milestone? I doubt it.

The next few months were comparatively quiet. We watched and waited. The Iraqi military and police had been overstretched by their efforts in Samarra, Fallujah and the election. Just when we should have been capitalising on our success, they pulled back into their bases and we had trouble getting them out again. The coalition force was also overstretched. We'd put off the rotation home of a large percentage of our US troops so that we had enough to get us to the election but now, as the 'muscle move' of troops out of Iraq tried to catch up with a delayed logistic schedule, the roads were jammed with vehicles and troops. As a result, we could not conduct operations to follow up our election success.

Our quiet satisfaction did not last long. On 16 March 2005 the Jafa'ari government came into being, and the parliament's first sitting was welcomed by several mortar rounds landing near the Tomb of the Unknown Soldier. In the seven weeks since the election, the insurgency had regrouped. The coalition was hampered by its logistics issues and the Iraqi Security Forces were dormant. Zarqawi soon found his voice again, and in April 2005 he started to attack the Iraqi people and military in a way that indicated that he knew where the threat to him was coming from — it was coming from Iraqis. He hoped to counter this threat by fomenting a sectarian civil war between the Sunnis and the Shias.

But it was not all gloom and doom after the exhilaration. Some weeks after I had left Iraq, the new Foreign Minister attended the Arab Summit in one of the Gulf States and joked in his speech to his fellow Arabs that Iraq promised not to export democracy to its neighbours. With such humour, perhaps there was hope yet!

February, March and April were hard for me personally. I was not as driven as I had been. My energy had always been the source of my success. People fed off me. I could start something and have as much energy at the end as I'd had at the beginning. But I drew my energy from the events around me, and now, with the election completed, I found that I had to drive myself every day and every hour.

I met my successor as chief of operations, a US Special Forces major general named Eldon Bargewell who was coming in from a US Army job in Europe. We went on a trip around the country together to familiarise him with Iraq. In Mosul we met Eldon's son, who was with a US reconnaissance unit out on the Syrian border. A good-looking young man, he had his patrol commander with him at the airport and his patrol mates in several Hummers outside. They stood there leaning against their vehicles, bristling with weapons, with that casual look that only real soldiers can ever achieve. He was as proud of his father as Eldon was of him.

When I saw these young soldiers just in from patrolling the Syrian border, I was reminded that several months earlier we had received a request from the Corps for permission to use claymore mines in that area. A claymore mine is like a big shotgun cartridge on four legs that you can prop on the ground. When you push a trigger it explodes in the enemy's face. It allows a small reconnaissance patrol, such as the one Eldon's son was in, to defeat a large-scale attack or give itself time to make a getaway. The request for claymores was made because these small forces operated in such isolation that if they were attacked they might be overrun before we could get assistance to them. The request was refused because of the name of the weapon — mine — and the connotations of that name. Regardless of what the claymore mine really was, it was called a mine and almost all the nations in the coalition, apart from the US, had banned mines. Therefore, in the coalition environment, the US did not permit their use. This was a brave decision and I admired Casey for taking it, especially when we knew that our opponent had not a single qualm about any weapons, including mines.

As I stood beside our helicopter at Mosul airport and looked at the young US reconnaissance soldier embracing his father, I realised that he was one of many whose survival might have depended on the claymore mine. Once again, I was reminded that every one of our decisions in Iraq had life-and-death consequences for real people, including our own sons and daughters.

Since leaving Iraq, I have had more time to absorb the significance of the January 2005 election. My other great experiences in assisting young democracies had been in Australia's part of the world: Papua

New Guinea, Indonesia, East Timor and the Solomons. None, not even East Timor, had to stand up for democracy against the murderous internal threat that the Iraqis faced every day. There were those who dismissed the election: the Iraqis, they said, had merely voted or not voted along sectarian lines. Of course they did. But many in my parents' generation also voted firmly along sectarian lines in the 1950s and '60s, causing a Catholic–Protestant rupture in one of the oldest and strongest democratic nations on earth. Yet within a decade, those narrow voting patterns dissolved, producing a much more inclusive democracy. If a similar change of attitude could occur in Iraq, even if it takes a generation, we should be very happy indeed.

Anyone who expected perfect democracy out of Iraq in its first attempts is living in a fool's paradise. My experience participating in the creation of other democracies told me that that is too much to expect: none of those countries got it right first off. Some of them still have not. Others are proudly moving forward, but have the potential to trip. Others took three elections before they voted in politicians who had a modicum of competence as national leaders. Our expectations of Iraq must be realistic. The act of voting is an important part of democracy, but elections alone have never promised to produce competent governments and democratic institutions. True democracy in Iraq will require our patience and vigilant support for many years to come.

CHAPTER 11

'Do not ever underestimate what you have achieved'

Coming home, April 2005

In addition to the daily routine of keeping the war going, my days during February and March were filled with the rotation of US forces, security for the new Iraqi government, and planning how to transition the fight to the Iraqis. Peter Palmer, my deputy in operations, was looking forward to going home just as much as I was, but he was going to have to do a little longer than a year. He was staying to provide continuity and to redesign the operations branch, part of a restructure that was being driven largely by the shortage of skilled US manpower. Given the demands on US personnel across the world, the 'big army' started to ask questions about exactly how much manpower the headquarters had and how we could reduce it.

The Iraqis were slowly taking a more active role, and we had to adjust to this. For example, since I had taken over as chief of operations, I had been managing 800 US soldiers, led by an extraordinary group of US Navy Special Forces, who protected the top five Iraqi leaders: the president, the vice-president, the prime minister and the two deputy prime ministers. I had been overseeing their gradual replacement with Iraqi bodyguards, and it had been pretty difficult. The US Special Forces performing this function were of the same quality as my special forces bodyguard, a standard which takes years to achieve even when you are starting from a very high base. We had to replace this world-class US bodyguard with newly trained Iraqis in a matter of months. This was as much about Iraqi sovereignty and pride as it was about our desire to use our special forces in other roles, but it involved risk. It would not have been a good look to have the newly elected Iraqi government protected by foreigners, but it would have been far worse to have had them killed. Yet again we were balancing risk.

As soon as we lifted our heads from the election, we started work on implementing General Casey's changes to the campaign plan, the most significant of which was to transition the fight to the Iraqis.

The one fact that was an issue in all our operations was that we didn't have enough good troops, but every general in every war has probably expressed that opinion. General Casey worked to solve this problem by creating more capable Iraqi units, and training the new troops was the responsibility of Lieutenant General David Petraeus. In the year I had been in Iraq, he had raised, trained and equipped almost 100 Iraqi combat battalions, some good, some still raw and inexperienced. The lack of seasoned combat leaders was the real problem. A large percentage of these Iraqi units now had at least some combat experience, but were still a long way from anything that approached the standard of US units. To strengthen them, General Casey was bringing in 5000 US junior officers and non-commissioned officers, and allocating them in teams of nine to each new Iraqi battalion. Called 'Transition Teams', these soldiers would live and fight with the Iraqis. They would help with training, and they would be the conduit through which we would pass the intelligence, fire support and logistics that the Iraqis would take years to develop themselves.

Taking 5000 key junior leaders out of any military, even the US military, causes an incredible strain, but the importance of having our soldiers with the new Iraqi battalions was about trust as well as skills. You only needed a few, but those advisers had to share not just the training, but also the combat. To train a unit and then stand at the barrack gate and wave goodbye as they marched off to fight does not build trust. The US understood this, placing so many of their young men and women in these units, where they were undeniably at great risk. Scott Davis, one of the 'roadside bomb twins' from my pipe repair days, now promoted to major, returned as a Transition Team leader with the first Iraqi tank unit, and was once again in the thick of it, again the target of many roadside bomb attacks.

General Casey had made his public comment about coalition troops being an antibody in Iraqi society, and we could all see what he meant. Despite our intentions, despite all our efforts, like an antibody, we drew a reaction from Iraqi society. President Bush had said that if the military commanders in Iraq wanted more troops, he would meet their requests. Casey had managed to get more troops during Fallujah and the election, and it had been a success. But Casey did not believe that more US troops was now the answer.

In the midst of the massive changeover of US units in Iraq, as old units left and new ones arrived, and as we waited for the government of Iraq to form around us, Casey held a meeting with his new commanders. He explained his new strategy in the biggest room in the palace at Camp Victory, with his principal staff lined up beside him, all waiting our turn to talk on our specialties.

'This year,' he said, 'our major focus will be to begin the transition of the counterinsurgency campaign to the Iraqis at the local, regional and national level. We need to use the post-election period to move towards this goal, and to deny the insurgents the opportunity to regroup following the decisive defeats they have been dealt since October 2004.'

Speaking with his words up on a giant screen behind him, under the heading 'Commanding General's Intent', he continued:

> The election has potentially changed the strategic calculation in Iraq for the better, both inside and outside. The Iraqi people have soundly rejected the former regime and foreign terrorist models as viable alternatives for their future, and the international community and coalition public may be more patient in supporting the mission. What we must do is to structure our plans to take advantage of the opportunities presented to us by the election to drive a wedge between the people and the insurgents and terrorists and to enhance the contribution of the Iraqi Security Forces to the counterinsurgency effort.

This was solid guidance on the campaign that stretched out in front of us, and Casey paused to let it sink in: we were learning, and adjusting to meet the reality on the ground. Casey knew that having set his campaign on this new course, the enemy might take a different view, which would in turn influence the application of our plan. After giving his broad guidance, he set out specific mission points. These were all expressed as 'action verbs', so that the new and continuing commanders would have no doubt as to what the commanding general wanted: 'begin the transition', 'empower the Iraqis', 'protect the population', 'consolidate our gains', 'deny sanctuaries', 'protect the new government', 'build confidence', 'avoid strategic surprise', 'sustain the momentum'. Heady stuff indeed.

Like a father conveying hard-won advice to his children, Casey then offered the commanders of the 60 per cent of his force that was new, many of whose troops had not yet joined them, a set of rules. These were listed on the screen as rules that you would break at your own risk. We had learnt them through hard experience, at the cost of many lives, including 900 of our own soldiers in the time I had been in Iraq. They reflected the continuing need to balance protection and success, where the lives of real people were at stake. General Casey's rules were:

Make security and safety your first priorities.

Help the Iraqis win, don't win it for them.

Treat the Iraqi people with dignity and respect.

Learn and respect Iraqi customs and culture.

Maintain strict standards and iron discipline every day.

Risk assess every mission — no complacency!!

Information saves lives — share it and protect it.

Maintain your situational awareness at all times — this can be an unforgiving environment.

Take care of your equipment — it will take care of you.

Innovate and adapt — situations here don't lend themselves to cookie-cutter solutions.

Focus on the enemy and be opportunistic.

Be patient. Don't rush to failure.

Take care of yourself and take care of each other.

The conference went on for several hours and was only one part of passing masses of knowledge to the new commanders. But you can only tell people so much — ultimately wars are learnt by getting out on the streets and doing them.

I was determined to make one final concrete contribution to the Iraq people. I still had overall responsibility for strategic infrastructure security. Approaching the election, the final series of infrastructure operations I had run were to keep the energy flowing for the elections. Despite persistent attacks, we did so. My staff used to joke that you can vote in the dark, so why worry? Now I could see a new group of people flowing in to replace our experienced team. It was obvious that they were likely to repeat the same mistakes that we had been making and learning from all year.

By February, the remains of the oil protection force put together during the CPA time under the Erinys contract was working for oil minister Ghadban. He was still ignoring them. He had also terminated the contract — the contractors were gone, so the force was beginning to disintegrate. In fact, we were now going backwards on infrastructure protection. Backed up by Jim Jeffrey and Ambassador Negroponte, I initiated the creation of a high-quality guard force whose job was to protect the strategic infrastructure. As a result of my urgings directly to Deputy Prime Minister Barhem Saleh, and despite deep opposition from those who were creating the Iraqi Army (well-intentioned, passionate opposition, but wrong), the Iraqi government approved the creation of this force at the end of February 2005, allocating US$500 million for its creation and US$130 million each year to sustain it. The money was to come from government oil revenue. It bought a force of 18 highly mobile and heavily armed battalions with six logistic support battalions, four brigade headquarters and one division headquarters, plus full supporting infrastructure. I had won the argument, on the basis that such a high-quality force should be able to pay for itself many times over in less than one year through increased oil flows.

I had one last argument to slug out. The Iraqi Army wanted to control the infrastructure force, but I knew that any local Iraqi military commander who was allocated a first-class force for something as unexciting as infrastructure security would immediately misuse it for other things, such as direct combat. I met few military commanders who paid anything more than lip service to strategic infrastructure security. They understood the pipes and the lines in their local area, but where electricity and oil actually came from seemed almost irrelevant to them. So if they commanded the force, it seemed highly likely that the people would miss out on their essential services yet again and the insurgency would enjoy yet another victory.

My view, strongly put, was that the new force had to be commanded centrally so that it stayed on the lines and the pipes. This became a furious and sometimes personal argument. On one side were the US Embassy, the Deputy Prime Minister and me. On the other were the Corps and the creator of the new Iraqi Army, Lieutenant General David Petraeus. David was an inspirational officer, a man who had the kind of command experience any soldier would respect. I admired David greatly, but we seemed to clash just about every time we came together. Because of this split, and because of the involvement of the embassy, Casey called a meeting only days before I left Iraq to try to thrash it out. I lost the argument and the infrastructure security battalions were allocated down to local commanders. I'm sorry to say that not much has improved in the provision of essential services to Iraqis over the last three years. In this respect, Iraqis are seeing few real compensations for the suffering they have endured since the invasion.

Less than a fortnight before I left, an ambush occurred that brought home the importance of the best tool the US military had: the individual soldier.

Salman Pak was an area just southeast of Baghdad, a stronghold of the insurgency. I had visited a Salman Pak electrical substation very soon after taking over the infrastructure security position, arriving unexpectedly and staying less than an hour. I met with its twenty or so local tribal guards and their families; the guards were equipped with only half a dozen AK-47s and a few rounds of ammunition. At the time, I had no idea of the reputation of the place.

On 20 March 2005, one of the most significant actions during my year in Iraq, involving up to 100 insurgents, took place. The ambush had a 'snatch party' equipped to take prisoners, it had a reserve position and it had an escape route and vehicles standing by to get prisoners away before a reaction force arrived. The insurgent force was very well armed with medium and light machine guns, RPGs and AK-47s.

Their target was a convoy of 30 contractor-driven 18-wheel semi-trailers moving south towards Kuwait from logistic bases around Baghdad. This convoy was one of a multitude of similar packets of vehicles moving at the time on this road. We referred to these truck drivers as TCNs (third country nationals). Like the benzene tanker drivers, they were mostly Jordanians, Turks and Sudanese. They had taken a road that went near Salman Pak, to confuse the enemy, but this time their luck ran out. The insurgents knew that if they stayed on this road long enough, some nice fat targets would pass, and there is nothing fatter than 30 18-wheelers. The danger for the insurgents was that the longer that they had this large force, which included escape vehicles, in an ambush position, the greater the chance of their being discovered.

Three of our 'gun trucks' escorted the convoy. The term 'gun truck' dated back to the Vietnam War, which was when it became common practice to protect supply vehicles by putting armour on any truck available and equipping each with a 50-calibre machine gun. The three escort vehicles in this convoy were not locally armoured trucks but Hummers that had been professionally 'up-armoured' — effective, but still far from impervious to attack. One Hummer led the convoy, one was in the middle, and one was at the end.

Some distance behind the convoy were three other Hummers carrying nine soldiers of the 503rd Military Police Battalion, 18th Military Police Brigade of the Kentucky National Guard, plus one medic. They had the radio call sign of 'Raven 42'. These three vehicles were 'shadowing' the convoy as a kind of roaming quick reaction force. Because they were not required to stay with the trucks, these three Hummers might avoid an ambush.

The ambush took place on a stretch of straight road in irrigated Iraqi farmland. The main road was sealed and carried a fair amount of traffic. There were the shallow irrigation ditches that cover that part of Iraq, some low scrubby cover and a few date palms. At one end of the ambush site, where a track ran off to slightly higher ground, there was a house, where the insurgents had parked seven vehicles. The car boots were open and the drivers were standing by to spirit away their intended kidnap victims. In addition, the insurgents were videoing the action, either for recruiting purposes or to use as proof that they were doing their job.

The ambush opened with a volley of machine-gun fire and RPGs. Most of the fire was aimed at the escort Hummer in the centre of the convoy. It caught fire and its three crewmen were wounded. Five of the cargo trucks were also set on fire and the convoy stopped in the killing ground, many of the trucks nose to tail. Four of the drivers were killed and seven were wounded in this initial 30-second-long burst — half a minute is a very long time to be shot at with automatic weapons from only tens of metres away. What the insurgents now had to do was snatch some hostages and get away before helicopter gunships or a ground quick reaction force arrived. What they had not counted on was Raven 42's three vehicles.

Raven 42 was commanded by a Sergeant First-Class Marshall P. Ware. His first two Hummers had three crew members each and the third had an extra crew member, a medic. Each vehicle was referred to as a 'team'. In the lead vehicle was its team leader, her driver and a gunner who operated a 40mm grenade launcher. This launcher could accurately blast out a stream of explosive 40mm grenades to a range of over a kilometre. It was not as useful in a close-in fight — where the enemy might be less than 50 metres from the vehicle. The gunner, standing through the hole in the Hummer's roof, was vulnerable to any sudden attack, but at least he could fight from behind some armour.

The second vehicle was the squad commander's. With him were his driver and a gunner named Specialist Casey Cooper. Cooper was well armed for either a close or distant fight. He had a 50-calibre machine gun on the vehicle's weapon mount; it fires large heavy bullets at a relatively slow rate out to a 2-kilometre range. In close, it could blast through a wall or trees or dirt bunds. As well, Cooper had a light machine gun that fired lighter bullets at a very high rate to an effective range of about 600 metres. This gun was down in the cabin of the vehicle. He also had a rocket launcher called an AT4 hanging on the back of his hatch. And of course, like all US soldiers, he had a rifle and a pistol. In the ensuing fight he was to use almost all of these weapons.

The third vehicle also had its team leader, a driver, a gunner, and the medic. This gunner had decided to mount a light machine gun on the top of his vehicle.

Sergeant Ware was a very competent leader. Events would show that he knew that detail is everything in tactics at his level, and that what makes a group of soldiers win is the battle discipline that leaders instil. He had insisted that each of his three vehicles was loaded identically, so that all his soldiers would know where things were in each of them. Each vehicle had a 'grab bag' of ammunition stowed in the same place so that in the heat of battle, anyone in the squad could take the nearest spare ammunition quickly. He had trained all members of his squad on all weapon types. Further, everyone had completed the advanced first-aid course that the US Army calls 'combat life saving'.

Raven 42 heard the firing and could see the dust and dirt as the trucks braked to a halt in the killing ground. Raven 42 drove straight towards the firing and the burning trucks. This in itself was an act of bravery that should never be taken for granted. The squad leader could have stopped and made radio calls and waited for reinforcements. But they drove their three vehicles into the ambush site. As they roared up on the road between the ambush and the burning vehicles, they came across members of the enemy 'snatch' squad who were sprinting up to the centre Hummer where the US crew lay wounded. Raven 42 put them to flight, killing or wounding several.

All insurgent weapons now turned on the Raven 42 vehicles, but they were moving fast, so the hits, while numerous, were not significant. Having passed all the convoy's vehicles and successfully stopped the snatch team, the squad leader could again have honourably driven on for a further hundred metres to a safe spot, made radio calls and waited for reinforcements. But he decided to turn his vehicles along the dirt track to outflank the ambushers. Once again, the insurgents saw Raven 42 as the major threat and fired all their weapons at them.

At this stage, one RPG hit the armoured lip of the door of the centre Hummer that contained both the squad leader and Specialist Cooper. Cooper was blown back and down into the Hummer; the squad leader, sitting in the front, thought Cooper was dead. At the same time, the gunner in the third vehicle was also hit. The commander of this vehicle and his driver both got out and started to return fire with their personal weapons. Again, this was an act of absolute courage: though they may not have been able to operate their personal weapons from inside the vehicle, at least the vehicle armour would have offered some protection. Once the crew of the third vehicle got out to fight, the entire squad was totally committed. But very soon both the third vehicle commander and his driver lay wounded beside their Hummer.

Things were not looking good for Raven 42. Gunners in the second and third vehicles had been hit and their guns were not operating. Two members of the third vehicle were being treated by their medic. The only weapon now firing at the enemy was the slow-firing grenade launcher on the first vehicle. The enemy well and truly had fire superiority and was manoeuvring to finish the three vehicles off with RPGs.

Once again great courage emerged. The driver from the first vehicle got out and ran back through the storm of fire to help the medic. The driver from the second vehicle, seeing that the third vehicle's gunner was down, got out and ran back to the third vehicle, got the machine gun operating and started to return fire. As well, Casey Cooper, in the second vehicle, realised that he was not as dead as he'd thought. He got back into his turret and started to operate the machine gun again. A 50-calibre machine gun has a very distinctive slow, thumping sound. Everyone would have heard this weapon rejoining the fight. But the fight was far from over. A group of insurgents was firing from a ditch very close to where the Hummers had stopped.

The squad leader saw the threat from the ditch. He moved forwards to the commander of the first vehicle, and they both assaulted the enemy in the ditch, moving at them and firing. Often the bravest act in battle is to move and fire. The enemy notices: as soon as you fire your one weapon, all of the enemy will fire back at you. The squad commander and his female colleague not only fired their weapons, they also moved towards the enemy in the ditch. The team leader of the first vehicle had a grenade launcher and used it to great effect. But after having moved ahead of the vehicles, the squad leader realised that they were going to need more ammunition than they carried, so he sent his first vehicle commander back to the Hummers to get more ammo while he fought on. Casey Cooper and the other gunners on the vehicles were supporting their commander's fight, but somewhere out there were 50 to 100 insurgents, all of whom now saw the two attacking soldiers as their best target. Cooper was using his heavy machine gun when appropriate and then grabbing his fast-firing light machine gun when he could find targets that were close in.

The commander of the first vehicle ran back from the ditch to get ammunition, but an insurgent stepped out from behind a tree and fired at her as she opened the door on the closest vehicle — the middle one, with Cooper on the top. Cooper could not bring either machine gun to bear quickly enough so he drew his pistol and fired at the insurgent, hitting him, and then moved back to firing the bigger weapons. The first vehicle commander found the grab-bags of ammo and ran back to the squad commander in the ditch, where the two of them killed or drove off the rest of the enemy close to the vehicles.

The enemy now realised that the tide of battle had turned against them. The weapons from the top of the three Hummers were operating well and the ditch had been cleared of enemy. The insurgents now tried to escape by moving back towards the house and cars. The gunner on the third vehicle and the medic — who had only been trained on the squad's weapons the day before — now fired AT-4 rockets at the house. Casey could not fire at the house because the first Hummer was blocking the way. So he dropped down from his turret, crawled into the driver's seat and drove around so he could get a better shot. His vehicle was badly damaged, but it got around the front of the other Hummer before the engine gave up. Casey returned to his turret and trained his 50-calibre machine gun on the seven escape vehicles, setting them all on fire.

This marked the end of the fight. The enemy dispersed and other military police Hummers arrived to assist Raven 42.

This was a significant small action, illustrating the courageous decisions that people at the bottom of the military tree made. These decisions are the real difference between winners and losers. Twenty-four insurgents lay dead on this little battlefield; six others were wounded, and two of them later died. One enemy was captured unwounded. As the battlefield was cleaned up, 22 AK-47 rifles were found, plus 123 fully loaded 30-round AK magazines and 50 empty magazines. The enemy left six RPG launchers and 16 rockets on the battlefield, 13 RPK machine guns and another three PKM machine guns, ten belts of 2500 rounds for the machine guns and 40 hand grenades. This was, by any measure, a serious fight, but it still only took about 20 minutes.

My description of this incident is based on reports that arrived at my headquarters during the day and on the 'incident report' that worked its way up the chain of command. I was inspired by this little action because it reminded me that everything we generals did relied totally on the fact that young soldiers were prepared to fight like this. In an unusual footnote, the intelligence officer of the military police brigade, extraordinarily proud of the diverse background of the soldiers of his brigade, noted that of the seven military police from Raven 42 who were not hit at the very start of the fight, two were 'Caucasian women', and of the five men, one was 'Mexican American, one was African American [the medic], and the others were Caucasian'.

This type of vicious little fight has been repeated countless times by US and coalition soldiers, and now also by Iraqi soldiers. But this particular group of young US National Guard men and women from the State of Kentucky, part-time soldiers, and many more like them, are the counterpoint to those few who failed us all in incidents such as Abu Ghraib, or the alleged killings at Haditha and the rapes at Mahmudiyah. I use this anecdote every time I speak to young Australian officer cadets. I challenge them as young professional full-time soldiers with a closing line: 'Are you as good as the Kentucky National Guard?'

For a year I found myself working at the centre of the most technologically advanced headquarters in the history of conflict. Yet the most important factor in anything we did was the human factor. People continually made the difference, whether those people were coalition soldiers, generals or diplomats, Iraqi ministers or prime ministers, US politicians or bureaucrats. And of course the human factor was as important for our enemy, in the form of figures such as the leader of al Qaeda in Iraq, Zarqawi, or the head of the Shia Mehdi Militia, Moqtada al Sadr, and each individual who was fighting. This was a conflict of ideas. It takes ideas or beliefs to call forth the kind of dedication and sacrifice that was being shown in Iraq, but it must never be forgotten that the holders of those ideas are always human beings.

In my year in Iraq, I was literally a card-carrying member of the US Embassy in Baghdad. On New Year's Eve I had attended a small dinner at the embassy to greet the Deputy Secretary of State, Richard Armitage, and found that I was the only non-American present. As an Australian in a foreign embassy, I shook my head in amazement. Having spent five years in our embassy in Jakarta, I found it very strange to be once again on the inside of an embassy looking out, particularly a US embassy!

I enjoyed good relationships with most senior embassy officers. I found Jim Jeffrey tremendously practical and supportive. Over the election, I worked closely with John Negroponte and the embassy officer responsible for political and military affairs, Ron Neumann. The talk was that after the friction between the CPA and the military in 2003 and 2004, Secretary of State Colin Powell had decreed that those posted to the US Embassy in Baghdad at the top level had to have military experience. If it was true, it seemed to produce results. Negroponte had been a young political officer in Vietnam, and Jeffrey and Neumann had both been combat officers there. Around the time I was leaving, so were Negroponte and one or two others; the team that had been together since the occupation ended was about to break up.

Late in my tour, I had regular discussions about 'current affairs' with the Australian Ambassador in Baghdad, Howard Brown. One Saturday late in March 2005, he brought with him a copy of a letter that Ambassador Negroponte had given him to send to the Prime Minister of Australia, John Howard. In part, it said:

Major General Molan excelled as a soldier-diplomat in the complicated political and military environment of Iraq. He melded seamlessly with senior coalition civilian leadership and consistently provided the wise counsel and strong leadership necessary to our success in creating a democratic, secure, and free Iraq. As a direct result of his untiring efforts to foster the conditions in which Iraqis could conduct free and fair elections for the first time in generations, Major General Molan literally made history and helped reshape the Middle East.

A consummate military professional, Major General Molan was the vital interface between the coalition and the nascent Iraqi Security Forces, helping to give them the leadership and confidence they needed to succeed. His identification of the protection of Iraq's infrastructure as a key strategic priority and his articulation of, and advocacy for, a specific Iraqi Infrastructure Protection Force has already started to pay dividends and is a major, strategic contribution to future Iraqi stability.

I was stunned that he would write to my prime minister. I was not part of an Australian force in Iraq, and much of what I had achieved had been as an individual. I had little significant communication with Australian officials in the time I had been in Iraq. What I was doing was invisible to my own military back in Australia. My experience in Iraq was a US experience within a US war, but I was always visibly Australian to them. Negroponte had seen more of what I had done in relation to the election and the infrastructure than had General Casey, who saw only the military side of my work. Negroponte had rung me late the night before he left to say farewell and to thank me for my work, but he had not mentioned that he had written a letter to the Australian Prime Minister. I dropped up to see Jim Jeffrey, who once again was Chargé d'Affaires. I asked him whether he had drafted the letter. He said no, the letter had been Negroponte's idea and his drafting.

General Casey had been extremely good to me in the nine months since his arrival. He was broadminded enough to accept me in the job of chief of operations — I was a coalition officer from a country that had only 311 troops in Iraq out of a total of 175,000. He could have had any two-star officer in the US Army. He had put up with much, and I'd done my best to repay his trust. He had been as tough with me as he was with his own people, and I had learnt incalculable lessons about high command from observing him.

A day or so before I left, I made a formal call to say farewell, even though I had seen him several times already that day. I was going to meet him over at Camp Victory, where he occupied the same office in the al-Faw Palace where I had first met General Sanchez 12 months previously. Joe Weber still occupied the office next door. Since then I had attended innumerable meetings at the long conference table, but this time we sat in the comfortable chairs. I had no thoughts in mind about what to say except to thank Casey for his trust in me, and to wish him well. I was going home after one year but he was to lead this war for several more.

We spoke generally, and then he asked me what was the one main observation I would make as an Australian after a year working in the coalition. I replied, 'The one thing that will stick in my mind is the lack of arrogance the US personnel have shown towards me. Of all the countries in the world that have a right to a certain amount of military arrogance, especially towards a small nation with an even smaller contribution in the coalition force, and one that is not offensively fighting, I would have excused a bit of arrogance from Americans. I was expecting it. But there has been none.'

Casey knew, as did many people in the headquarters, all about the often intense 'disagreements' I'd had with other generals as our priorities conflicted. We had only just come from the final infrastructure security meeting, after all, where Casey himself had had to pull David Petraeus and me apart! But these were not manifestations of US arrogance towards a little country at the end of the earth. These disagreements were what you would find in any collection of generals involved in life-and-death issues. These were human attributes, not US attributes. Casey had either ignored them or sent Joe Weber to kick our backsides. The key part of running a coalition is making everyone feel wanted, and Casey did that exceedingly well.

Time came to part, and his closing comment was sobering. 'Do not ever underestimate what you have achieved,' he said to me with a final handshake.

He handed me a copy of a letter of commendation he had written to Peter Cosgrove and turned back into his big office to continue to fight the war. He had been in Iraq since mid-2004, and would hand over command to General Petraeus in February 2007. General George Casey deserves a fair share of the credit if we win this war; and if we lose, it will not be his fault.

I sat down in Joe Weber's office next door and read Casey's letter to Peter Cosgrove:

Having just witnessed the historic elections here in Iraq, I wanted to write to thank you for sending your very best officers to support our important efforts here. It has truly been a great honor and privilege to serve with them in this Coalition.

I would like to draw special attention to Major General Jim Molan's efforts as my chief of strategic operations (STRATOPS). Jim's performance and strategic vision have been brilliant. The recent election, and its multitude of attendant tasks, was a perfect capstone for all he has done here.

There can be no mistake. Jim has been a driving force here in this Multi-National Command and absolutely critical to my mission.

At that evening's shift change, I was in the operations centre to make my official farewell. The evening shift change was normally packed, with close to 200 people in the room, because staff overlapped during their handover. But this night, the steps leading up through the tiers were jammed and the gallery up the back where the colonels worked was also full.

Two or three times a week we had farewells; people were always coming and going. I paused to take it all in. This operations centre was the focus of our lives. Computers glowed and phones quietly buzzed at each desk. Conversations took place everywhere. Groups formed and re-formed around certain desks as people came in and out looking for information. Sometimes information was actually shouted from one section to another, but mostly it moved by computer.

Among the hundreds of people who had come through this operations centre, some people were good at certain things, and others were good at different things. In this situation, dealing with reservists from many countries, you did not know what people could do until you tried them out. I had found that not a single one of these fine people lacked dedication. The Americans were patriots in a way that only Americans can be, and I admired them for it. The only thing they lacked was leadership, which was where I came in.

And now I was saying goodbye; it was my turn to be farewelled.

The official farewell was like a family affair. This room was our home. A few times a day, we let ambassadors and generals and other staff in for briefings, but the evening shift change briefing was our in-house time. This was our time to examine how we had gone during the day. This was when I trained up new people and, when necessary, publicly kicked arse. On this occasion, my last night in the operations centre, the farewell was to start with that great American tradition of a 'Roast', after which I was to make a reply and gifts would be presented. Then I was to leave, and the war would go on as though I had never been there.

As would be expected, the Roast focused on anecdotes and my regularly used sayings, especially those I had used to 'encourage performance'. Also mentioned was my 'relatively infrequent' use of strong language. Steve Hashem, the brigadier general who ran civil affairs, started off, reading from a script he had prepared. As I stood there beside him, he brought back a crowd of memories and raised many laughs. He didn't remind us of the long hours, the exhaustion or the underlying death and injury we all dealt with each day. Instead he talked about some of the tensions that existed and the pressures that bore down on us, and how we reacted. This was not a time to dwell on old arguments. This was a time to laugh and to forgive. He said:

Many of you have just recently joined the coalition and the operations centre. For the new people, the General Molan that stands before us now is not the General Molan of a few months ago. Those of us who have been around for a while preceding the elections went through some pretty intense times. That being said, I have been waiting for this opportunity for about eight months now. I have worked with General Molan since last September and have suffered more than my fair share of floggings. Actually, he has mellowed out significantly over the last several weeks after the elections. I'd like to share a few of our collective experiences with you about Major General Molan, one of the most colourful characters in MNF-I as well as the author, as General Casey has often said, of the famous Molan Plan or Strategic Energy Plan, the central theme of which was to beat the Ministries into submission by relentless pressure.

Steve then went through some of my more memorable quotes, getting a laugh out of every one. It made me think that when you are very tired, when you are desperate to laugh at something, it is amazing what you will find funny. I did go through a mild patch after the elections, when I thought I could relax the pressure on everyone a little bit. In a particular meeting that I used to have with my colonels to make sure what I had directed was being done, normally a pretty tense affair, I ran out of things to badger them about. When it came my turn to talk, instead of the usual 20 or so tasks, I had only one or two. I then said to the colonels: 'Guys, that is all I have today to beat you with, which is a great disappointment to me.' And one of the most experienced of them, Mark Lowe, quipped back, 'Sir, what have you done with the real Major General Molan?'

Some of the quotes Steve attributed to me I did not remember. Not that it mattered. I probably said them and it was great fun anyway. Doing things correctly is what staff work was all about. It was all about achieving a result. Steve quoted me as saying to one of our oil experts, 'Harry, you have 24 hours to finish this task.' Two hours later the phone rang and I said, 'Harry, you have 12 hours to finish this.' Three hours later, poor Harry got a call from Steve Gliddon, 'Harry, General Molan wants to see your final product in five minutes, and by the way, he wants to know why you're late.'

Our existence was a constant series of tense episodes. Casey did not deserve to have me come into his office and present him with crap. And if I did, he would never have accepted me blaming the staff. It was right that I absorbed the impact from Casey, but I then needed to encourage my people to produce the goods. I used to say to people that if you cannot manage, if you cannot get ahead of events, you will never have time to lead because your life will be one long series of crises. But then operations in wartime are all about crisis management.

Very little that we ever did was sequential. In his Roast, Steve reminded me that everything was Priority One. Once he claimed to have said to me, 'Sir, we have about 20 priorities here. I need your guidance on establishing priorities.' Supposedly (and quite likely), my reply was, 'They're all important. They're all number one. I want to see everything immediately in the next 30 minutes.'

Hearing this and seeing how much merriment it was causing in the operations centre, I realised how often I'd been a demanding — even tyrannical — boss. Leadership can sometimes rely in part on fear, but I like to think that if fear was all I had to motivate them, these guys would not have worked for me for a year. It never became an issue, but as a coalition officer bossing up predominantly US and UK officers and soldiers, I had absolutely no formal authority over anyone in the headquarters, absolutely none.

One of my continual bugbears was people not reading the orders we put out, called 'fragmentary orders' or FRAGOs, and then complaining to us that we were not telling them what was going on or what to do. It was the bane of my existence, and my fellow generals were the worst at not reading orders and then complaining to Casey. It is quite likely that, as Steve claimed in the Roast, I once said to one of my own staff, 'Colonel Lowe, I am determined that someone in the Multinational Force is going to read this FRAGO and if no-one else is, it's going to be you.'

But although I sounded tough and probably quite frequently was, Steve was generous enough to admit that 'every once in a while, and more often than you would think, he would compliment people on doing a good job with a resounding, "Well done, mate!"'

My reply to Steve was a little less light-hearted. I'd made some notes, which I normally did not do when speaking to my staff, but because I owed these guys so much I wanted to say the right thing. I stood where I had stood for the past year, at the front desk with my back to the screens, looked up at the two shifts assembled before me, and began.

I told them how I had been privileged four times in my career as a soldier to accompany countries some of the way down their road to democracy. I had been a platoon commander in Papua New Guinea in the mid-1970s, I was on the streets of Jakarta in the middle of Indonesia's fight against Suharto's tyranny in 1998, I had been in the middle of Dili with five of my brave and resourceful attaché staff when the East Timorese made the heroic choice to separate from Indonesia, and I had been commander of the evacuation of our citizens from the Solomon Islands when their journey to democracy hit a pothole. And now, with these 200 or so staff, 175,000 members of the coalition, and 130,000 Iraqi soldiers and police, I had been honoured to play my small part in Iraq's first step towards democracy. I pointed out that in the operations centre there were still a few of us who had arrived as reinforcements at the height of the April 2004 fighting when, as the old saying goes, we were 'up to our armpits in grenade pins', cut off from Kuwait, mired in Fallujah and fighting across most of the south of Iraq. I continued:

Yet, as a soldier, and in a military sense, I leave at a time when we have achieved so much. We have moved from CJTF-7 to MNF-I. We have concentrated a significant part of the HQ in the embassy. We have now fought in Fallujah a few times, Najaf a few times, Mosul a few times, Baghdad and Basrah all the time. We have created an army. We have kept the leadership alive. We have kept the lights on in Baghdad and the oil exports flowing. We had an election. The only thing I really failed to achieve was to truly beat the Oil Ministry into submission!

In the year that I have been here, like you all, I have had three jobs and nine offices but only one home, and this has been it, and you have been my family.

I cannot adequately express to you my gratitude for the support that I have received from you guys in this room. You are the operators; you make things happen around here. I have asked for a lot from individuals here and from 'y'all' as a group. I hope that I have been fair, I think that I have shouldered my share of the burden, and I thank you for accepting my authority. But what is most important — together we have achieved extraordinary things for Iraq and for those nations that hold the common values of democracy and freedom.

Iraq tended to bring out the Churchill in us all! But my words were accurate. We may not win this fight, but those who were doing the fighting knew what we were fighting for.

On my final day in Iraq I attended my last BUA. At the end, Casey, who was over at our side of the vidcon, presented me with the United States Legion of Merit. The Legion of Merit is described as being awarded for 'exceptionally outstanding conduct in the performance of meritorious service'. The words of the commendation, read out by Joe Weber, were:

Exceptionally meritorious service as Deputy Chief of Staff, Strategic Operations, Multi-National Force–Iraq, in support of Operation Iraqi Freedom. His outstanding dedication to duty, coupled with his knowledge and skill at integrating and synchronizing critical battlefield effects across the strategic continuum, contributed directly to the success of this Coalition's mission. His decisive leadership, initiative, and insight into strategic and operational concepts and plans were instrumental in translating thought into action. This was particularly evident in bringing to bear all elements of strategic power towards achieving success in combat operations in Najaf, Tal Afar, Samarra, and Fallujah. He aggressively implemented the Commanding General's guidance to fight to the elections. MG Molan's penchant for synchronizing election preparations, to include the coordination with a host of agencies and governments, directly and positively impacted on the Independent Election Commission Iraq and the Iraqi Government's preparation and execution of the country's first truly democratic election. His actions are in keeping with the finest traditions of military service and reflect great credit upon himself, the Multi-National Force–Iraq, and the Australian Defence Force.

On 2 April 2005, almost a year to the day since my arrival, I drove along Route Irish for the 120th and last time. At the airport, I farewelled my US bodyguards, who would stay on and look after my successor, Eldon Bargewell. Two of my Australian bodyguards accompanied me to Kuwait and then headed home to Perth. The other two stayed with Steve Gliddon in Baghdad to tie up loose ends. I said farewell to Steve, expecting him to follow me in a few days, but Iraq said farewell to Steve in its own inimitable manner — he developed a strange illness only days after I left, keeping him in-country for an extra few weeks.

I had already returned my trusty rifle in Baghdad, and in Kuwait I handed back my pistol and ammunition, my helmet (the most comfortable I have owned in more than 30 years of soldiering), and my body armour. From Kuwait, after the obligatory long wait for a connecting flight, I flew to Dubai and then direct to Sydney, courtesy of a business–class seat on Emirates.

Fourteen hours later, I arrived in Sydney. After another longish wait in line, a customs officer asked me if I had brought any souvenirs home from Iraq. I replied that I had nothing at all, only later thinking up all the clever answers I could have given him.

I arrived home in Canberra mid-morning. Anne and the children met me at Canberra airport and Peter Leahy, the Chief of the Army, met me at my house in Duntroon to welcome me home.

I spent a week in Canberra attending debriefings in various parts of Defence and the intelligence community. Casey had requested that Australia replace me as Chief of Operations with another Australian general, but in our written reply we had expressed our regret that we did not have officers available with the operational background necessary — this was a view that surprised me. In Canberra, I was asked in one of my debriefs: 'Jim, what is the most significant thing that Australia could do to influence how this war is being fought?' I was staggered. Trying with all my might to stay in control, I answered, 'You should have replaced me with another Australian general.'

Most US units, before being reintroduced into home society, have a few days somewhere — known as 'decompression' — when they are quarantined from others, drink their first alcohol in a year, and are allowed to blow off steam. Thinking of this reminded me that my group in Iraq had been required to attend a psychological debrief at Camp Victory before I left Iraq. It was conducted by a well-intentioned young officer who had no frame of reference that would help him understand what we had been doing for the past year. I gained the impression that, having risked our lives to attend this debrief, it was being conducted not for us, but for the 'system'. It was most unsatisfactory, so I had cut it off and we had all travelled back along Route Irish to the Green Zone, more 'compressed' than ever.

After the debriefs in Canberra, Anne and I went for two weeks to our favourite part of the world: Caloundra, on Queensland's Sunshine Coast. We had the first week by ourselves and then the children joined us for the second. Caloundra provided the very best 'decompression' that I could ever experience.

CHAPTER 12

Playing Casey in Germany

Lessons for the long war

There are many postscripts to my year in Iraq. As I was leaving, the Americans invited me to what was called a Mission Rehearsal Exercise for the V Corps headquarters, which was to deploy from Germany back to Iraq in December 2005. The Corps headquarters was home-based in southern Germany, and was still commanded by Lieutenant General Ric Sanchez. This was to be the final teaching and testing exercise to determine their readiness for war.

The exercise took place in Germany in August 2005, four months after I had left Iraq. This group, with new staff and a new commander, was preparing to run the seven coalition divisions and now ten Iraqi divisions fighting the war at the tactical level. It was the next link in the chain of command below General Casey's headquarters.

Ten other Australians and I, all with recent experience in Iraq, went to the Grafenwoehr training area in Bavaria for a month. Bavaria was outstandingly beautiful in high summer, a delightful contrast to the Iraqi flatness and heat.

I hadn't seen General Sanchez since mid-2004, so we had a lot to talk about. He was a gracious host, and as I watched him train his headquarters, he repeatedly demonstrated his enormous operational experience — he is a great example of the technical military competence that the US Army expects and gets from its senior officers.

I spent a few minutes contemplating the irony of this exercise: so much effort went into preparing the Corps headquarters for its tactical role in Iraq, yet comparatively little effort was ever put into preparing the strategic headquarters that commanded them. Although it is passé to quote dead German generals, one of them once said: 'Strategy without tactics is the slowest route to victory, while tactics without strategy is noise before defeat.' The exercise in Germany reflected some of this wisdom.

My role in this computer-based exercise was to play the part of my ex-boss, General Casey, as commanding general of MNF-I. The exercise was big by any standards, but particularly for an Australian. We were electronically linked to smaller units in Germany and to two division headquarters in the US, all about to deploy to Iraq. We were also linked to Iraq itself, using real daily data from actual events. There may have been 5000 players and support staff involved. This was a sophisticated 21st-century exercise, lifting real-time events in Iraq from the military intranet and weaving them into the puzzle that the Corps staff had to solve. I had not been on such an activity since the 'Warfighter' exercise that had such an effect on me in the mid-'90s. Returning as someone considered an 'expert', I felt I had come full circle.

My mentor from Iraq, retired General Gary Luck, was the senior mentor in this exercise, working his magic for the benefit of the inexperienced Corps staff. My sparring partner from Iraq, Peter Chiarelli, was to command the new V Corps headquarters, but he was there for only a few days as an observer, as he had not yet taken over. There could not have been a better choice, given his success in very difficult conditions in Baghdad. But I felt for Pete, who must have had very little recovery time since returning home in April 2005 as commander of 1st Cavalry Division. He told me what a big decision it had been for his family, to have him spend another year in Iraq after surviving a very violent first tour.

Joint Forces Command, a relatively new body which sits outside the US Army, Air Force and Navy, ran the final phase of the Mission Rehearsal Exercise. The Americans had learnt through hard experience that 'jointness' cannot be achieved by the three services themselves, no matter how well intentioned they are. If you ask the army, navy or air force to lead joint exercises or operations, whatever 'jointness' there is will always be dominated by the lead service. Following the attempt to rescue hostages at the US Embassy in Tehran in 1979, and the spectacular failure on an Iranian airfield known as 'Desert One', the US Congress had forced the issue of how the traditional services worked together, and Joint Forces Command was a result. The US part of MNF-I may have looked like an army force, but in fact it was a joint force, with large joint, or non-army, components in its fire support, its intelligence, its logistics and its command.

For many years in various command positions I had concentrated on how a military should fight as a joint force — it was a passion of mine. I had a chance to apply those lessons when I commanded the Deployable Joint Force Headquarters in a major exercise against the US 7th Fleet in 2001, and I had tried to pass on what I knew to senior students when I was commander of the Australian Defence Colleges. Now I had practised it for a year in Iraq on a real battlefield and my appreciation of its value and its difficulty had been confirmed.

The ADF has no equivalent to the US Joint Forces Command. We have no single body that is uniquely and solely responsible for creating joint fighting capability, and I see this as a serious deficiency. We have bodies and individuals that are responsible for using joint forces when deployed, and we have bodies that are responsible for defining and then acquiring the equipment for our joint forces, and then sustaining them once deployed. However, we have no-one who has the means to 'create' the joint force before its deployment. I believe that because each service in the ADF is so small, we have an even greater need to work jointly than does the US military — it's just not obvious because we are so much less active than the US.

The exercise in Germany ran 24 hours a day for a few weeks, with the odd day or so between phases to confirm lessons learnt. We carried out remedial training in these lay-over days and, although the pace was busy, it was like a holiday compared with Iraq. I knew many of the key members on the re-formed V Corps HQ who had been in Iraq with me. Several had now been promoted and were going back. I also knew many of the staff running the exercise. Peter Palmer, my ex-deputy, was now Deputy Commander of the US Army's 1st Division (known as the Big Red One), which was also stationed in Germany. Peter had been pulled into the exercise because of his expertise in training.

My involvement as 'General Casey' was limited to a few hours each day. Early in the morning, I received the kind of briefs that I had spent so long giving to Casey myself. I then played Casey's reaction to those briefs, knowing what his strategy was and how he would have reacted. After that, I spent some time each day with the exercise administrators, reviewing what we had achieved and what we should concentrate on in the next period of the exercise. I then came back into the game from late in the day until early evening, giving my best impersonation of a US commanding general.

Unlike my time in Iraq, I spent most nights away from the operations centre, and had a few hours in the middle of each day where I was free from the day-to-day worries of a war. At last, I could think. I began to formulate and re-formulate what my experience in Iraq meant for me personally, and what it might mean for the ADF and my country. Between bouts of playing Casey in sunny Germany, I set myself a number of questions. As I jogged around the tank tracks in the German pine forests or enjoyed balmy Bavarian evenings, I worried that my own military was not asking the questions I thought should be asked to gain the most out of my experience. After each mind-clearing jog through the pine forests, I made notes. By the end of the exercise, I had tabulated a large number of lessons.

Personally, I took away from Iraq a feeling that, as a general, I was up to every challenge put to me. In all the ways I could think of, I was able to perform in a world-class shooting war to a world-class standard. I was fortunate to have spent my first month understudying Tom Miller, then three months in an unconventional role looking after strategic infrastructure security. During the latter period, I had less need for 'technical' knowledge of equipments and procedures, and more for initiative, drive and a willingness to take on responsibility and make things work. Having gone through this 'apprenticeship', I was ready for the bigger responsibilities of chief of operations once Casey arrived. Perhaps self-indulgently, I concluded that I should be happy with my performance. My bosses in Iraq expressed their satisfaction with my service. The operations I ran and the targets I prosecuted were not only successful efforts; just as importantly, they withstood the very high level of legal scrutiny in the US system.

The next question was slightly more complicated and less self-indulgent. It was: Did I perform capably to a world-class standard *because* of the preparation for senior rank provided by the ADF or *despite* the ADF?

Before I left for Iraq in April 2004, I had been running that segment of the ADF responsible for formally educating potential senior joint commanders. Even then, I had widely and publicly expressed my dissatisfaction with the Australian system of professional military education and, supported by Peter Cosgrove and several of the service chiefs, I had been able to convince the ADF via our committee system that changes were needed to emphasise generalship for a joint force. I had based these changes on the UK and US models and adjusted them for Australian needs, and in all this I had been assisted by a retired officer of great ability, Peter Abigail. I received approval and funds for these changes only months before I went to Iraq, but many of the changes were sidelined as soon as I left: some were later revived, but only partially. In my view, the ADF's senior professional military education system still does not emphasise 'operational art'. Even if, through some miracle, the changes I recommended in 2003 suddenly came into being, it would be years before they affect Australian generalship, and we have already lost too many years. Perhaps unsurprisingly, I did not, in the end, feel that my performance in Iraq owed a lot to the Australian professional military education system.

'Operational art' is all about the use of military forces in conflict and is sometimes referred to as generalship. It has elements of science: things you can learn and point to, things you can touch and be trained on. But it also requires experience and intuition. Intuition in the military is priceless. It is created within senior commanders by all their many military experiences, but most importantly, it is created by 'doing'. The 'doing' can be fighting real wars or being involved in advanced training exercises. The experience that creates intuition can also be passed from one generation to another by mentors. Our warfighting tradition in Australia has strengths at the lowest tactical level, but we have failed to keep abreast of conceptual debates and developments about how commanders use forces on a battlefield at the level above tactics.

This is understandable. Australia has not actually run many campaigns in its military history. We have handed either sizeable (and very capable) military forces over to fight under the direction of our allies, as in the two world wars, or we have made smaller contributions to various campaigns, such as Korea, Malaya, Vietnam and now Iraq and Afghanistan. One exception was East Timor, where Australia led a large multinational force, but the level of combat was very low so many of the stresses on commanders were absent. The longer that senior Australian field commanders do not have recent experience of planning, commanding and actually manoeuvring our own joint forces on a battlefield, the more important it is to emphasise training, education and what experience we can gain from our allies.

I make an important distinction here. I am not saying that Australia's military leaders lack competence. What I am saying is that our professional military education system is not helping our senior officers to be competent joint operational (field) commanders, because we are not investing in the necessary professional military education at the senior end. I also feel that the standard of joint competence we set for ourselves is skewed too far towards humanitarian operations, peacekeeping and peacemaking and away from warfighting. Of course they are important, but Iraq confirmed my long-held belief that even a small country such as Australia needs to be up to world standard in the fighting part of operations. Every soldier's bone in my body tells me that modern counterinsurgency operations in what may be a long war will require the ADF, not just our Special Forces, to fight jointly, as well as do all the other clever things that are necessary in a three-block war.

When I make this point, I am often asked why Australian forces, apart from our Special Forces, need to be good at joint warfighting as well as humanitarian, peacekeeping and peacemaking operations. It may seem a strange question to ask, but of the countries that committed troops to Iraq, most limited their use to non-offensive or non-combat roles, many for the simple reason that they were not capable of fighting a modern insurgent force in a city. They wanted to show commitment, but left the fighting up to the US and the UK.

It might be logical to think that Australia as a small country should always take its lead from countries much larger than ourselves, therefore joint warfighting is not relevant. My answer is that, first, government tells us in its regular defence guidance that we should be able to actually fight and to fight jointly and therefore probably expects that we can. Second, we are putting a vast amount of money into buying the materiel to enable us to fight. When it all arrives in ten years' time we will have the equipment to fight jointly — we just need to match that with fully competent field generalship by the time that we get the equipment. And third, although we will almost certainly always fight as part of a coalition, Australia is different from some middle powers in that government expects us to lead coalitions as well as to fight under others' plans and leadership. Finally, it is often the enemy that decides how intense and complicated a fight will be, not Canberra-based strategic experts and military and civilian bureaucrats. It is the arrogance that precedes a fall to believe that we are 'only' likely to fight a bunch of insurgents and terrorists in future counterinsurgencies, and therefore we need only prepare small army, navy or air force contingents that we give to allies to fight under their direction. What price Australian sovereignty? Ironically, in Australia's case it is not much more expensive to prepare for joint warfighting because most of it is about establishing the intellectual capital in the minds of future leaders — we have already contracted to buy the expensive equipment.

With a few exceptions, the ADF has been well led strategically over the last few years, and remains well led strategically today. Our deficiencies lie in what might be called 'operational generalship', not in the essential (and very difficult) 'Canberra generalship' or 'strategic generalship'. By 'operational generalship' I am referring to how air, ground and maritime forces fight as a single joint force led by

Australian senior joint commanders in sophisticated joint operations in modern, sustained combat.

Australia has had good field commanders, and we do not have to go back as far as Monash to find them. Australian battlefield commanders were inspirational in the two world wars. Even during the Korean and Vietnam wars we still had commanders at high levels who actually commanded the troops in combat and were not just looking after Australia's national interests. But much of Australian command has been exercised at the tactical level; there have been few instances of Australian generalship at the operational level in big, complex conflicts for at least half a century.

If our future commanders are not steeped in the operational art as it applies to all forms of joint operations, then our soldiers in our capable units are likely to be in the wrong place, at the wrong time, with the wrong equipment fighting the wrong war with the wrong strategy.

Peter Cosgrove ran a masterful campaign in East Timor — I was there and I watched him on the ground in Dili with admiration — but the level of opposition fell below what one would call 'warfighting'. Our troops were involved in several clashes in East Timor and were ready for much more, but it was not the kind of close combat that is underway every day in modern urban counterinsurgencies. In the Solomon Islands, the ADF's commitment was small and, thanks to competent civilian and military leadership, no combat occurred. Our involvement in Iraq in 2003 and earlier in Afghanistan involved some very effective combat by our Special Forces, very competent maritime operations in the Northern Arabian Gulf, and air force participation in combat operations. Our ongoing operations against the Taliban in Afghanistan certainly indicate that our Special Forces are extremely competent at the tactical level. Our force in southern Iraq is as ready as you can get a ground force for certain aspects of combat, but it is a very light force and has not been tested in sustained combat.

The ADF has deployed other generals and brigadiers overseas on operations in the last few years. But they were either staff officers like me or 'national commanders', not commanders who made the plans and manoeuvred the forces on a battlefield. National commanders have great responsibilities to look after the interests of Australia and its troops who operate under the foreign control, but they do not control troops on the battlefield.

Notwithstanding the success of our special forces, the ADF has not been involved in serious, joint, sustained combat since Vietnam. We have not practised 'operational generalship' in a fighting war for at least that long. I focus on generalship for a number of reasons: I am one; I had a unique exposure to world-class military operations as a general; and, most importantly, the general is still the only individual who can lose the war. Because we do not have the battle experience, our professional military education and training system should compensate by being of an even higher standard, and it is not doing that.

So my considered view is that we need change. This may not be apparent to some in our society, mainly because the ADF is a victim of its own success. Our troops have met all the requirements of the governments that have sent them to war since 1999, with very few casualties. We in Australia luxuriate in what I describe as wars of choice and choice within wars: we choose the wars we will fight in, we choose the timing of our participation, we choose the geographical area of our participation (and so control the level of likely combat), we choose the kind of operations we will conduct, and we choose when we come home.

There is nothing wrong with this, as long as circumstances permit. It indicates successful diplomacy and costs us few lives. But how long can we keep doing it? If the answer is forever, then my lessons from a fighting war are irrelevant. But if there is even a 1 per cent chance of Australia having to fight a war involving sustained combat (and I think we could say it is many times greater than 1 per cent), then I suggest that the ADF study those who are gaining experience of fighting now, and start with a review of operational generalship. The consequences of getting it wrong are too horrendous to contemplate, and the Australian people would never forgive us.

Shortly before the end of November 2006, Defence gave me permission to speak at a civilian think-tank known as the Kokoda Foundation. My fellow speakers were the retired US Marine General Anthony Zinni, an ex-commander of Central Command and long a critic of how the Iraq War was being run, and Rich Armitage, the Deputy Secretary of State to Colin Powell with whom I had dined the year before in the US Embassy in Baghdad. The question we were asked to address was fundamental: What needs to be done to ensure that the next generation of Australia–US combined operations can be conducted to the greatest effect? It was an interesting discussion because it came just before the US mid-term elections in which the Republicans lost control of both the congress and the senate, and the war in Iraq was said to be the major issue. It was also before the US President's January 2007 'Strategy on Iraq' statement.

I took the notes I'd made in Germany and looked for one main point that would encapsulate everything I learnt in Iraq. I rejected the obvious one: Don't get involved in a counterinsurgency unless you intend to win! The closest I could come to an original idea was to say that success in counterinsurgency lies simply in carrying a significant proportion of our own citizens and the target country citizens with us.

Just about everything else flows from that one requirement. Counterinsurgencies are not short, sharp manoeuvres that result in victory and are followed immediately by a parade in front of a grateful nation. Counterinsurgencies are all about attrition of mind, spirit and body, and no-one wins quickly. If you do not have a significant level of support at home, your people will not have the endurance to win. If you do not have support from the people in the country in which you fight, the insurgents will win. This fact affects policy, strategy and tactics. In my speech to the Kokoda Foundation, I acknowledged that in our Iraq engagement it appeared that the coalition had failed to carry most of the population of most of the countries involved. Is it because the endeavour is evil? I don't believe so. Is it because Iraq is unwinnable? No, the Iraq War remains winnable (and I attempt to define 'winning' later). Will it be easier to keep the support of the US population with fewer US casualties? Probably.

Just before the forum, being something of a masochist, I had listened to a BBC phone-in program on Iraq. One caller grabbed my attention as she spoke about life in Baghdad at the height of the sectarian violence. She was an Iraqi ringing from the Karada neighbourhood, not far from the Green Zone.

She spoke emotionally of the disruption of her life by coalition troops who were searching for kidnapped US soldiers. Many Iraqis are kidnapped and killed each day, she said, and that doesn't spark such a strong reaction from the coalition forces. Iraqis' daily tragedies, she said, tended to be overlooked. She had supported the overthrow of Saddam, but now she saw no benefit, just death and disruption. Finally, she was asked if the US should leave. She said no, the US could not leave now or there would be a disaster, but the US must solve the problem that they had created and then get out.

For this Karada lady, the low value she felt was placed on Iraqi lives, the disruption to her daily life, and the lack of benefit to Iraqis were overwhelming. She was not complaining about some strategy, or expressing a view about right and wrong, or about abstract concepts such as democracy and values and military effectiveness. And who can blame her, after more than three years of this?

I mentioned the Karada lady to the think-tank. I acknowledged that my actions had disrupted her too. I'd moved aggressively through her neighbourhood with my bodyguard and armoured vehicles. Some of her neighbours in Karada even attacked my convoy with an RPG, but I am sure it was nothing personal. But that was not this lady's problem. Our enemy in counterinsurgency is not the people; our enemy is hiding among the people and using them as a shield. The people are intimately involved in modern urban conflict, and it's inevitable that sometimes they will see our actions as being careless of their safety. That means that the current and future challenge for Australian–US counterinsurgencies (the topic of our think-tank seminar) must be the people and their attitudes.

My greatest disappointment, I told the forum, was that the coalition had not been able to fully protect the Iraqi people, their economy or the process of reconstruction. We may not have failed entirely in supplying some essential services, but the Karada lady would not have been impressed that I managed to get six hours of power into Baghdad each day instead of none or two. She is living our failure, and her attitude is the key to our present and future success.

I have often wondered what would have happened in Iraq if several hundred thousand coalition soldiers had stopped the looting, nipped the insurgency in the bud in late 2003, achieved security in the cities so that jobs, education and other essential services could be resumed, and found, then killed or captured the terrorists before they could get established. But that is fantasy, and soldiers deal with reality.

Those of us who fought in 2004 and 2005, the second year of the war, had the theory of counterinsurgency fixed firmly in our minds and reflected in our plans. But the reality of making it work was different, and that reality is the Karada lady. We couldn't put the theory into practice effectively because of the immediate demands of current combat. As long as the enemy kept fighting us across Iraq, we couldn't protect the economy, the infrastructure and the people at the same time. Therefore we could rarely do the clever hearts-and-minds part of counterinsurgency. Essential services and reconstruction were key parts of our campaign plan, but I only ever gained coalition attention to address these at moments of absolute crisis, and then not for long. Coordinating what we did across the entire country was the most difficult thing I have ever attempted, and only on two occasions (at the November 2004 battle of Fallujah and at the January 2005 election) did I come even reasonably close.

It is now generally accepted that there were not enough quality troops in Iraq to do the job in the first few years of the war. The coalition had enough troops to protect the Iraqi leaders, carry out operations against the insurgent leaders, and protect ourselves. We had enough to win the big battles and to conduct some training of the Iraq security forces. But we did not have enough to establish a presence in all key areas, nor to protect the infrastructure and reconstruction, nor to maintain a reserve fighting force. This shortage disrupted all continuity. No clever or innovative tactics could ever fully compensate for it. General Casey's idea of providing the extra troops by creating Iraqi forces was correct at the time, and remains correct. The recent surge of 25,000 US troops is a start, and over the time that the surge has been effectively applied, the Iraqi Security Forces have also grown significantly and increased in experience and quality, but they still have many problems. If the war is ever to be won, though, it will be they who ultimately win it, when the surged troops have gone home.

The second major point I made to the forum was the need for both a consistent and agreed counterinsurgency policy and strategy, and infinite flexibility in tactics. One should lead to the other. The way President Bush intended to run the war over his last period in office was contained in the 'Iraq Strategy Review' published in

January 2007. It generally ignored the preceding Baker/Hamilton
Review, and I applauded him for doing so. I could understand the
desire of the Baker/Hamilton Review to recommend the
withdrawal of troops and an increased emphasis on diplomacy, but I
could not reconcile that with the viciousness of the enemy, which
the review also acknowledged. The review stressed the special
responsibility towards Iraq that the US had because it invaded, but
went on to say that withdrawal of troops before success should be an
option. If we who invaded have any responsibility, it is to not leave
the Iraqi people to al Qaeda.

Personally, I consider withdrawing US forces from Iraq a
catastrophic mistake, so I support President Bush's overall strategy.
Strangely, though, what struck me most about the so-called new
strategy put out by the White House was the degree to which it
continued a straight line of strategy from our August 2004 Iraq
campaign plan through the November 2005 public document called
the 'National Strategy for Victory in Iraq' to the 'Iraq Strategy
Review' published in January 2007.

The strategic situation for the US in Iraq has always involved
three options, all of which are expressed in the popular mind by the
number of troops engaged. The first is to remain engaged in order to
win — that may require more US troops or the creation of more
Iraqi troops, or both. The second is to withdraw from Iraq because
defeat is inevitable — withdraw all troops fast and leave the Iraqis to
it. The third is a mix of the first two — withdraw slowly and limit
military engagements because failure may occur sometime in the
future. Bush stuck with the first strategy and provided the necessary
troops from both the US and Iraqi sources.

This continuity, I suspect, was the basis on which General Casey
stated that he does not see the war as 'slow failure' but as 'slow
progress'. Iraq needs a consistent strategy and that is what it seems to
be getting, but it will still take time. Within this strategy, however,

there is an almost infinite number of optional tactics and techniques: engage diplomatically with neighbours or freeze them out; use US troops or use Iraqi troops; operate from big centralised bases or from small neighbourhood bases; engage with the Sunnis or keep them separate; allow Iraqis political freedom or take over the whole show and run it for them. Tactics must be used when appropriate, and dropped when not. In this world of imperfect knowledge, it is often the case that no-one will know if a tactic will even be initially successful, but a promising tactic can always be tried, and discontinued if it does not work. And of course, tactics that work today may not work tomorrow.

Throughout 2007, the level of support for the Iraq War in the US fell even more. But in our media-driven society, history shows that support for any war will wax and wane over time, fuelled by the casualty rate and also by the political cycle. In the face of this, President Bush continued to prosecute the war, and even increased troop commitments, despite Democrat control of Congress and anti-war opinion polls. These were determined actions for a president often lampooned by his detractors. I still ask myself: Is it the mark of a true leader of a democracy that, on occasions and within constitutional bounds, he must be prepared to ignore the apparent views of the people? Was it Churchill who carried the British nation in its darkest hour against a strong view that some accommodation must be entered into with Hitler? In these situations, the right or wrong of any course of action can only be judged in retrospect.

So, having spoken to the Kokoda forum about reconciling a broad sustained consensus that carries your people with you, having a consistent strategy applied over time, and democratic leadership, I limited myself to about ten points.

I said that despite the importance of technology, leadership is still the most critical aspect of modern conflict. I thought of the extraordinary leaders I had seen in Iraq. Early mistakes are inevitable:

in fact, trial and error is the norm, even with good leaders. But societies that send people to war must not see trial and error as failure. I believe that no society should skimp on preparing its civilian and military 'generals'. In a sovereign democracy, generalship is not something that should ever be left to chance.

For counterinsurgency, I said, you certainly need sufficient combat troops, but you also need enough specialists for 'war among the people', such as military police, human intelligence, detention specialists, biometric specialists, and civilian affairs personnel. But as well, you must have forces who have the skills and the attitude to conduct the three-block war, but who are also resilient enough to be swung into more demanding conventional assault operations, such as Fallujah. The question will always be: Are they to be foreign or local troops? Almost certainly, in the case of failed states, in the future they will be our soldiers, until the local troops are capable.

I spoke about the need for professional headquarters to support the leader. If you rely on the famous military principle of 'ad hoc-ism', you will pay in the long run. General Sanchez suffered from this, and we worked to avoid it with General Casey. It has been a popular view for most of my military career that the ADF has too many headquarters and too many peple working in them, a view more likely to be held by those who have never commanded. It is certainly possible to have too many headquarters in any military, but leaders are the key, and both civilian and military leaders need the best professional support. I believe we have finally provided the right headquarters at the strategic level in the ADF; we just need to do it at the next level down as well.

Stabilising a country takes time and costs money, whether there is an insurgency or not, and I suggested that East Timor is a prime local example of that. We should all understand that the military normally does not produce results initially or quickly, and that it rarely produces them cheaply. The initial stages of any conflict will not be handled perfectly. We are in what the Australian author Coral Bell calls the 'Jihadist War', and the first few years of the war in Iraq went about as well as history would indicate most serious wars went in their initial stages. In fact, at the start of 2008, Iraq may even be going better than most.

I suggested that none of us should be surprised if the enemy surprises us. Our enemy doesn't have perfect knowledge and the worst does not always happen, but often the insurgents in Iraq seemed to know intimately what our options were, and they worked to our weaknesses. It was when things were going better for us at the end of 2005 that the enemy ignited the sectarian violence that, in turn, required the troop surge. Perhaps we assumed that the enemy would never be so lacking in humanity as to attack his own people with such a vengeance. The enemy assumed that by escalating the violence, he would prompt us to leave. We used to refer to the IRA as hard men, but they were 'pussies' compared to this lot, and it took a long conflict to bring all sides in Northern Ireland to compromise. I risked making a statement of the blindingly obvious when I reminded the conference that no-one will compromise when they think they can win!

No-one needed to tell the conference that counterinsurgency is not just a military activity, nor is it only about fighting. In Iraq, the role of the military (coalition or Iraqi) is to protect the people, protect the electoral, constitutional and political processes, protect the economy and establish a level of security that can ultimately be taken over by local forces. Nothing occurs until there is security, and security is very hard to establish in an urban environment against the kind of enemy we face. But the sectors of our societies outside the military must also carry their burden, and just as we did not have enough US troops in Iraq, we also did not have enough State, CIA, Homeland Security, and other personnel either.

I offered the truism that when you have to fight, you must be able to fight effectively. Because combat is so ugly, many people in our society want to find another way of resolving issues, but often there is no other way. It sometimes seemed that the only group not concerned about the ugliness of combat was our enemy, who relied on violence as his prime tactic.

In Iraq I had learnt never to expect success in information operations, so I was rarely disappointed. It is very hard to use information as a weapon, and harder still to measure its effectiveness. You must keep using information, however, for a variety of reasons, not least of which is to establish a public record. In my view, we were only ever mildly successful in information operations in my time in Iraq on two occasions: the second battle of Fallujah, and the January 2005 election.

Modern counterinsurgency is essentially joint, not army-only. Any military that considers itself modern and competent must be able to conduct a sophisticated level of joint operations where the three traditional services (and everyone else who contributes to operations) work together intimately. In Iraq, we face a daunting, fast-learning, adaptable enemy, and we must expect to face similar enemies in the future. As I said, techniques that took the IRA ten years to develop are being mastered by this enemy in one year. Any force that considers itself capable of 21st-century counterinsurgency must be inherently joint at the operational and tactical level.

I stressed the need to get the doctrine right. Doctrine is military experience written down, and it must have authority to shape what the military will become and will do. US counterinsurgency doctrine adapted to the current war by learning and re-learning. In the ADF we need good doctrine across a range of situations: humanitarian, peacekeeping, peacemaking, counterinsurgency, warfighting. Not only must our doctrine be right, it must also flow down with authority into every aspect of our military.

Even the lowest level of troop density for modern counter-insurgency operations, especially against a jihadist enemy in cities, will require the use of part-time forces. This is because no country in the world can maintain enough full-time forces. The US Reserve and National Guard had trouble meeting combat requirements in the high-intensity 1991 Gulf War. They do not have that problem now in most operations in Iraq. US part-time forces fight as coherent units, and they are impressive.

I concluded my segment of the conference by saying that there is no silver bullet that will give us instant and easy success in any counterinsurgency. Perhaps the closest thing we have to a silver bullet is national resilience: an expression of the will of our people over time. We need time because we learn and improve, and if we have the will, we can find the resources to win most conflicts. In the case of the jihadist war, where we are fighting proponents of a distorted view of the Islamic religion, we occupy the moral high ground and we must be confident of that position. If we are uncertain about what we stand for and about the righteousness of any cause on which we embark, then we will not know what we are fighting for, and we will lose.

In the New Year's Honours list in 2006, I was awarded the Distinguished Service Cross for 'distinguished service in command and leadership in action'. It was a significant award, not often given, and I was greatly honoured. A small picture of my face appeared on the front page of the *Sydney Morning Herald*, dwarfed by a very big picture of Nicole Kidman, who was also being honoured that year, in a slightly different field. For obvious reasons, very few people noticed the picture of me. Jokingly, Anne expressed the hope that that was as close as I would ever get to Nicole Kidman.

CHAPTER 13

Epilogue

Sow and reap

Because of the nature of the wars we fight today, I find it hard to envision any soldier in the foreseeable future enjoying the indulgence of a victory parade. Wars do not seem to have a neat and tidy end any more. My comrades and I have not marched in victory through any streets — we have no victory to declare in Iraq. The nature of war, especially 'war among the people', is such that there will rarely be definable victory.

But there can still be defeat.

I felt good about our progress in Iraq throughout 2004 and 2005. Nothing about it was neat and tidy and we did not at any stage approach perfection, but I came home cautiously optimistic. I had an incentive for optimism. Having seen our enemy, I had a better idea of what could happen if we were defeated in Iraq — the effect on the whole of the Middle East, the global consequences of a humiliated US, and the impact of emboldened Islamic extremism in my part of the world.

From the safety of Australia, I thought that General Casey probably had reason to be satisfied by late 2005. Not only had he conducted the three elections, but an army and a police force had been created,

Zarqawi was being closely pursued and would be killed by a strike of several JDAM bombs in 2006, and Iraqis were participating in greater numbers in the running of their country. Although the delivery of essential services to the people was still poor, just about every other economic indicator was looking positive. But the fight was far from over, and 2006 was a bad year. My 'constructive paranoia' should have warned me that the moment we patted ourselves on the back, our enemy would adapt. In January 2006, the Golden Mosque in Samarra was destroyed, heralding the emergence of full-blown sectarian conflict. Rightly, in my view, General Casey stuck with his plan of transitioning the fight to the Iraqis, more US soldiers were put into Iraqi units, and in mid-2006 US soldiers moved back into Baghdad to assist their Iraqi comrades. Al Qaeda recovered from the loss of Zarqawi and increased their indiscriminate attacks on the Iraqi people. Not only did the Iraqi Police and Army fail to counter the onslaught, but undisciplined and badly led elements actually participated in the killing. The number of US casualties increased and the involvement of Iran, directly or indirectly, brought a new dimension to the fight. All of this was of course reported by the world media. The slaughter of Iraqis in sectarian violence continued for the rest of 2006 and my cautious optimism was severely tested.

I am writing in early 2008, nearly three years since I left Iraq. The intervening period has given me some perspective on my involvement in the war, on what the war is, and on what it means to Australia. I have watched the continuing struggle with more than a passing interest. In just about every public discussion in which I have been involved, at least half the audience have not supported the war in Iraq, mainly because of the way it started, not because of what it is now. I understand that sentiment, and even the outrage, but I also know how it can distort our present and future policy.

I have never publicly stated whether or not I supported the invasion of Iraq. To me, the invasion of Iraq is now history and you might as well ask me if I supported D–Day in 1944. The 2003 invasion was history, even in 2004, when I arrived in Iraq, and it is even more so now. The legality and morality of how we, the coalition, found ourselves in Iraq is very important, but it is a vastly different issue from what we must do now. Of course we must learn from our past actions, but it is dangerous to spend our time beating our breasts in regret while our enemies concentrate on defining the future by winning the present. I believe the coalition is legally and morally correct in what it is doing in Iraq today, and we should have the confidence in the values of our own societies to say so. Just as the end does not justify the means, what may have been an initial policy error could indeed be seen as a tragedy in itself, but only our enemies want it to end in policy paralysis. Whether it is comforting to say so or not, the values of our society are being challenged by extremist ideas, and at some stage our society must take a stand. I do not know if Iraq is the place to make that stand, but I do know that in Iraq I saw evil in a form I had not seen anywhere else, and values that are inimical to everything that has shaped our society since the Enlightenment. What is most important is how we manage this war now and in the future.

Since I left in April 2005, there have been many significant events for Iraq, and the struggle continues. The electoral and constitutional process was completed during 2005. Eight million of the 14 million who were eligible voted in the first election. Media reports told me that 12 million, including Sunnis, voted in the constitutional referendum, and then more than 12 million voted in the final election in December 2005 which chose the Maliki government. Prime Minister Nouri al-Maliki has not yet fulfilled our hopes, despite the extreme efforts made to put him in place. But we should not be surprised at that. Indonesia did not get its democratic leadership right first go. Democracy has never promised to produce competent governments immediately, but in the case of Iraq there is little time to experiment.

I have faith in US generalship because the generals I know are competent and moral. Like all of us, they are not flawless, but these are men and women who deal with issues of enormous complexity. The commander in Iraq who replaced General Casey, General David Petraeus, is a fine leader and his surge of 25,000 extra troops since late 2007 seems to be producing results. I did not agree with the media endorsement of him (when he replaced General Casey) as a saviour, the 'Ulysses S. Grant of the Iraq War', and I would like to think that he would not believe it either. It casts aspersions on General Casey, and I find that difficult to accept.

The US doctrine on counterinsurgency (identified by the alluring title of *Field Manual 3-24*) was produced by two of the most experienced soldiers from the Iraq War so far: David Petraeus and Marine Lieutenant General Jim Mattis. It is a solid doctrinal base for present and future conflicts involving insurgents. It is the result of what has been learnt and practised on and off in Iraq over the last few years. But neither the generals nor their doctrine will have any dramatic new answer to the war. Again, winning this war will take time. If the current strategy in Baghdad and the Sunni triangle is successful, it will take us back to roughly where we were at the end of 2005, ready to transition the fight to the Iraqis. General Petraeus will know that this was just before the attack on the Golden Mosque in Samarra, and the start of the sectarian phase of the war. Where will our enemies take the war if they again feel that they are being beaten in Iraq? How will they surprise us next time?

It is my contention, with full knowledge of all the errors that we made, that we had to go through the 2003–06 period to get serious about this fight. In 2006, as the violence increased, I often stated my fear that we were going to be defeated in Iraq before we had begun truly to fight.

The fact that the enemy changed the nature of the war is an important point that is often missed, because people accept the popular wisdom that we have been losing in Iraq since the invasion. That is not true. We have been winning and losing in Iraq — at different times, sometimes at the same time, and in different places. We were not winning in 2007, and perhaps we are not losing in 2008. But we can still win overall. It was our successes in 2005 that forced our adversary to risk his sectarian violence strategy. To visit such extraordinary violence on your own people, even for an inherently violent body such as al Qaeda, is not without risk. The Sunnis who are turning away from the insurgents and the terrorists are proof of that.

I can now see that the war in Iraq is not one single fight. Even at this stage, in my opinion, it has had four quite distinct phases. We decisively won the first: March to April 2003, the invasion. We disastrously missed many opportunities in the second: April 2003 to August 2004, the emergence of the insurgency. We won (or at least did not lose) the third: August 2004 to January 2006, the creation of institutions. And we lost the fourth: February 2006 to January 2007, the shift to sectarian violence. President Bush's Iraq Policy Review in 2007 marked the start of a fifth phase, which until his elevation to Commander, Central Command, was being led by General Petraeus. I hope historians will rate it a successful phase and perhaps title it the 'Comprehensive Response'. If it is successful, and the enemy is reduced to a level that can be handled by the Iraqis, the coalition can withdraw the bulk of their troops. What is left of *the* Iraq War will become *an* Iraqi war and then, let us hope, the Iraqi peace.

There is a plan for Iraq, and I believe it can be successful. Any plan is still only 10 per cent of the required effort, though. Execution is 90 per cent. As chief of operations in Iraq, I planned a bit, but generally I lived and breathed the execution of others' plans. I know how execution overrides everything else. Once the experts had planned, and I had executed, it was then up to the soldiers' courage and initiative, and they did not let us down.

It is fair to ask the question: Why should President Bush's new strategy work now when the perception is that other plans have not worked? Maybe that perception is wrong. I see the surge of troops in 2007 and 2008 as a continuation of strategy: it is the second time in Iraq that US troop numbers have been increased by this amount. As we approached the second battle of Fallujah and the first Iraqi election, General Casey asked for and was given an increase in troop numbers of 30,000, taking us from roughly 125,000 to 155,000 US troops for about six months. We could not have successfully conducted the first Iraqi election in January 2005 without those extra troops. As I have recounted here, it worked well the first time and it looks as if it may have some effect this time.

The big challenge is still to give security, prosperity and governance back to the Iraqi people. Everything depends on security, and a key part of security is created by militaries that can fight. I was part of a force that could certainly fight, but we had trouble delivering services to the people, despite the emphasis we put on this in every plan that we made, and despite the demands of our subordinate commanders and the cries of the people. It was not that we were ignorant of what we should do; we were just limited by a lack of resources. Unfortunately, there is still insufficient energy flowing into Iraqi cities, and a lack of emphasis on competent troops to protect the infrastructure.

The daily headlines screamed defeat for some time after the surge began, but the papers seem to have gone silent now, in early 2008, as the levels of violence fall. For a long time, much of the information delivered to the public would have us believe that the sacrifice of human lives was occurring, without any gains that would make that sacrifice worthwhile. In making mature judgments about the war in Iraq, we must be able to see past the daily headline.

The US has had close to 4000 soldiers killed and 28,000 wounded in Iraq since 2003. This is a major conflict by any measure.

Because every death and injury is a tragedy, it is particularly difficult to gain perspective. In World War II the US lost 300,000. In the Korean War, 36,000 US soldiers died. And in Vietnam, the US lost 54,000. I have heard that the Iraq War would cost US$2 trillion if it ran for ten years. This is a sum of money that is beyond my comprehension, but I am told that it would only be 1.1 per cent of US GDP over that period. In terms of treasure, this could still be a comparatively cheap war in dollar terms. But no war is cheap in lives or treasure if you end up losing.

The estimate of Iraqi casualties when I was there, before the sectarian violence really bit, was in the order of 30,000 killed, and is now estimated to be perhaps as high as 90,000. Almost all of that horrific total were killed by insurgents and terrorists, but I would never agree with anyone who argues that this is the price the Iraqi people should be prepared to pay to be free of Saddam. One of my responsibilities as chief of operations was to coordinate with all our other military operations the search for mass graves by the Regime Crimes Commission in Iraq. By the time I left, we had found 300,000 bodies in mass graves from Saddam's regime. He murdered unknown thousands of his own people, not including those he killed in the wars he started. I am not able to judge the validity of *The Lancet*'s figures of 2006 that 650,000 people have died as a result of the war in Iraq. It is a surprisingly large number, and does not accord with estimates by the US, the UN or the Iraqi government or others, such as Iraqbodycount.org, who follow the toll closely. Whether or not it is correct, though, it still does not represent an argument to abandon 27 million Iraqis to the terrorists.

The country of Iraq and its people are important in themselves, as well as in terms of what they mean to the world. Despite the fact that the tree of freedom is being watered daily with their blood — on some days a deluge — the Iraqis should be given their chance at freedom. They deserve this as much as the Indonesians or the East Timorese or anyone else. After three elections, they have earnt it.

I have said that I did not know much about Iraq in early 2004. What I quickly learnt about the Land of the Two Rivers, the cradle of our civilisation, was that civilisation itself was being threatened there. I was reminded once again that there is still truth in the hackneyed saying that freedom is not free, but must be purchased and re-purchased with effort, blood and sacrifice. In Iraq I witnessed sacrifice and courage, dedication and professionalism, cruelty and barbarity, success and failure, often in the same day, even the same hour.

None of us can ever be sure if ultimate victory will be ours. As the surge of US troops has some effect in Baghdad we have cause for greater hope, but I held silent hopes after the first election in 2005, and then much greater hopes at the end of 2005. It may sound callous, but I rarely permitted myself to focus on the cruel and inhuman day-to-day slaughter of innocent Iraqis, or on the sacrifice of our soldiers. I felt their pain, but my focus had to be elsewhere. As my prime minister directed me, I fought to protect the Iraqi people.

There is a difficult road ahead for Iraq and for the supporters of the Iraqi people, but the journey must soon be led by the Iraqis themselves or they will lose their chance at freedom. This could be the last chance for a long time for anything that approaches a democratic future for Iraq, and they must seize the moment. Casey often paraphrased Lawrence of Arabia: 'Help them to do it; do not do it for them.'

But we should not turn to another strategy, such as total and precipitate withdrawal, just because things are tough. There could be a time when we leave the Iraqis entirely to sort it out for themselves, but it is not now, not in 2008. The trick, as Casey said and wrote often, is to not rush the Iraqi government and its security forces towards failure. This haste was evident when I first arrived in April 2004.

There has been extraordinary sacrifice in Iraq and it is legitimate to ask what we are likely to get from it. What, in short, is 'winning'? In my view, we should be content if we have created in Iraq a sovereign country that has its own form of democracy. We should be happy if Iraq becomes more economically independent and brings some prosperity to its long-suffering people. We should be ecstatic if the new Iraq is inclusive of its minorities, understands human rights, and can defend itself internally. We should be delirious with joy if Iraq is not a threat to its neighbours and stands beside us in the war on terror. None of these will, however, be achieved perfectly. My year in Iraq reinforced a view that those who demand perfection are constantly disappointed.

The campaign plan in Iraq was part of the long-term global war on terror. Secretary Rumsfeld was quoted as saying that the average insurgency in the 20th century lasted nine years. The insurgency in Iraq started in about August 2003, so my year in Iraq straddled the first and second years of the life cycle of an insurgency that probably still has many years to run. As I write in 2008, by the law of averages, it is just over halfway through.

We have certainly 'sown the wind' in Iraq. Regardless of why we find ourselves there, regardless of how tough it is at times and the cost that we need to pay in lives and in treasure, if we 'lose' in Iraq the whirlwind could truly be ours. General Petraeus says Iraq is the central battlefield in the struggle against extremist Islam, and I find it hard to disagree with him on that. Given the extra resources we have now put into the fight and their apparent success, I now feel that at least we will not lose before we have really begun to fight. But, as General Casey would say, our peoples need continual resolve, and this will still be a long fight. Every time we get close to some acceptable form of victory, our enemy will try to change the nature of the struggle. War has never been just an extension of politics by other means; war also creates its own politics. If the coalition or the

US are seen to be defeated in the Middle East, then there are likely to be consequences for Australia in our part of the world that we don't want.

In Iraq I watched the impact of a relatively small number of battle-hardened foreign fighters from previous jihadist conflicts. They led inexperienced volunteers from Saudi, Jordan, Sudan, Egypt, Chechnya, Afghanistan, Pakistan and from Islamic communities in Europe. Some came to fight, some came to be martyrs. If we are defeated in Iraq, I can only wonder about the outflow of experienced fighters, emboldened by success against a superpower, and the impact of only a few on the accommodating tropical Islam of Indonesia, the most populous Islamic country in the world — but still a new democracy.

My Prime Minister and the Chief of the Australian Defence Force sent me to Iraq with certain directions. To the best of my ability, I fulfilled them. As an Australian general in a coalition force, I planned and ran a multitude of operations, military and non-military, culminating in the elections. We found and dealt with terrorists who offered Iraq nothing but a return to the Middle Ages. I carried out my duties as directed by my military and civilian coalition superiors to their apparent satisfaction, and I acted legally and morally. I gave no cause for our allies to have anything but the highest regard for ADF personnel. Australia was shown as unified with other nations in the coalition and as an active, responsible and committed partner. In my actions I gave no comfort or solace to those who were working against the new Iraq. I fought my way to the election.

It was an extraordinary year for this Australian general.

Several months after I came home, I finally received my few boxed possessions from Iraq — they had been shipped by the cheapest and slowest means possible. As I unpacked them in the old stable at the back of my house in Canberra, I saw a square box that the Chief

Electoral Officer, Dr Adil, had given me at a farewell just before I left Iraq.

Steve Gliddon had suggested the farewell; I was against it, because I just wanted to go. But he insisted, and he was right. Most of my Iraqi friends came to my office at the back of the operations centre in Saddam's palace in the Green Zone. Ali's mother produced Iraqi sweetmeats, and Steve produced a most unmilitary china tea service from which we sipped Iraqi tea. It was an extraordinary few hours. The tension was gone, we spoke in many languages, we congratulated ourselves and we toasted in tea the future of Iraq. Each Iraqi group — the military, the police, the intelligence and the IECI — presented me with gifts. Many of them I was unable to open at the time, but I thanked them each profusely through Ali. One of my guests protested my thanks, saying in English that if the coalition had not come to Iraq, he would never have seen the inside of the palace in which he now stood. After several hours, Steve and my bodyguard escorted the last of our guests out of the palace, and their gifts were packed away, including Dr Adil's box and a flat stiff object.

Months later in Canberra, both were still gift-wrapped, with a card written in Arabic. I unwrapped the box and found an impressive Baume and Mercier wristwatch. Delighted, I took it into the house, put it on, and showed Anne. Then I turned my attention to the flat object. I lifted it out of the freight box and saw a note stuck on it, written by Steve Gliddon.

'Sir,' Steve's note said. 'Have a look at this. It appears to be Ballot Paper number nine. A great honour.'

Steve had obviously noticed the significance of the presentation as he packed it up to send back to Australia.

It was indeed Ballot Paper number nine. After the election, someone had told me that the first eight of the 20 million printed and individually numbered ballot papers were to be presented to the eight commissioners of the IECI. These were eight courageous and patriotic Iraqi men and women who risked everything for a concept of freedom that many claimed was not understood by Iraqis. The commissioners understood freedom and deserved their ballot papers. But for Dr Adil to give me Ballot Paper No. 00000009 was an honour of which, unfortunately, I was unaware at the time, and which I would never have thought possible. What we in our campaign plan called a 'milestone', the first Iraqi election on 30 January 2005, many Iraqis saw quite rightly as the first step to true freedom. Here was their message: they thought I had played a part in creating an Iraq that had a chance of actually being free. And now an Australian general, standing in an old stable in a wintry but secure Canberra several months later, had been reminded of the privilege that was his.

List of Acronyms

AC-130	armed Hercules aircraft
ADF	Australian Defence Force
APC	armoured personnel carrier
BUA	battle update assessment
C-130	Hercules aircraft
CCCB	CENTCOM Component Commanders' Brief
CDE	collateral damage estimate
CENTCOM	US Central Command (Qatar)
CG	Commanding General
CJTF-7	Combined Joint Task Force 7
CPA	Coalition Provisional Authority
DESC-I	Defense Energy Support Centre, Iraq
ERPRO	Emergency Rapid Pipeline Repair Organization
FRAGO	fragmentary order
HMMWV	high-mobility multi-purpose wheeled vehicle (Hummer, HumVee)
IGC	Iraqi Governing Council

IECI	Independent Electoral Commission of Iraq
IED	improvised explosive device
JDAM	Joint Direct Attack Munition
MNF-1	Multi-National Force–Iraq
PNG	Papua New Guinea
Psyops	psychological operations
RMC	Royal Military College
RPG	rocket-propelled grenade
SAS	Special Air Services (Regiment, ADF)
SECDEF	US Secretary of Defense
SUV	Sports Utility Vehicle (four-wheel drive)
TACSAT	tactical satellite communication evening update
vidcon	video conference
XO	executive officer

Cast of characters

John Abizaid	General (US Army)
Dr Adil Al-Lami	Chief Electoral Officer, IECI
Mowaffak al Rubaie	National Security Adviser
Aiham al-Sammarae	Iraqi Electricity Minister
Ali al-Sistani	Grand Ayatollah (Shi'ite)
Iyad Allawi	Prime Minister, Iraqi Interim Government
Eldon Bargewell	Major General (US Army)
Chuck Betack	Colonel (US Army)
Brad Bellis	Captain (US Navy)
Brian Boyle	Colonel (US Army)
L. Paul (Jerry) Bremer III	US Ambassador
Howard Brown	Australian Ambassador to Iraq
Ken Brownrigg	Colonel (Australian Army)
Harry Callicotte	Major (US Army)
George Casey	General (US Army)
Dick Cavasos	General (US Army – retired)

Peter Chiarelli	Major General (US Army)
Jim Conway	Lieutenant General (US Marine Corps)
Peter Cosgrove	Chief of the Australian Defence Force (2002–05)
Tony Cusimano	Lieutenant Colonel (US Army)
John Custer	Brigadier General (US Army)
Adam Damiri	Major General (Indonesian Army)
Sandy Davidson	Brigadier General (US Army)
Scott Davis	Captain (US Army)
John Defreitas	Brigadier General (US Army)
Garth Derrick	Colonel (British Army)
Tom Duhs	Colonel (US Marine Corps)
Barbara Fast	Brigadier General (US Army)
Dick Formica	Brigadier General (US Army)
Thamir Ghadban	Iraqi Oil Minister
Steve Gliddon	Major (Australian Army)
Al Goshie	Lieutenant Colonel (US Army)
Falah Hasan al Naqib	Iraqi Interior Minister
Steve Hashem	Brigadier General (US Army)
Jim Hawkins	Colonel (US Army)
Noel Henderson	Captain (Australian Army)
Angus Houston	Chief of the Australian Defence Force (2005–)
Don Jackson	Colonel (US Army)
Ibrahim Jafari	Iraqi Prime Minister
James Jeffrey	US Deputy Head of Mission, Iraq

Matt Jones	Major (Australian Army Corps HQ)
Abdul Kadr	Lieutenant General (Iraqi Army)
Shayk Kalidh	Chief Imam, Fallujah
John Kisely	Lieutenant General (British Army)
Peter Leahy	Chief of the Army (Australia)
Erv Lessel	Brigadier General (US Air Force)
Mark Lowe	Colonel (US Army)
Gary Luck	General (US Army – retired)
Pat Malay	Lieutenant Colonel (US Marine Corps 3/5)
Jim Mattis	Major General (US Marine Corps)
Mark McQueen	Lieutenant Colonel (US Army)
Tom Metz	Lieutenant General (US Army)
Tom Miller	Major General (US Army)
Des Mueller	Lieutenant General (Australian Army)
John Negroponte	US Ambassador to Iraq
Ron Neumann	Ambassador US Embassy in Iraq
Bob Newman	Colonel (US Army)
Peter Palmer	Brigadier General (US Army)
David Petraeus	Lieutenant General (US Army)
Aden Khaled Qalir	Major General (Iraqi Police Service)
Bob Pricone	Colonel (US Army)
Mike Regner	Colonel (US Marine Corps)
Donald Rumsfeld	US Secretary of Defense (2001–06)
Barhem Saleh	Iraqi Deputy Prime Minister
Saleh	Major General (Iraqi Army)

Ricardo (Ric) Sanchez	Lieutenant General (US Army)
John Sattler	Major General (US Marine Corps)
Dr Mohammed Shakir	Director General of Health, Iraq
Steve Summersby	Major (Australian Army)
Joe Weber	Major General (US Marine Corps)
Jim Xinos	Squadron Leader (Royal Australian Air Force)

SAS bodyguard:

Dave

Drew

Harry

Henry

Kaz

Lockey

Mac

Paul

Ryan

Stodds

Thommo

Whitey